SUE.
HAPPY BIRTHDAY
MAY YOU BE VERY BLESSED
IN ALL THAT YOU DO
LOVE
JANET.
xx

PRESENTED TO:

SUSIE, PETER, JESSICA
& BABY No. 2

FROM:

JANET, JACO, JULIA & JENNI

DATE:

10 OCTOBER 2000

NEW BEGINNINGS

366 daily devotionals inspired by God's love and compassion

Solly Ozrovech

CHRISTIAN
ART
PUBLISHERS

Originally published by Christian Publishing Company
under the title *Elke môre nuut!*

© 2000
First edition 2000

English edition © 2000
CHRISTIAN ART PUBLISHERS
P O Box 1599, Vereeniging, 1930

Translated by Haidee Kotze
Cover designed by Christian Art Publishers

Scripture taken from the *Holy Bible,* New International
Version®. NIV®. © 1973, 1978, 1984 by International Bible Society.
Used by permission of Zondervan Publishing House. All rights reserved.

Set in 12 in 15 pt WeidemannBook by Christian Art Publishers

Printed and bound in Hong Kong

ISBN 1-86852-620-8

00 01 02 03 04 05 06 07 08 09 – 10 9 8 7 6 5 4 3 2 1

DEDICATION

This book is dedicated to the congregation of Kroonheuwel-North in
general, for a mountaintop-experience in 2000, and to Annemarie
Swart in particular, for her exceptional hospitality and friendship.

$\mathcal{A}$ WORD TO THE READER

My heart is steadfast, O God, my heart is steadfast; I will sing and make music. Awake, my soul! Awake, harp and lyre! I will awaken the dawn (Ps. 57:7-8).

There are thousands of people in our southern country who spend time with God in the early hours of the morning. It is a special time of silent seclusion that helps us to find the strength and inspiration for a full and busy day ahead. This book, written in an accessible style that is easy to comprehend, wants to make a humble contribution to help make this time with God meaningful and dynamic. Of course, the Scriptures are always the point of departure, and there is no substitute for the Word of God. Therefore I appeal to you first to read the passage from Scripture, before continuing with the daily devotional and the prayer. We pray that, in this way, the Holy Spirit will open the Word to you. The best time to meet God is early in the morning, so that we may devote the best of our time and mind to Him.

Because of the Lord's great love we are not consumed, for his compassions never fail. They are new every morning ... (Lam. 3:22-23).

Soli Deo Gloria

~ Solly Ozrovech ~

January

Prayer for the New Year

Holy God, Creator of new things,
  we thank You for the experience of the dawn of a new year.
Help us to discard the old ways of the old year and
    to walk a new path in the new year,
    to wait faithfully for your blessing in solemn and
    prayerful patience.
Together with the old year we want to lay down our old sins.
In the new year, through the strength and mercy of God,
    which we have experienced so often in the past,
    we want to crucify the "own I" on the cross.
In the old year we have had many troubles, and therefore we plead
    that in the new year You will grant us contentment with our lot,
    so that we will look forward to every new day with confidence,
    and venture forth with God at our side.
May your bountiful blessings accompany us in the new year:
    peace and quiet for our heart.
May there be flowers aplenty on our path and
    may our joy as well as our grief be hallowed by God.
In the Name and for the sake of Jesus Christ.

Amen.

*I*N SAFE KEEPING

"I am with you and will watch over you wherever you go ... I will not leave you until I have done what I have promised you" (Gen. 28:15).

---

*H*ere we find a wonderful, all-encompassing promise for the first morning of a new year. The old year is behind us with all its burdens of guilt and sin, its sorrows and disappointments, its dark days and difficult hours. Now, because of the eternal faithfulness of God, we may enter the new year with this declaration of the gospel, this joyful message, which continues to resound in our ears. May God allow it also to permeate our deepest heart.

We are heading towards an unknown future, and despite what we have left behind in the old year, we will not be free of troubles and worries. We are, after all, human children with much anxiety and little faith. This is why we stand terrified and weak before the unknown.

However, now the almighty God comes and reads the fear and worry in our eyes, and speaks to us as He did to Jacob, the one-time drifter: "Don't be afraid. I am with you. The promises that I have made I will keep." These words fall like heavenly music upon our ears.

Through Jesus Christ this God is our God. If we believe, we are God's redeemed children through Christ, and we will never have to doubt his eternal faithfulness. God has spoken these words, and each promise will be consummated in our lives if we but wait patiently for Him.

I thank You, Lord my God, that regardless of whether I lie down or get up, You continually watch over me. When I venture upon unknown paths, You support me with your strength. Thank You for always being faithful and that the night will never become so dark that your light will become invisible to me.

God is always with us; why will we not always be with God?
~ William Ullathorne ~

Don't lose your way

Show me your ways, O Lord, teach me your paths; guide me in your truth and teach me, for you are God my Savior ... (Ps. 25:4-5).

There are very few of us who haven't been lost at some point in our lives, usually because we took a back road. It was Langenhoven who said: "Never take a back road, because there is a reason why the highway doesn't run along there." Maybe we attempted an unknown road by car or foot, and suddenly realised that we had lost our way. At that moment our greatest need is for a road map or a friendly helper to guide us back to the right road. If we refuse to accept advice in such circumstances, we run the risk of only worsening our situation.

It is the same in life. You set out on a project or an action that swiftly turns out to be mistaken; or you have to make a choice and it becomes apparent that you have chosen the wrong option. Or maybe you have to make a decision, but you can't, because your perspective is obscured and forces beyond your control make it difficult for you.

Throughout the journey of life we must lay every decision we have to make before God. Then, wait in the quiet of his presence for Him to give you guidance, so that you can be sure that you are setting forth in faith, and know that you are not alone because Jesus the living Christ will be there to guide you on the right path. It would be the height of folly to ignore this fact on your journey into the new year.

Lord Jesus, Governor and Finisher of my faith, help me not to follow my own heart, but to wait quietly for your guidance so that I will walk the right path.

There is a time when we have to decide firmly on the direction we wish to take, or otherwise circumstances will make the choice for us.
~ Herbert V. Prochnov ~

How will I know the right way?

I will instruct you and teach you in the way you should go; I will counsel you and watch over you (Ps. 32:8).

Who will need to grope their way in the dark if the faithful God will be our Guidepost? Even if we have to pass through torment and strife, we will arrive at the right destination, as long as God's Word remains our truth: "I will teach you everything about the path that you must travel."

The question is whether we will follow the heavenly Guidepost; whether we want to be taught by Him. Unfortunately there are so many of us who do not want to allow Him to teach us, even if we piously say that we do. We have said it so often in the past, and yet we don't truly want to see the Guidepost planted in the ground before us. We want to walk our own path without any interference. Isn't it then understandable that we end up being disappointed and with our hopes dashed to the ground?

Today's text contains another powerful word of comfort: "I will keep watch over you." Is this truly a word of comfort to us? Will it be a relief to us, knowing that God's eyes are upon us? He pays attention to the path that we are walking. May the thought of this keep us from wandering onto a wrong path and prevent us from committing deeds and speaking words that do not demonstrate love.

The eyes of God will be upon us. May this, which is intended as eminent consolation, not become a sentence to us.

We praise and thank You, o God, that we may entrust the path of our lives to You. When we call upon You in faith and trust, You are always there to support us and show us the right way.

Those who insist on seeing with complete clarity before making a decision will never decide.

~ Henri Frederic Amiel ~

Your developing prayer life

But grow in the grace and knowledge of our Lord and Savior Jesus Christ ... (2 Pet. 3:18).

Of the spiritual luggage that you will carry with you into the new year, prayer is one of the most important components. Some people maintain that prayer is easy. Others believe that it is difficult. If you are trying to develop a growing and meaningful prayer life, you will know that both these statements contain some truth.

With the best intentions in your heart you set aside time for a peaceful time of prayer, but just as you are preparing yourself, something intrudes upon these precious moments: a telephone call, a knock on the door, a sudden reminder of something you should have done. You can be sure that the devil will leave no stone unturned to prevent you from praying.

It would be a good idea to take these things that distract you and enfold them with your prayers. Take the disturbances that the devil places in your way and change them into subjects for prayer.

Prayer is not a static entity, but a dynamic, pulsating force that needs to be used continually if it is to retain its power and fulfil its function of leading you into a more intimate relationship with God. If your prayer life is weak and ineffectual, you become like a motor battery that hasn't been used for a considerable time: it cannot fulfil the task for which it was created. Recharge your prayer batteries through disciplined prayer and feel how God starts working in your life once more.

Lord Jesus, consummate Supplicant, let me discover the wonder and the power of prayer anew through the inspiration of the Holy Spirit. Sanctify my prayers and make me faithful in my prayer life.

Persevere in prayer, but be grateful that God's answers are wiser than your prayers.

~ William Culbertson ~

Your faith will be tested

" ... However, when the Son of Man comes, will he find faith on the earth?" (Lk. 18:8).

How will one be able to face the future without faith? As the writer of Hebrews says: *Now faith is being sure of what we hope for and certain of what we do not see* (Heb. 11:1). In the final days of the old millennium many things were said and written about the world as it is at present. Violence continually erupts and signs of permissiveness, lawlessness and anarchy are commonplace. We often hear the clarion call reminding us that we live in the last days and that the Second Coming of Christ is at hand. There is nothing more that humanity can do to prevent the destruction of the world. These are some of the things that are so often said offhandedly.

Regardless of whether there is any substance to these predictions, and despite the fact that chaos *is* rampant, we are not allowed to abandon the standards set by Christ. The fact that the world is in a desperate state does not give Christians the right or an excuse to give up in the struggle against the forces of the evil one.

Our Christian commitment lasts for a lifetime. Despite the evil one's efforts to undermine the Church of Christ, despite the pressures building up against the Christian faith, it remains your duty to exalt the Name of Christ. Through his strength you must hold on to everything that He has taught, so that when He returns, you will hear these words from his holy mouth: " ... *'Well done, good and faithful servant! ... Come and share in your master's happiness!'"* (Mt. 25:23).

When the days of trial come, Lord my God, strengthen me in my faith so that I will not fail in truly being your faithful witness.

I do not merely want to possess a faith, I want to have a faith that possesses me.

~ Charles Kingsley ~

*W*HEN THINGS GO WRONG, PRAY!

"I revealed myself to those who did not ask for me; I was found by those who did not seek me. To a nation that did not call on my name, I said, 'Here am I, here am I'" (Is. 65:1).

*W*hen things go wrong, there are always those who question the existence of God. In the midst of the chaos of personal tragedy we hear their cry of distress: "If there is a God, why does He allow such things to happen?" The brutality of war or the death of a child is used as the basis of an argument in which the love of God is denied. Time and again God stands as the accused, as if He is simply allowing the tragedy to happen. God's love is denied and the sceptics flourish by using these arguments to drive people further and further away from God's protective love.

God's immutable promise to his children has always been, and will always be, that if they only turn to Him in prayer, He will hear their voices and answer their prayers. Jesus promised: *"... whoever comes to me I will never drive away"* (Jn. 6:37). The almighty God challenges his children and says: *"... return to me with all your heart ... Rend your heart and not your garments. Return to the Lord your God ... "* (Joel 2:12-13).

Whatever your worries, however desperate your situation, turn in sincere prayer to God and gratefully accept the guidance that He has promised.

When I am tired and overburdened, weak and unbelieving, Lord Jesus, I turn to You in prayer so that I may receive new strength and vigour. Help me in this through your Holy Spirit that prays in me.

Prayer is the breath of the reborn soul, and without it there can be no Christian life.

~ Rowland Hill ~

*T*HE GLORY OF TODAY

This is the day the Lord has made; let us rejoice and be glad in it (Ps. 118:24).

*W*e can't change the past and the future is a mystery to us. Therefore the present is of crucial importance. By fully living in this moment we can bring homage to the past and prepare ourselves for the unknown future.

People realise the importance of the present in different ways. Some people are continually involved in big plans that they want to accomplish at some point in the future, and any sacrifice in the present is worthwhile because the future is bright with possibility. The serious student will sacrifice his sport and social life to realise his dreams. But wise is the student who manages to keep his eyes fixed on future ideals while enjoying the accumulation of knowledge for the sake of the satisfaction that it provides him in the days of his preparation.

There was a time in the history of Christianity when the present was scorned and only the future was of any value to the serious believer. It was a "pie in the sky when you die" approach to life and faith. Currently, this religious philosophy is on the wane and the truth is dawning increasingly on people: that Jesus Christ, who is our perfect Master in the art of life, is not only involved in the heaven after life, but wants to establish heaven in the hearts of people here and now.

When you venture forth on the path of this new year with Jesus Christ, the present is filled with his glory and life becomes indescribably beautiful and good.

Heavenly Governor, though the future is unknown, I confidently place it in your almighty hands, so that I may enjoy the present joyfully.

Do you love life? Then do not squander time, because it is the stuff that life is made of.

~ Benjamin Franklin ~

What do we owe one another?

Let no debt remain outstanding, except the continuing debt to love one another ... (Rom. 13:8).

If we consider the matter carefully, we all have so much to be grateful for to the Lord. Despite the fact that we become dejected and pessimistic when things go wrong, we must also realise that God's mercy and love for us are infinite. He granted you life and the freedom of choice to do with this life what you wish. You may be blessed with a happy family who loves you deeply. Even the most dejected person will, if he ponders the matter seriously and honestly, inevitably find something for which he can thank and praise God.

How do you prove your gratitude for the bountiful grace in your life to God? No money, no commodities, no hours of service can be sufficient payment for his love that is so great that He bestows all these benefactions upon you, and then also ultimately sacrifices his life for you.

Love can never be repaid sufficiently, because it is an article that is simultaneously precious and priceless. You cannot measure the magnitude of it; it cannot be weighed to determine its value. Love can only be passed on and shared.

Here you have the only way in which you can acknowledge the great love that God has for you: by sharing it with each person whose path crosses yours on your pilgrimage into the future.

Help me, o Holy Spirit, to understand the lesson of true love as God has taught it to us through Jesus Christ. Grant that my every thought, word and deed will be an act of love for You.

Take away love and our earth becomes a tomb.
~ Robert Browning ~

FOR DAYS WHEN EVERYTHING GOES WRONG

... " ... 'To whom do you belong, and where are you going, and who owns all these animals in front of you?' ... " (Gen. 32:17).

When the one drab, humdrum day follows the other with tedious regularity and it seems as if your life has no meaning or purpose, it is easy to develop the attitude that nothing in life is worthwhile.

If this is your unfortunate experience, it proves that you are busy losing your grip on life – or that you have already lost it. Life must have purpose and significance if you are to live meaningfully. How is it possible to develop such a depressed attitude? Maybe you have been doing the same work for years, and as far as you can see you will be doing it for many years to come. What, you may justifiably ask, is the use of thinking that circumstances will change? You feel as if you are trapped in a dead-end street from which you will never be able to escape.

One of the facts of the Christian rebirth is that it changes your attitude towards life. While you previously lived without hope or expectation, Christ now plants new hope in your heart and makes all dejection and despair disappear. When you truly start living in Christ, you look with new eyes of understanding and love at life.

This new concept of life that is conveyed by Christ gives life meaning, so that you will never again have to ask: "Is it worthwhile to live?" When the powerful thoughts of Christ fill you and the Holy Spirit's strength saturates your spirit, you realise the rich quality of your faith, and you will never again question the meaning of life.

Lord Jesus, You came so that we may have life in abundance. Please keep me from forgetting to come to You in dark days, so that my life may be infused with significance and meaning once again.

Do not fear that your life will come to end, but rather that it will never truly begin.

~ John Henry Newman ~

What would Jesus do?

Therefore, brothers, we have an obligation – but it is not to the sinful nature, to live according to it (Rom. 8:12).

The temptation to act in a normal, human manner in any given situation is always present. Consequently, the sharpness of the tongue will also always be inclined to make a painful and caustic remark. Meanness will inevitably manifest itself, with the sole purpose of winning points. A prolonged feud may result from a refusal to forgive some trifling matter. It is fairly accurate to say that most of the world's ills have their origins in the weakness and inconstancy of human nature.

To overcome the temptation to take revenge or to react in a way that will damage your relationship with someone else, first calm down and think before you do or say something. Consider the way in which Jesus would handle the situation. The Scriptures contain many instances of the hostility, ridicule, false accusations, humiliation and rejection that He had to suffer. And despite this, He said and did nothing without love.

Regardless of how strong the temptation is to react in anger in any situation, stop for a moment and allow the Spirit of God to flow through your heart and spirit. In so doing, you will know that you will not be the cause of someone else's hurt. Through the love that you show you will emerge from the circumstances as a victor in Jesus Christ.

Heavenly Teacher, help me through the Holy Spirit to restrain my tongue and my emotions. Grant that I will always manifest your tolerant love.

I have a great need for Christ, I have a great Christ for my needs.
     ~ Charles H. Spurgeon ~

*W*HAT ARE YOU STRIVING FOR THIS YEAR?

"But seek first his kingdom and his righteousness, and all these things will be given to you as well" (Mt. 6:33).

*T*ales of people who started out with nothing and made a great success of life make for inspiring reading matter. People tend to find immense satisfaction in their achievements, but the fact remains that they are part of the human race and have therefore been created in the image of God. It is only by admitting this fact that they may be saved from foolish conceit. Successful people need salvation just as desperately as those who have made a failure of life.

Have you noticed how success can change a person's entire personality? If financial success becomes an obsession to the extent that all other things are excluded, people lose the ability to understand and love their fellow man. Of much greater importance than acquiring success and money is developing an honourable character.

The most reliable builders of character are the laws of God, as portrayed by the living Christ. If you share your life with Him, your character will be formed after his image. An old hymn pleads: "I want to be like Jesus, so humble and so soft. His words were always friendly and his voice was always soft."

This should be the goal of every child of God, be he rich or poor, successful or unsuccessful. To aspire to the highest and best in Christ is your calling and responsibility in the year ahead.

Merciful Master, I praise You for the fact that the more I live in You, the more I develop, thanks to your Holy Spirit, a balanced set of values and a pure spiritual consciousness.

To desire the kingdom of God unconditionally, at all times and under all circumstances, this is the kingdom of God inside of you.

~ Francois Fenelon ~

Enchanted by the peace of Christ

"Peace I leave with you; my peace I give you ... Do not let your hearts be troubled and do not be afraid" (Jn. 14:27).

At some point in our lives we all yearn for peace and inner calm. The general uncertainty of our world creates a sense of restlessness; illness, death, insecurity and domestic disturbances cause worry and strife in our minds. The list of our troubles is endless, but the results are always the same: anxiety and stress.

Many people experiencing such emotions seek professional help. The psychiatrist's couch and sedatives become an accepted way of life for them. Others, who lack willpower, turn to drugs and alcohol in an attempt to erase the reality of the present. Still others suffer in silence while life slowly loses all its meaning and significance for them. They continue living in a void that is bereft of everything worthwhile.

The only way to handle all the pressures and tensions of life is to possess a faith that is firmly anchored in Jesus Christ. Your relationship with Him cannot be a transient matter or a question of convenience. You have to practise a permanent experience of unity with Him in your entire way of life. Hold on to Him in all situations; talk to Him, however desperate you may be; know for certain that He is always with you. Even though it may be difficult for you to comprehend his peace, you will recognise it when it flows through your being, allaying all your fears.

Help me, Lord Jesus, to hold on to You, thus receiving your peace in every situation in my life. Let your peace flow from me to all my fellow human beings.

The essence of peace is God; the secret of peace is trust.

~ J. B. Figgis ~

The Holy Spirit is of cardinal importance

"The Spirit gives life ... " (Jn. 6:63).

Every human being develops physically. What is not as common as physical development is intellectual development. It requires effort and discipline. There are those who refuse to accept the challenge to develop mentally, simply because of their laziness. While all people do not have the same intellectual ability, there are many people who do not optimally utilise their abilities. The spiritual dimension is neglected or ignored because it cannot be determined or analysed that easily.

And yet the spirit that is in you is of cardinal importance. If the spirit in you is strong, your physical and mental powers are influenced by its vigour. A strong spirit stimulates the intellect, and physical shortcomings may be regulated and even overcome through its power. Such a powerful spirit is the result of a living communion with Christ. To live in harmony with Him and to grow in the awareness of his living presence develops your thoughts and spirit and allows you to grow spiritually. This is pre-eminently the work of the Holy Spirit.

Jesus Himself developed spiritually, intellectually and physically. If He had to go through this process of growth, how much more do we need to go through it? The tragedy of modern Christianity is that many disciples who have accepted Jesus Christ as Saviour have stopped growing, because they have not given the Holy Spirit a central place in their spiritual lives. Stagnation results in spiritual death. Through the Holy Spirit we must continue to grow in Jesus Christ.

God, help me never to stop growing spiritually. Make me mature in body, thought and spirit by remaining true to Jesus, the True Vine.

Every time we say "I believe in the Holy Spirit" we mean that there is a living God who is willing and able to permeate the human personality and change it irrevocably.

~ J. B. Phillips ~

For Days of Sorrow

... (T)he Lord will be your everlasting light, and your days of sorrow will end (Is. 60:20).

There is nothing that we, as powerless humans, can do when God decides to take away a loved one from us through death. Regardless of how strong you are spiritually, you always experience profound sorrow during those moments of immeasurable powerlessness and irreparable loss. Despite the fact that the Scriptures assure you that the death of the body is the passageway to the eternal glory of God, your human feelings of sorrow and loss dictate your grief at that moment.

In moments like those God lovingly calls to you to turn to Him and find peace in Him. The living Christ, who assures you that you will ultimately be reunited in Him, waits to lead you tenderly from your sorrowful darkness towards his wonderful light and the house that He went to prepare for you and your loved ones.

While it may be true that words sound hollow in your deep sorrow, it is just as true that the Spirit of the loving Christ can and will console you if only you would open your heart to Him. Allow Him to support you in your sorrow and to lead you on his path. Invite Him into your life and He will light your way and fill you with his peace. Then you will be able to start living on the sunny side of life once again.

Thank you, Lord Jesus, that You conquered death and that I and my loved ones will also be resurrected because You were resurrected. Let me not grieve like those who have no hope.

Sorrow is a fruit; God does not allow it to grow on branches that are too weak to carry it.

~ Victor Hugo ~

To DO GOD'S WILL ACCORDING TO GOD'S WAY

Teach me, O Lord, to follow your decrees; then I will keep them to the end (Ps. 119:33).

There are many servants of the Lord who diligently serve Him, but who keep the love of their hearts from Him. These people serve the Lord in many different ways, but often these are ways of their own choice. When they are challenged to a form of service that demands more sacrifices, they merely work harder and more dedicated at their own choice.

While all work done for the Lord benefits the one doing it – no one can work for the Lord without being blessed – the only work that is truly beneficial is the work done according to his holy will.

The problem is to know what the will of God is for you personally. However, if you have compassion for others' physical and spiritual problems and needs, it will help you to understand God's way better. When the suffering of others compels you into compassion as well as action, you are most surely acting within the will of the Master. Christ was always profoundly touched when witnessing other people's suffering, especially the suffering of the innocent. If you become aware of someone else's spiritual distress and you offer your heart, thoughts, spirit and voice to God, asking Hom to enable you to help, you will be astonished at your own responses while God is using you in his service.

I am willing, Lord, to do your work according to your way. Let your Holy Spirit guide me not to follow the path of my own heart, but to wait prayerfully so that I will know the path on which you want to send me.

We only have to obey. There is guidance for every one of us, and by listening humbly, we will hear the right words.

~ Ralph Waldo Emerson ~

Into the Future with Christ

" ... Be strong and courageous. Do not be terrified; do not be discouraged, for the Lord your God will be with you ... " (Josh. 1:9).

We usually step into the new year with mixed feelings. Aware of the failures of the past, you go towards the future with a certain degree of hesitation. Will the failures of the past be repeated this year and will that soul-destroying monotony remain with you this year?

What the new year holds will depend largely on yourself. You may try to side-step its challenges and continue in the same old rut that you have been in for so many years. Alternatively, you can jump at the opportunities that the new year presents you with, and start with a completely new lifestyle and approach to life.

There are two ways of handling the challenges of the new year. You can approach it in the same way as in the past: resolute to do better, but in your heart convinced that you will be back in the same old rut of unfulfilled expectations and doleful failures before the end of January. Alternatively, you can go to meet the new year with the full realisation of who you are, but also with the conviction that you serve a wonderful God who desires only victory and fulfilment for you.

God invites you to enter into a partnership with him. He offers you not only the gifts and grace of an intensified spiritual life, but also the privilege of being a saved child of God through Jesus Christ. If you step into the new year with trust and faith in Jesus Christ, nothing in the future can hold defeat or failure for you.

Holy Lord Jesus, because You have given me your Spirit, I can face the future with courage and confidence. For this I praise and thank You from the depths of my heart.

Courage does not exist in being blind to dangers, but seeing and conquering them.

~ Jean Paul Richter ~

The Light on Your Way

And God said: "Let there be light," and there was light (Gen. 1:3).

When a year has rushed to its end and we look back upon the road travelled, we tend only to see things like adversity, violence, disasters and strife. When we then look towards the future everything seems gloomy and pitch dark, and we fear the future. There is no getting away from the fact that the past leaves much to be desired. As a result many people feel that they can expect no better from the future, and this makes them despondent.

If this is your heart's disposition towards the new year that stretches ahead of you, it is very likely that you will not be disappointed. What we expect in our hearts usually happens to us. You must think and believe positively in order to obtain positive results. As you travel through the new year, you will have to live on the reserves of your faith. You must call into remembrance all the great deeds of God throughout the centuries and place your trust in Him to lead you on his perfect path.

The prayer of your heart should be every day: "Lead me, o Light of the world!" Even today Jesus Christ is still the Light of the world and He has promised that those who follow Him will never walk in darkness. There is no darkness that He cannot illuminate. He invites you to continue this year's journey in his company. Take his hand in faith and trust and experience Him as the light of your life.

God of light and truth, thank You that your Son has illuminated my life so that I may walk towards the future in faith and trust. Be my light, even when darkness falls around me.

In the darkness we have no choice. It is the light that enables us to see the difference between things, and it is Christ who gives us light.

~ C. T. Whitmell ~

A LIFE OF VICTORY

... (F)or everyone born of God overcomes the world. This is the victory that has overcome the world, even our faith (1 Jn. 5:4).

---

*M*aybe you are one of those people who find life in its entirety an immense struggle. Everything you undertake ends up in frustration and possibly in failure. This unhappy situation may lead to diminished self-confidence, so that you shrink back from new endeavours and start accepting the false perception that nothing you undertake will succeed. Even before you have started you have given up on yourself.

Self-pity is like a devouring cancer in your life. It consumes your belief in yourself and in what you can achieve. When you pity yourself, you are your own worst enemy. Self-pity creates self-centredness and once this disease pervades your thoughts and spirit, your whole world becomes centred on yourself. Such a person is usually egotistical and fails to find the purpose and meaning of true life.

The only way to avoid a life of self-inflicted limitation is to accept the discipline of faith. It is inspirational and elevates you above self-interest, thereby imparting a deeper and broader perspective on life. It enables you to admit that it is only through the strength and influence of the living Christ, through the Holy Spirit that lives in you, that you are able to constructively deal with the problems and failures that come across your way. Through faith in Christ you can live on conquered ground from day to day. Do this, and the beautiful flowers of the new year will unfold before you.

Holy Master, I thank You that I may live victoriously because I believe that You are my Saviour and that the Holy Spirit lives in me. I thank You for every victory that I win over myself.

The first step on the road to victory is to identify the enemy.

~ Corrie ten Boom ~

Do not scorn the day of small things

"Your beginnings will seem humble, so prosperous will your future be" (Job 8:7).

Many people are so excited by the big and important things in life that they fail to see the apparently unimportant matters that carry the seeds of true greatness. There are many industrial and business ventures that originated in a backyard or a simple kitchen. They all started with an idea, were inspired by knowledge and made possible through hard work and an iron will to succeed. Never in the history of mankind have there been more true tales of humble people, motivated by an idea, who created something out of nothing.

There are people who find shelter in the false perception that everything worthwhile has already been thought of by people who are cleverer than they are, and that it is therefore not worth the trouble to start something new. Nothing could be further from the truth. The world is full of ideas that are waiting to be exploited. But how?

Many people find it strange to think that contemptation is the channel for creative thought. True Christianity is involved in every facet of life, and if it is to be effective it must encompass your entire life. True Christianity can never be confined to the inside of the church. All constructive ideas have their origins in God, the great Creator. Those who wait for Him in a spirit of excited anticipation, who are sensitive to his guidance, will receive new ideas. This will lead to a practical manifestation of our faith and to spiritual growth.

Father, make me sensitive to your perfect guidance, in my spiritual as well as practical life. Fill me with holy idealism, only in your honour.

To ask new questions, to ponder new possibilities, and to approach old problems from new perspectives, require creative imagination and are signs of true progress.

~ Albert Einstein ~

Don't try bargaining with God

"Do not test the Lord your God as you did at Massah" (Deut. 6:16).

You cannot try bargaining with God. There are people – some in complete innocence – who in their prayers tend to offer God something in exchange for the fulfilment of their requests. Despite the fact that there may have been instances where people *did* receive what they had asked for, it remains an undesirable practice that can easily have a negative influence on your faith.

It is imperative that you realise and accept the fact that everything you are and everything you have, comes only through the grace of God. Because He loves you He provides in all your needs according to the wealth of his mercy and the all-powerfulness of his will. It is also essential that you will accept that you belong to Him. You have been redeemed through the sacrifice of Jesus Christ on the cross, and now you belong to Him. From these facts it becomes clear that you cannot bargain with Him on the basis that you will do something for Him if He will give you something in exchange.

The right approach in your prayer life is to lay all your concerns and requests before Him and then to wait faithfully. Accept that whatever He ordains for you will be good, and acknowledge it as being within the will of the Father.

If this is your attitude in your prayers, you will experience the peace of God that flows from faith in and acceptance of the will of your heavenly Father.

Your will for me, o Father, is only good. Therefore I will wait patiently for your answer to every prayer that I send up to You. Keep me faithfully at your feet so that your plan with my life may come to fruition.

All of heaven waits to help those who discover the will of God and do it.

~ J. Robert Ashcroft ~

*S*CRIPTURAL RELIGION

"Why do you call me, 'Lord, Lord,' and do not do what I say?" (Lk. 6:46).

*W*hy is it that so many good, churchgoing people in our time experience a sense of disappointment and failure that borders on despair? They have faithfully attended church throughout their entire lives and honestly feel that they truly love God in their own way. Despite this they suffer from spiritual malnutrition. There is something important lacking in their spiritual experience.

The answer may lie precisely in the fact that they love God in their own way, instead of in the scriptural way. They have created a form of Christianity that fits neatly into their lifestyle. This private and personal version of Christianity turns them into masters of compromise. They find excuses not to forgive; they are selective in who they want to love; their business negotiations are controlled by whatever suits them at that moment and not by scriptural principles.

Scriptural Christianity starts with an act of repentance and confession. This implies a complete about-turn and an awareness of the presence of the living Christ. Scriptural Christianity means complete obedience to God and to the standards set out by Christ. These standards are found in the New Testament, and the Master commands us to keep them.

Such a demand is not unreasonable, because when He calls us He also equips the new disciple with his Holy Spirit. When we are empowered in this way, Jesus Christ guides us into the fullness of life.

Thank You, Lord Jesus, that You came so that we may have abundant life. Keep me from seeking my spiritual salvation outside the Scriptures.

Obedience to God is the infallible proof of our sincere love for Him.
~ Nathaniel Emmons ~

Divine Protection

They remembered that God was their Rock, that God Most High was their Redeemer (Ps. 78:35).

There have been countless occasions in history when it seemed as if all were lost and all hope extinguished. Circumstances were such that people and even nations were forced to admit defeat in an unequal battle against the superior numbers of the enemy.

Even so, there have been even more cases in which deliverance came to people and nations in answer to their prayers. God has saved people and nations from obliteration in miraculous ways, and has enabled them to overcome dangers and transform humiliating defeat into glorious victory.

These cases, both personal and historical, should serve as a constant reminder of the victorious omnipotence of God in all spheres of life. No circumstances are too small or too big for Him, and no prayer will remain unheard or unanswered. This is the extent of God's unfathomable love for his people and his world.

Where you now go to meet a new, unknown year in which adverse circumstances may threaten to overwhelm you, or fear may make your heart tremble, remember that Christ has given his life for you. Turn to Him and lay your fears at his feet, because only in Him will you find deliverance from your distress.

Lord my God, You are a safe fortress to me; a shield against every calamity that threatens to befall me. You promised to be my keeper who will not slumber or sleep. In this knowledge I step with confidence into the unknown.

God is the one without whom we cannot live.

~ Leo Tolstoy ~

GO WITH GOD

When his master saw that the Lord was with him and that the Lord gave him success in everything he did, Joseph found favor in his eyes ... (Gen. 39:3-4).

---

*I*t seldom happens that two people experience the presence of God in their life in exactly the same way. It is one of the great mysteries and joys of the Christian faith that the triune God manifests Himself in so many different ways to his children, to each according to his personal situation, circumstances and needs.

The Christian disciple is often discouraged when hearing of the refreshing and astonishing experiences of others who have felt the touch of Jesus in their lives, and who have experienced unforgettable moments of ecstasy in which they knew without a doubt that they were in the presence of the risen Christ.

If you have experienced these feelings of discouragement, which can so easily make you despondent, don't allow it to influence your relationship with God negatively. You are a very special person to God. Not only are you his unique once-off creation, but you are his child, and as your heavenly Father He knows your needs better than you know them yourself. As a result the omniscient, loving Father will always be with you in a special way intended to fulfil your unique needs.

All that is expected of you is to wait quietly for Him and to know that He is God.

Faithful Father, I find peace and quiet with You and rejoice in your lasting presence in my life. May I step into the future with your loving hand upon mine and with faith in my heart.

The essential meaning of faith is to take someone at his word.
~ David Watson ~

He knows and He understands

He did not need man's testimony about man, for he knew what was in a man (Jn. 2:25).

Because Christ understands your weaknesses doesn't mean that He condones your sins. He, who was tempted like us in all respects, has called you to a life of victory through the strength of his immanent Holy Spirit. Unfortunately those things which people call "weaknesses" for convenience's sake, and which are really just sins, rob our spiritual life of its growth and vigour. These things create an obstacle between our spiritual life and Christ.

As far as Christ is concerned there are no insignificant sins, because all sin separates the human being from the Master. As soon as there is a weakening in people's relationship with Christ, they will always find trifling excuses to defend their apostasy.

Christ never tries to gloss over sin. He understands human weakness and frailty, offers forgiveness, and purifies us, saves us, and gives us the spiritual strength to live victoriously.

Christ looks beyond man's sin and sees what he can become through the power of God's Holy Spirit. He does not see us as struggling, failed and imperfect beings, but as channels of the grace of God who do his will in the sphere of life where He has placed us. Because He knows what people are like, He knows their potential and desires to lead them to the perfection that God has ordained for them.

Holy Jesus, please look beyond what I am and inspire me to be what You know I can be. Let me never hide behind my weaknesses while your Holy Spirit is available.

Sin is not painful because it is forbidden. It is forbidden because it is painful.

~ Benjamin Franklin ~

Be wary of false prophets

They want to be teachers of the law, but they do not know what they are talking about or what they so confidently affirm (1 Tim. 1:7).

There is an increasing confusion in the thoughts of the average Christian. He is confused by the variety of interpretations of the Scriptures. All over the world there is a conflict of opinions among the leaders of denominations, churches and sects, who place their own interpretations on the Word of God and preach their religious convictions accordingly.

For example, much is written and read about liberation theology, or the socio-political gospel. The issue of surrendering to Christ differs from one group to the next. In this situation there is a real danger that the man on the street will become so confused and disillusioned that he will soon be completely lost for the church of Christ.

The foundation of our Christian faith is love: *"For God so loved the world that he gave his one and only Son ... "* (Jn. 3:16). The unavoidable requirement of the Christian faith is complete surrender to Jesus Christ, because a love so divinely wonderful demands all – body, mind and spirit. Any doctrine that is not founded on love and surrender, is not centred on Christ and does not give all the glory to God, is false and only worthy of rejection. The Scriptures seriously warn us against false prophets. Let us pay heed to this warning.

Lord and Master, amidst conflicting doctrines I commit myself inextricably to your pure gospel of love.

Not everyone who speaks in the Spirit is a prophet, but only he who follows the example and principles of Christ.

~ William Temple ~

*T*HE MIRACULOUS POWER OF PRAISE

My heart is steadfast, O God; I will sing and make music with all my soul. Awake, harp and lyre! I will awaken the dawn (Ps. 108:1-2).

*W*e often use prayer to thank God for what He has done for us, to lay our needs before Him, and to confess our sins and shortcomings to Him. It is sad, but true, that we often neglect to express our praise of Him in prayer.

Never underestimate the power of praise in your prayer life. If someone impresses you, you speak words of praise towards him or other people. Good artists, sportsmen, musicians and singers are showered with praise. There is always a rapport between the giver and the receiver of praise.

Why shouldn't we then shower the benevolent God with praise? Think of all the remarkable things that He has done; the miracles that flow from Him; the extraordinary extent of his love. Ponder for a moment the wonders of the universe and creation; of human life and achievement – and praise and glorify Him. More than anyone He is worthy of our love and thanksgiving.

If you concentrate on praising and glorifying God, you will create a very special relationship with the living Christ, which will transform your prayer life and intensify your love for Him. Through your praise you will become a stronger witness for Him.

Great and wonderful God, we want to exalt your Name without end, and praise and glorify You for all the wonders of your love and grace that You give to us even though we don't deserve it.

Praise is the product of a singing heart. It is the inner person who is delighted in the love and grace of God.

~ Basil Hume ~

WHEN KNOWLEDGE BECOMES WISDOM

The fear of the Lord is the beginning of wisdom; all who follow his precepts have good understanding ... (Ps. 111:10).

Knowledge is a wonderful thing and one can never have enough of it. Anyone who specialises in a particular field of knowledge so that he may serve his fellow human beings more effectively deserves our gratitude and appreciation. The collection of knowledge keeps the mind active and vigorous. The Scriptures declare that the Lord is a God of profound knowledge (see 1 Sam. 2:3). A thirst for knowledge is actually a yearning for a deeper understanding of God and his ways.

Knowledge in itself is insufficient unless it is aligned with God; not necessarily in a purely spiritual manner, but with an all-encompassing love for life, which transforms knowledge into wisdom as a consequence of an intimate understanding of God.

Unfortunately there are people who are intellectually brilliant, but who fail to create meaningful relationships with their fellow human beings. They cannot control their behaviour and emotions and are often poor partners because they lack understanding and appreciation.

The Word of God teaches us: *The fear of the Lord teaches a man wisdom* ... (Prov. 15:33). To honour God and to build an intimate relationship with Him through Jesus Christ is the first step in transforming knowledge into inspired wisdom. Therefore maintain communion with God through prayer, Bible study and contemplation.

God of wisdom, make me wise in your ways, through the Spirit. Let me wait for You constantly so that I can develop an intimate relationship with You. Preserve me from knowledge without wisdom.

Wisdom is the ability to deal successfully with life's crises. People may accumulate knowledge, but wisdom is a gift that comes from God.

~ Bob Jones ~

Are you seeking Jesus?

But Herod said, "I beheaded John. Who, then, is this I hear such things about?" And he tried to see him (Lk. 9:9).

In our time there are many people who, like Herod, tirelessly try to find Jesus. They seek Him in worship, contemplation, prayer and Bible study. People go into retreat and seclude themselves from the world, or attend conferences, seminars and workshops in an attempt to encounter the Son of God. Thousands attend evangelical gatherings in the hope of finding Christ in the ecstasy of worship or in the drama of divine healing and conversions.

There are also those whose erstwhile living faith has lost its fervour, and who feel the need to renew their attempts to get back to the Christ who meant so much to them before. Many achieve success in this mission and enjoy the wonder of new communion with the Master. Others fail and their spiritual life remains barren, stark and desolate; their faith fades and they drift further and further away from Him.

If you sincerely and earnestly seek Jesus, there is one certain way of finding Him: seeking Him among people. Wherever there is distress you will surely find Him and He will be with you in any deed of compassion that you perform. The Christ that you seek lives in the hearts and minds of people and in the smile of gratitude when you bestow love and compassion on others. It is here that you will meet the Master you are seeking.

Beloved and compassionate Master, it is when I serve others with love and thoughtfulness that I am repeatedly surprised by meeting You. Thank You for manifesting Yourself in this way to insignificant human beings.

It is in silence that God is found and through mysteries that He manifests Himself.

~ Frederick W. Robertson ~

*B*E A JOYFUL *C*HRISTIAN

Do everything without complaining or arguing (Phil. 2:14).

*T*he Christian's life is a life of service and submission. It may be that you are called to work among people in distress, or that your calling is administration, preaching or another form of service. Whatever it is, it will demand that you invest your time and yourself in the service of Christ.

Unfortunately many people have the habit of performing their task for Christ with a negative attitude. They will do their work and often do it exceptionally well, but they are unpleasant people with poor interpersonal relationships. This spoils the quality of their deeds, which should have been manifestations of compassion or mercy in the Name of Christ. The result is that people hesitate to approach them because of the attitude that they encounter.

You must always remember that whatever task you are assigned to do for Jesus is to be done in his Name, and therefore your attitude will have a positive or negative influence on the Christian faith. To ensure that you reflect the glory and love of God in everything that you do, you must do it in the strength of the Holy Spirit. Follow the example of love, compassion, understanding and humility that Christ set in his ministry. In this way your discipleship and service will be fruitful and effective, and fulfil its ultimate purpose to exalt God.

Master and Guide, I newly dedicate myself and my strength to your service. Make me a joyful servant because I find my joy in You.

Joyfulness is the unmistakable sign of the presence of God in our lives.
~ Leon Bloy ~

Live One Day At A Time

" ... For today the Lord will appear to you" (Lev. 9:4).

We all sometimes become impatient with ourselves. You may have been a Christian for many years and occasionally thought about deepening your prayer life and being more earnest with your Bible study. However, other things came up and claimed your attention. Your noble aspirations failed and were eventually pushed so far into the background that they were almost forgotten.

It was not your intention for this to happen, and on numerous occasions you were determined to do something positive and constructive about it. But despite your best efforts you slipped back into the old rut, once again tasting the bitter taste of failure and disappointment.

If you are determined to reaffirm your spiritual goals, don't start by making impressive vows that you know will be difficult to live up to. Learn the secret of living one day at a time and offering your very best to God throughout that entire day. Even then you will still have a sense of dissatisfaction because your best seems so inferior next to God's holiness and perfection. The secret of living one day at a time for God is to do so in the strength of the living Christ. Put aside time for Christ in the early hours of each day and utilise this time optimally. It will place the entire day in the right perspective, and you will discover that as you experience every day in his presence, your spiritual life will grow and become meaningful.

Holy God and through Jesus Christ my heavenly Father, I want to live each day in your holy presence so that I may grow spiritually and become stronger every day.

The great law of moral conduct, besides God, is to respect time.
~ Johan K. Lavater ~

Grow through humility towards confidence

... (R)ather think of yourself with sober judgment, in accordance with the measure of faith God has given you (Rom. 12:3).

We will never really know how many people harbour a negative opinion of themselves. If they serve on a committee or take part in a discussion, they are reluctant to express their opinions. Ideas are held back because they fear what others may think or say. Because they feel that they are inferior, they restrain their initiatives and live their lives filled with unspoken ideas – and the world is the poorer for it.

In the eyes of God you are of immeasurable value. God does not create nobodies. It is your privilege and your duty to develop your character and personality to its fullest potential. But how is it possible to be liberated from inferiority and to live free from limiting fears?

Accept the scriptural truth that it is possible to live in harmony with God through Jesus Christ who lives in you. Once this truth has taken possession of your mind and has become a motivational force in your life, you will be renewed to the point of understanding what life really is. You will no longer retreat from daily challenges, because you will know that this new strength that you possess is not of your own making, but the product of the Spirit of Christ that works in you. Through your humility you will grow towards God-centred self-confidence and your life will be filled with thanksgiving and praise.

Thank You, my Saviour and Friend, that I may rejoice: I can do everything through Him who gives me the strength. I want to sing your praise and my thanks!

If there were no humility upon the earth, we all would have committed suicide a long time ago.

~ Thomas Merton ~

February

*H*oly God and through Jesus Christ my heavenly Father,
  You are the God who created the universe, but also my Father.
I thank You for your grace that I may believe the invisible
  and may be sure of the things that I hope.
I believe that You sent your Son, Jesus Christ, to the world
  to reconcile mankind with You
  and also to become my Redeemer and Saviour.
I believe that He lived, died and was resurrected
  to be the guarantee that through faith I too will live eternally.
I believe that through his Spirit He still today lives in his children
  and that I too can be a dwelling of the Holy Spirit.
I worship You, Lord Jesus, as my Redeemer, Friend and Saviour.
I worship You, o Holy Spirit, as Immanuel, God in me.
I thank You that I may believe that death is
  merely that luminous portal through which
  we will walk into the brightly lit glory of God
  that we call heaven.
I thank You for the example of thousands of believers from all ages
  who light the path before my feet.
Help me to serve your church on earth faithfully, thereby contributing
  to the advent of your kingdom.
I pray this in the Name of Jesus Christ,
  the Name before which every knee will bend
  and every tongue confess that "Jesus is Lord."

*A*men.

PUT CHRIST FIRST

So I say, live by the Spirit, and you will not gratify the desires of the sinful nature (Gal. 5:16).

If we were truly honest with ourselves, very few of us would be able to deny that it is extremely difficult to live a good Christian life and to act in the way that Jesus expects. As a matter of fact, it is written in the Gospels that our Master Himself said this, and He never promised that it would be easy to follow Him. He explicitly warned us about the problems, dangers and opposition that his disciples would encounter.

One of the greatest obstacles on the Christian path is our human nature with its desires, accepted practices, presumptions and many other things that monopolise our time and attention. These things sneak into our lives, and whether we realise it or not, they relegate Christ to an inferior place in our lives.

It is needless to point out that this is an unacceptable state of affairs, and no person who bears the title of Christian can allow it. And yet, in his own deceptive and cunning way Satan continues to tempt us to follow our own desires, to the detriment of our faith.

To prevent temptation it is essential to open up your entire life to the influence of the Holy Spirit. Deliberately invite Him to take control of your life. He will undoubtedly assist you in overcoming all evil, and help you to live the Christian life to which you have been called.

Lord Jesus, from experience we know that if we wait prayerfully for You, your Holy Spirit will give us the strength to resist every temptation. For this we thank and praise your holy Name.

Obedience is the fruit of faith; patience is the blossom of the fruit.
~ Christina Rossetti ~

GOD STILL PERFORMS MIRACLES

Still, many in the crowd put their faith in him. They said, "When the Christ comes, will he do more miraculous signs than this man?" (Jn. 7:31).

Is your religious mind broad enough to expect miracles? One of the great tragedies of modern Christendom is that it has become so ordinary that it is no longer expected that miraculous events will occur. People attempt to explain everything in terms of logic, and we deny the reality and efficacy of a childlike faith.

Miracles happen every day – it's just that many people prefer to call it coincidence. Sick people recover as a result of faithful prayers; guidance is given in unexpected ways; a social miscreant is transformed into a law-abiding citizen through the acceptance of spiritual powers that he cannot fully explain; great distress is relieved in miraculous ways. Many people witness God's work in the lives of human beings. This truth is so genuine that only those who refuse to acknowledge and praise God for his goodness fail to see these miracles.

Jesus Christ is still an essential force in this world. Even though there are those who wish to relegate Him to only the spiritual and religious life, He is still the Lord of all life. He manifests his full glory in every sphere of human thought and action. Those who acknowledge his reign and who place their trust in Him, experience the miracle of the workings of the Holy Spirit of God in their lives. In doing so, you too will discover that the time of miracles is definitely not past.

Holy Father in heaven, because You bestowed your Holy Spirit upon me, I daily see all the miracles that You perform in your omnipotence.

But for a miracle, I would not have been a Christian.
~ Augustine of Hippo ~

Who controls your life?

You, however, are controlled not by the sinful nature but by the Spirit, if the Spirit of God lives in you (Rom. 8:9).

Are you in control of your own life, or are you controlled by changing circumstances, variable moods and other forces beyond your comprehension or control? It may be possible that you say and do things that are not true to your nature. Paul says: *... When I want to do good, evil is right there with me* (Rom. 7:21). This is a very common human experience. You therefore need an external force that is larger than yourself to control you when you cannot control yourself.

The nature and temperament that you have inherited is often a slave to destructive habits, and when you are constrained by such bonds, your whole spirit is in slavery. Even though your spirit tries to assert itself, it finds that it cannot enjoy the freedom which it intuitively knows to be its birthright. However, here is a wonderful truth of Christian principles and experience: *... (W)here the spirit of the Lord is, there is freedom* (2 Cor. 3:17).

When the Holy Spirit of God takes possession of your life and expresses Himself through your spirit, you will discover that your life gains new meaning and significance and is filled with spiritual strength that enables you to grow to maturity in Him.

Thank You, Lord Jesus, my Redeemer and Saviour, that when your Holy Spirit fills my life I am governed and guided by Him.

When you must make a choice and don't, this in itself becomes a choice.

~ William James ~

Faith is Productive

... "According to your faith will it be done to you" (Mt. 9:29).

There are people who manage their faith as if it were a commercial product; something of which they either have a lot or have little, depending on the circumstances of the moment. In times of stress and tension they yearn for more faith, but don't quite know where they can acquire this miraculous force.

However, the fact is that you *have* faith and that your need is not for more faith, but for a change in the quality of the faith that you already have. Perhaps you have had faith in the wrong things for too long a time. Perhaps you have had more faith in failure than in success; you long for inner victory but are convinced that you will fail. Your actual faith isn't really a religious question; it is what, from habit, you expect life will give you. This daily expectation, which is merely another facet of faith, is what really becomes evident in your practical life.

You will agree that it is important to maintain an attitude of expectation in life: to expect only the finest and the noblest in the secure knowledge that what you expect will be realised in good time.

How is it possible to expect the best when standards are dropping so quickly and the outlook seems so grim? Only the person who has faith in God and his plan for the final redemption of the human race can step into the future with courage and tranquillity of spirit. This enormous truth brings a reassuring purpose in your life and enables you to go towards the future with confidence.

With steadfast faith in You, my God and Father, I step into the future with confidence and peace of mind.

Knowledge is a truth that is maintained in the mind; faith is a fire that burns in the heart.

~ Joseph F. Newton ~

*W*ORK WITH GOD

But as for me, it is good to be near God ... (Ps. 73:28).

*E*very one of us desires what is best for us. We feel that we have a vested right to receive that which belongs to us. Unfortunately so many of us have never tried to define exactly what it is that we regard as our "right", and as a result we are often unhappy and complaining throughout our pilgrimage through life.

This inner desire that seems to be so unattainable, and the awareness that there is something that we seek but cannot define, unconsciously make us lower our expectations of life, especially regarding that which is our "right". "I have the right to happiness," and "I have the right to financial independence" are but two of the rights claimed.

Often these demands are made without stopping to think about how they may be achieved through personal involvement. Many people demand happiness, without giving it; others demand financial independence without being careful in their financial transactions. In the fulfilment of our expectations and demands God surely has the right to our co-operation as well as our prayers.

Our text for today contains an amazing and practical truth. When God occupies the first place in our lives and his laws govern our daily lives, the demands of our lives become of secondary importance. Then it is no longer a question of what you demand from life, but rather what you can contribute to the fulfilment of his holy will in your life. Then you will experience a life of profound joy and true satisfaction.

While I seek your gifts with a yearning heart, o Father, I offer You my humble and willing co-operation in the fulfilment thereof.

In this world those things that grow naturally to exist for a long time are the slowest to reach maturity.

~ Vincent de Paul ~

ARE YOU THE JUDGE?

"Do not judge, or you too will be judged" (Mt. 7:1).

Most of us tend to jump to hasty conclusions and consequently also often judge other people. A simple comment may be misunderstood, or someone's behaviour may be interpreted inaccurately. You may try to avoid an unkempt person because you think that he is a drunkard who is just begging again. A snippet of news that is recounted incorrectly grows as it spreads and soon the issue or person concerned is discredited. It just goes to show how easily human nature tends towards the condemnation of others.

In some cases it is sensible and necessary to judge others. However, it is of crucial importance that you do so very carefully. You must investigate the surrounding factors in every situation and judge fairly and impartially.

In all likelihood you will find that things are not always what they seem, and that the person who is being condemned is not always entirely to blame for his faults and errors, or that he is not the person you imagined him to be. There may be a completely natural explanation for his behaviour or actions, which calls for your understanding and love.

In all your interactions with other people you should look for positive and commendable aspects and try to place yourself in their position. Try to act towards them as Jesus would have done. Then you will undoubtedly not judge someone wrongly.

Loving Lord Jesus, help me always to look at my fellow human beings through your eyes and with your love.

It is much easier to be critical than to be right.
~ Benjamin Disraeli ~

Service yields fulfilment

... Today, if you hear his voice, do not harden your hearts ... (Ps. 95:7-8).

There are many people in our world who are dissatisfied with their lot. Some feel that life is merely monotonous existence; others complain that they achieve nothing in life; yet others are so busy finding fault with everything that they fail to see the good things in life; and then there are those who are only interested in themselves, and consequently become lonely.

The one sure path to fulfilment is to serve God among his people. There are people who need a helping hand, who seek companionship, or a friendly word of advice. There are others who yearn for encouragement or recognition. A few moments of your time can make an immense difference in their lives. Opportunities to serve God in this way come along all the time. All you need to do is open your heart to God and remain sensitive to the voice of his Holy Spirit. He will touch your conscience and guide you towards those in distress.

When this happens you should not hesitate. People often refrain from acting because they fear that they are incapable, or that their helpfulness will be misinterpreted. If you are willing to allow the living Christ to use you, you can also be sure that He will lead you to those He wishes you to serve lovingly. In addition, the Holy Spirit will put the words in your mouth and grant you the capabilities to perform your task. In this way your life will become dynamic and meaningful.

Fill me with your abundance, o Holy Spirit of God, until my heart overflows and streams towards those who need my ministry. Lord Jesus, keep your love burning in my heart, because without it I cannot do your work.

In Jesus Christ service to God and service to the smallest of his children is one and the same thing.

~ Dietrich Bonhoeffer ~

CHRIST LIVES TODAY

"He is not here; he has risen ... " (Lk. 24:6).

Here we find a dynamic truth that imbues the Christian faith with strength and life. A gospel without the resurrection of Christ may be a beautiful philosophy, but it will lack the essential ingredient that elevates Christianity from a religious philosophy to the positive experience of a living faith.

When Jesus walked the earth with his disciples in the glory of his resurrection, it was not a passing mystical experience only granted to a privileged few. He promised to be with his disciples in every generation. The Spirit of Christ is just as alive and present in your life today as in the lives of the first disciples. He is the timeless Christ.

The first disciples had the privilege of knowing Him in his physical presence. Modern disciples do not have this privilege, but He becomes a living reality to those who discipline themselves and wait patiently and in silence, with their thoughts focused on his presence. This experience of knowing the living Christ is more than a psychological or emotional response to an intense, religious longing, although both these dispositions may be present. To believe that you are in the company of Christ fills you with a presence and a strength that is real and pertinent to your life.

If you live in the awareness of Christ's presence, you become increasingly sure that life is not a drab and lonely pilgrimage, but an exciting and satisfying adventure that you share with your living Master.

I thank You, risen and glorified Lord Jesus, that I may experience your living presence and share my life with You. It provides me with courage and strength for every day.

Jesus Christ changed all our sunsets into daybreaks.
~ Clement of Alexandria ~

Don't be partial

"Do not show partiality in judging; hear both small and great alike ... " (Deut. 1:17).

*I*n your public or business life, is your judgement influenced by social status? Are you more interested in people who occupy positions of authority than in those who are typified as "ordinary people"? When you are confronted with the opinion of an important public figure as opposed to the opinion of a relatively unknown person, whose interpretation are you more likely to accept?

These questions speak to the conscience of every honest and sincere person, because there are few people who can say in all honesty that they are not in the least influenced by the opinions of important people. The opinions of a prominent businessman are newsworthy while the opinions of ordinary folk are completely ignored.

By getting caught in this trap you deprive yourself of learning the full truth. You owe it to your fellow human beings and to yourself to consider all viewpoints and to give equal attention to both sides. Otherwise you will not be able to make a well-balanced judgement.

Jesus Christ gave no exclusive preference to anyone and He had time for people from all walks of life. No one is greater than the all-seeing, all-knowing God in Jesus Christ. If the Master could do it, how much more do we owe it to each other not to be partial?

Help me, impartial Lord Jesus, to keep an open mind and to listen to all people, regardless of their social status or wealth.

It is only through the mystery of self-sacrifice that one can find oneself anew.

~ Carl Gustav Jung ~

God is immutable

He set the earth on its foundations; it can never be moved (Ps. 104:5).

In every sphere of life it is essential that something will remain constant in order to ensure stability. This applies to the fields of mathematics and science, but also to your everyday life where you need a standard upon which to base your way of life. The lack of something constant will inevitably lead to confusion and chaos.

As far as the day-to-day life of mankind is concerned, the Lord Himself established something constant. Through the prophet Malachi He said: *"I the Lord do not change ... "* (Mal. 3:6).

People come and go; times change; fashions are in vogue one moment and passing fads the next; moral standards, behaviour and principles appear to vary from one generation to the next. As a result, there is a very real danger that you will become confused, and find it difficult to know how you should live your life and what exactly is expected of you.

Follow the way of the Master to overcome this problem and to free yourself from feelings of doubt and guilt. He set an example for your entire life and if you hold on to it, you can be assured of a life of peace and fulfilment.

Holy and almighty God, help me to build upon the Rock of ages, because all other soil is uncertain and nothing but sinking quicksand.

There are three things known only to God: the beginning of things, the cause of things and their outcome.

~ Welsh proverb ~

The Mighty Hand of God

For the wisdom of this world is foolishness in God's sight ... (1 Cor. 3:19).

Throughout the ages people have claimed the honour of making the greatest discovery of all times. Looking back we see the wheel, fire and the power of steam, followed by electricity, the telephone, radio and television. Great leaps of progress have been made in the spheres of science, mathematics, medicine, atomic and nuclear power, and now we live in the age of the computer.

While we should by no means disparage the wonders of these discoveries, it is essential not to overlook the omnipotence of God in this world of so-called human achievement.

It would be worthwhile to take a little time to quietly ponder how mankind would have fared without the assistance of the Lord. Just as He created people, He also provided them with knowledge and abilities. The expertise of scientists, engineers and doctors did not appear out of nothing, but is the result of God-given talent. In the same way the omnipotence of God can destroy anything which man undertakes (or abuses), if it is against his holy will.

Despite all the excitement over human achievement throughout the ages, we must never neglect to notice the mighty hand of God in all things.

Holy Father, throughout the ages your almighty hand protected and guided your flock. Thank You that we may experience your presence and omnipotence in everything.

There is nothing in the universe that God cannot do.
~ Marcus Tullius Cicero ~

Light from the Darkness

When all the people saw this, they fell prostrate and cried, "The Lord – he is God! The Lord – he is God!" (1 Kgs. 18:39).

Today, as in the days of Elijah, it takes an earth-shattering experience for some people to recognise the existence and omnipotence of God. People become used to a way of life that has little or no space for the Lord: they immerse themselves in their work or their chosen lifestyle.

Regardless of this, God moves in mysterious ways to manifest his wonders. These ways may be drastic. Therefore we should not judge the Lord with our senses, but trust Him for his mercy. Behind the severe ways in which He sometimes acts lies a heart full of unfathomable love.

Perhaps you have experienced adversity or tragedy, or maybe your burden seems unbearable and your problems irresolvable. At times like these, don't give in to the temptation of throwing in the towel, but turn to the living Christ in faith. He was a human being just like us. He knows all about your situation, understands your distress, and is waiting to come to your assistance.

To draw people to Him, Christ underwent the torment of crucifixion. As He did then, He who leads you out of distress still sometimes uses negative circumstances to draw you closer to his heart. Accept this assurance and live in peace under the certainty of his love.

Blind disbelief is doomed to destruction, o Father. Everything that it does is in vain. But You, wonderful God and loving Father, have a perfect plan with every life.

I saw that there was an ocean of darkness and death, but a boundless ocean of light and love washed over the ocean of darkness and death, and in it I saw the eternal love of God.

~ George Fox ~

Guard Against Subtle Temptations

"Be careful that no one entices you by riches; do not let a large bribe turn you aside" (Job 36:18).

The extremely dangerous consequences of compromising on your principles can never be overemphasised. Time and time again one hears of decent people who give in to temptation and as a result lower their moral standards. The consequences are usually disastrous, for themselves and for their families.

Initially the suggestion to compromise on your principles may appear quite innocent. You accept a small gift for an apparently insignificant favour; a suggestion that you bend the rules somewhat or turn a blind eye may be made in jest at a lunch or dinner to which you have been invited as guest.

When the suggestion that you deviate from the right course is made or even just insinuated, you should be on your guard. What starts as a trifle may soon start growing covertly, and before you know it, it will have become uncontrollable and you will find yourself in a trap from which you will struggle to escape.

Jesus made it clear and distinct that He will tolerate no compromise. He set the example for a good and virtuous Christian way of life. Follow in his footsteps and resist everything that is contrary to his principles. Only then will you live in tranquillity and inner peace.

Holy Spirit of God, help me to stand firmly against the temptation to lower my Christian standards. Let me live according to the will of the Master.

Every moment of resistance against temptation is a victory.
~ Frederick W. Faber ~

DON'T PUT YOURSELF DOWN

No, in all these things we are more than conquerors through him who loved us (Rom. 8:37).

There are people who constantly degrade the gifts that God has given them, so that these gifts eventually become useless. Others bemoan the fact that they are so ordinary that they have no gifts at all. Both these attitudes cause God great sorrow.

God has given each person at least one gift. It may initially be barely noticeable, but it is there and waits to be discovered and developed. You have the responsibility to first discover that gift which God has given you, and then to develop it to its fullest potential.

Initially you will experience problems and you will find numerous excuses why these gifts cannot be utilised: you are too busy, there is no time, you are under too much work pressure. But the main reason may not be immediately apparent to you. The truth of the matter is that you are scared of starting to work on God's gifts, in case you fail and cannot complete your task. Someone whispers in your ear that you are not up to the challenge, and you accept this lie at face value, without even attempting to prove it wrong.

God would never give you a gift that you cannot bring to fulfilment through effort and dedication. At first it may seem to be beyond your natural abilities, but God grants you the grace and the strength to become spiritually strong, and to develop and fully unfold the gift that He has given you.

Thank You, Lord my God, that You foresee everything I need to develop the gifts that You have given me to their fullest potential.

If you want to be respected by others, it is important to respect yourself.

~ Feodor Dostoyevsky ~

God is in Control

Then Job replied to the Lord: "I know that you can do all things; no plan of yours can be thwarted" (Job 42:1).

In every sphere of society and in every successive generation you will meet hardened pessimists who find little or nothing that is right with this world. They see no hope for the future and wherever they go they create an atmosphere of gloom and dejection. This attitude finds precipitation in their personal life and as a result they become mean-spirited and negative.

In the midst of this atmosphere of despair it is beneficial to take a few minutes to ponder the greatness of God. Look back over the years and you will find example upon example of the wonderful ways in which God has transformed despair into vivacious hope; changed sorrow into joy; allowed victory to grow from defeat.

Of all these examples the one that towers above all the others is the way in which God used the horror of Jesus' crucifixion to manifest the wonder of his forgiving love in the glory of the resurrection. To those of little faith Golgotha was the end of a sorrowful road, but Easter Sunday ushered in the beginning of a wonderful new life: God's plan for the redemption of mankind had been completed.

When things around you appear dark and terrifying, hold on to the promises of God. Remember the mighty deeds that He has performed, and continue in confidence and with the certain knowledge that He is wholly in control.

Almighty God and loving Father, my heart's knowledge that You are in control allows me to be courageous even in dark days. Guide me on your path and keep my faith strong.

We are the conductors, God is the electrical current. Our only existence is by letting the current flow through us.

~ Carlo Caretto ~

Unite behind Jesus

Is Christ divided? ... (1 Cor. 1:13).

In an era in which the church of Christ is under constant threat, there are two main problems within the Christian community: indifference and dissension. The evil one undermines the principles of Christ in many ways, as is evident from the manifold instances of dissipation, immorality, drug addiction and violence in our society. At a time when Christians ought to be united against such evils, there are indications of poorer church attendance, to such an extent that some churches have to be closed down. Doctrinal and denominational differences are driven to extremes, to the detriment of the united voice of the churches.

The church has been under fire throughout the ages and will be for as long as Satan attempts to destroy the living Christ's work of redemption. Time and time again he has made vicious attacks on the church averted only by a small but valiant band of Christians.

Until Satan is finally destroyed, as prophesied by Scripture, you can be assured that he will not abandon his attempts. Therefore it is imperative that those who call themselves Christians will stand united against him. Instead of fighting each other, we should fight him.

It is the duty and privilege of everyone who bears the Master's Name and who is fortified by the strength of the Holy Spirit to be diligent in their worship, to set aside all their differences, and to stand united against anything that is intended to disparage the glory of the triune God.

Lord, grant that your followers on earth will stand united in our attack on the evil forces that threaten us. Help us not to allow insignificant differences to divide us, thus allowing the evil one to reign supreme.

Fortunate are those who know that discipleship is simply a life that flows from grace ... And this grace simply means discipleship.
~ Dietrich Bonhoeffer ~

*H*ANDLE YOUR PROBLEMS IN THE STRENGTH OF CHRIST

My flesh and my heart may fail, but God is the strength of my heart and my portion forever (Ps. 73:26).

*T*here are a variety of factors that may cause you to feel despondent, weak and helpless. These factors cover a wide spectrum of issues, but their effect on your mental, spiritual and physical wellbeing can be very destructive, should you allow circumstances to overwhelm you.

There is no getting away from the fact that Christians must endure problems and setbacks. Indeed, Christ warned us of this, and most of his followers were severely tried when their faith was put to the test.

The joyful assurance that you receive from Christ is that He will never abandon or forsake you. In addition, He will provide you with the ability to successfully cope with your circumstances through his strength and faith.

To some people this may sound like an unattainable and idealistic dream, but you can transform it into a glorious reality. You have the assurance that the heavenly Guide will always be with you. All that is expected of you is to accept his word in faith, and to remain in his company. Lay your fears, worries and hopes before Him. Do this, and you will experience the peace that passes all understanding.

Holy Lord Jesus, my ability to handle my problems emanates solely from my unconditional faith in you.

Through perseverance the snail reached Noah's ark.
                    ~ Charles H. Spurgeon ~

ARE YOU EASILY HURT?

"Remain in me, and I will remain in you ... " (Jn. 15:4).

Perhaps you are one of those people who go through life being continually hurt by other people. You may have become so sensitive about what others think and say that your entire life has declined into a wretched existence. If you allow this state of affairs to continue, it may have serious consequences for your whole personality. The challenge lies in the fact that you are responsible for deciding whether this situation will continue or not.

God left you with the responsibility of choice. You choose your thoughts and attitudes. You decide whether you are going to live on the pinnacle of true life or in the valley of despair. It may be that you mistakenly think that these circumstances are created by matters beyond your control. However, in reality it is the power of your thoughts that make you the person you are.

This thought could seem overwhelming if it weren't coloured by the realisation of a Higher Power. As our thoughts control our deeds, so is it possible for the Holy Spirit to control our thoughts. If you allow the Spirit of Christ into every aspect of your life, He takes control of your thoughts, and you discover that the petty injuries and possible insults that have been thrown at you no longer have the power to hurt you. The strength of the Holy Spirit in you is more powerful than any torment or insult hurled at you.

Thank You, Lord Jesus, that You live in me through your Spirit, and that You give me the strength to stand steadfastly against the small-minded insults that I have to endure. Help me always to stay in You.

What other people think of me becomes increasingly unimportant to me; what they think of Jesus as a result of my life becomes increasingly important.

~ Cliff Richard ~

Is sanctification your goal?

... "I am God Almighty; walk before me and be blameless" (Gen. 17:1).

Throughout the world the focus is on excellence and perfection. In the arts, science and business everyone aspires to ways of perfecting methods and machinery in the name of progress. In many cases perfection in terms of material things has become such an obsession with human beings that they have allowed moral and spiritual standards to decline or to be abandoned altogether.

The beauty of God's creation is ravaged by pollution and waste materials while human machinery just keeps rolling on. Deadly weapons are manufactured because one nation wants to rule over another. Personal and ethical values have taken the back seat to monetary profit. This is the price exacted by progress.

There is only one kind of perfect life that is worth living, and this is the life that Christ sets out for us. Nothing else can give you true fulfilment and satisfaction, because life in Christ is eternal and constant.

Whatever your task, if you aspire to true excellence and perfection, you have to ensure that God is your guide in all your endeavours. Dedicate everything you do to Him; remain within his will; maintain the standards that Christ has set. If this is your goal, you will achieve a degree of excellence that nothing and no-one else can offer you.

Lord God, You who are consummately perfect and who want your children also to achieve perfection, grant that I will never relinquish the ideal of perfection, because your Holy Spirit works in me constantly.

We have to be holy in the way that God wants us to be holy. God does not expect you to be a Trappist monk or a hermit. He asks you to sanctify your work and your everyday life.

~ Vincent Palotti ~

Live in fellowship with Christ

God, who has called you into fellowship with his Son Jesus Christ our Lord, is faithful (1 Cor. 1:9).

God has given you a wonderful privilege. He has called you to share in the life of Jesus Christ. When the full meaning of this divine gift dawns on you, the implications are almost too great to envision.

To share in the life of Jesus Christ implies unlimited possibilities, but also great responsibilities. Connected to so much omnipotence and wisdom, your understanding of God is deepened, your vision of what your life can be is expanded and you become aware of the enduring presence of Christ. But such intimacy with the Master creates certain responsibilities. The quality of your life has to be in accordance with the expression of your faith. The characteristics of God must be reflected in your life through love, complete honesty, unselfishness and purity of purpose.

To express the Spirit of Christ to the best of your ability you should develop a vision of what you can achieve for the Master. You are no longer restricted by secret fears and uncertainties, but can move confidently forward in the empowering strength of the living Christ.

Christ offers Himself to you so that you may share in his life and share your life with Him. But this offer only becomes a reality when you accept it in faith. You may have the knowledge of this glorious truth, but until you have made it your own you will not experience the strength and joy of the presence of Jesus Christ in your life.

Lord Jesus, I invite you anew to come into my life and to do your work on earth through me. I now open my heart and life to You.

Should you be arrested for being a Christian, would there be enough proof to convict you?

~ David Otis Fuller ~

*T*HERE IS A LESSON TO BE LEARNT IN EVERYTHING

It was good for me to be afflicted so that I may learn your decrees (Ps. 119:71).

*D*espite all your positive thinking and creative prayers things still happen to you that you would rather have avoided. Consequently, you start wondering where you failed, what you did to land yourself in such a situation.

This can be a time of futile self-accusation in your life, and you may covertly feel either that God disappointed you, or that your faith wasn't strong enough. The psalmist has a unique way of looking at his tribulations. He believes that God wishes to teach him lessons through these hardships and that God has a message for him in every situation. As a result he uses his time to search for the lesson rather than pitying himself or complaining about the circumstances through which God wants to teach him the lesson.

Of course, when tribulation strikes in your life you should do everything in your power to remedy it, and not simply foolishly and passively regard it as the will of God. This is the difference between calamity and blessing. It is often in moments of tribulation, when negative forces threaten to overwhelm you that you discover a new facet in the loving character of God. You learn that a short spell spent in the valley of despair can enrich your life in a wonderful way through positive and constructive thoughts and meaningful conversation with God.

Master and Guide, thank You for the lessons that I too have learnt in tribulation. Sustain me through every situation in life, be it prosperity or adversity, and let me embrace the lessons that You wish to teach me.

The strangest truth of the gospel is that salvation is brought about through suffering.

~ Milo L. Chapman ~

What words can do

Nor should there be obscenity, foolish talk or coarse joking, which are out of place, but rather thanksgiving (Eph. 5:4).

The language you use reflects the quality of your spirit and is the measure according to which others evaluate you. If your words fortify and inspire others, you will always have friends. People will enjoy your company because of the blessing that they receive from your words.

Never underestimate the power of the spoken word. Not only does it manifest who you really are, but it also has an immense influence on others. If bitterness and hate dominate your words, or if you are driven by a compelling need to hurt and humiliate others, words become instruments which can inflict irreparable damage.

There are people who cannot speak their thoughts except in vulgar or blasphemous terms. God's Name is taken in vain. Such utterances not only indicate an impoverished mind, but also an immature spirit.

By using words in the right way you can help to heal injured hearts that have been battered by inconsiderate people. When communicating with others you should always choose your words carefully. Using the following miracle-working words every day can make a world of difference: "I love you and I appreciate you."

Set a guard over my mouth, O Lord; keep watch over the door of my lips (Ps. 141:3).

Our words are a reliable indication of the state of our souls.
~ Francis de Sales ~

*P*EACE IN THE MIDST OF CHAOS

But in keeping with his promise we are looking forward to a new heaven and a new earth, the home of righteousness (2 Pet. 3:13).

*I*n times of crisis there are people who tend to lose all courage and hope, and threaten to collapse in what they perceive to be a lost battle against insurmountable problems. This experience may take place in your personal life, or be prompted by the state of your country or the world. Its causes are numerous, but the results are always the same: the future always seems dark and even hopeless.

To everyone who believes in Him Jesus offers a life of abundance. This promise encompasses your situation here and now and until all eternity. Because He conquered sin and death, Christ has prepared a place for all the faithful in the eternal glory of the kingdom of God.

In your present life the Lord offers you his Holy Spirit if you surrender yourself to Him. It is his Spirit who gives you the ability to handle life's problems successfully in the certain knowledge that He will not forsake or abandon you. As Paul says: ... *If God is for us, who can be against us?* (Rom. 8:31).

Whatever your circumstances may be, remember that Jesus is constantly at your side to guide and help you. Place your trust in Him as He leads you, and remember that He is busy guiding you towards God's eternal kingdom where there is only harmony and peace.

Beloved Leader, I know that this life's struggles and problems will soon pass, and then I will enter into the eternal peace of your kingdom.

Where there is peace, there is God.
                    ~ George Herbert ~

*T*HE REWARD OF THE RIGHTEOUS

Do not fret because of evil men or be envious of those who do wrong
... Trust in the Lord and do good ... (Ps. 37:1, 3).

*M*any disillusioned people believe that it is not worthwhile to do
good. This may concern their own life or the lives of others, but they
can quote example after example to justify their standpoint: someone
who always managed his business honestly, a person of impeccable
integrity, who is now experiencing serious financial trouble, while others whose business methods are particularly dubious, are prospering;
the death of a loved and only child, while so many other children grow
up to be honourable citizens despite the carelessness of their parents.

Never lose sight of the fact that life does not begin and end with the
earthly existence that we are experiencing now. The tribulations and
suffering that you experience now, the way in which you conduct yourself, your attitude towards others – all these things prepare you for the
eternal life that still lies ahead.

Whatever happens here and now, always remember that the ultimate judge is the almighty God. Always aspire to satisfy Him and behave in ways that are agreeable to Him. Even though you will suffer for
a time, you can be sure that God will reward you for the way in which
you lived here on earth and the way in which you reflected Jesus in
your everyday life.

Lord and Master, I will hold on to the guidelines and standards that
you have set for my life, so that I will please You in all things.

The ability to choose between right and wrong is within the reach of
us all.

~ Origen of Alexandria ~

*T*HE POWER OF THE SPOKEN WORD

A word aptly spoken is like apples of gold in settings of silver (Prov. 25:11).

A single word can make a vast difference to a person's life, and it is therefore of the utmost importance how it is said. Some people have a gift for words. By saying the right word at the right time they can radically change someone else's life by filling them with a sense of pleasantness and well-being. However, it is equally true that an inappropriate word at an inopportune moment can have a destructive effect on a person's life.

There are times in people's lives when they yearn for a sympathetic or encouraging word, when the display of loving interest and compassion can make an immense difference and brighten their dismal day. A word of appreciation or advice is never wasted; even constructive criticism or a loving reprimand can be beneficial to the recipient.

It is important that you will never be afraid to speak, but at the same time you must, through the strength of the Holy Spirit, choose your words and your timing very carefully. Be sensitive to the mood of the person you are talking to, guard against unnecessary flattery but also against crassness, be sincere in what you say and say it with the love of Jesus in your heart. In so doing you will infinitely enrich not only the person you are talking to, but also yourself.

May the words of my mouth and the meditation of my heart be pleasing in your sight, O Lord, my Rock and my Redeemer (Ps. 19:14).

Small keys can unlock great locks. Simple words can reflect great thoughts.

~ William A. Ward ~

Do you sometimes feel unsafe?

Surely God is my salvation; I will trust and not be afraid. The Lord, the Lord is my strength and my song; he has become my salvation (Is. 12:2).

We are all under some kind of pressure. The state of the world has penetrated all of our homes and has created a fear of the future. It seems as if the world is heading for disaster, which nothing and no one can prevent. This external pressure causes internal tensions, and feelings of fear and insecurity become an integral part of countless people's lives.

God's omnipotence and redemptive power are much more than mere religious clichés. It is an experience that may be enjoyed by all who place their faith and trust in the living Christ and entrust their lives unconditionally to his care. To do this is not an act of self-denial or an unwelcome discipline that adds to the burdens of your life, but a voluntary act that gives you confidence and assuages fear.

If your faith is focused on Christ and you are guided by his principles, you not only conquer all destructive fears, but you also become aware that He equips you with spiritual power and strength. It is unnecessary to feel weak and insecure if you know that He loves you and promises you his assistance. Always remember the promise of the Scriptures: *The eternal God is your refuge, and underneath are the everlasting arms ...* (Deut. 33:27). Hold on to this promise: God will never disappoint you.

I place my trust in You completely, holy Father, and it fills me with confidence, which banishes all uncertainty and fear.

There is a natural, elemental home instinct in our soul, which makes us turn instinctively towards God as a flower turns towards the sun.
~ Rufus M. Jones ~

WHEN YOUR CONSCIENCE SPEAKS

... "I heard you in the garden, and I was afraid because I was naked; so I hid" (Gen. 3:10).

There are times in our lives when we are bowed down under the burden of guilt, and many of us find it exceedingly difficult to reconcile with our consciences. The causes of this are too numerous and varied to mention. The most common are those deeds containing half-truths, deception, jealousy and falsehoods, to name but a few. Some of these are very insignificant and yet the human conscience will remind the wrongdoer in no uncertain terms of his transgression.

Because it is connected to feelings of guilt and shame, many people will try to conceal their mistakes by instinctively turning their backs on them and trying to shut them out of their thoughts. Others try to justify their behaviour. They think that this will help to calm the storm that is so often the result of wrongdoing.

One thing is absolutely certain: however hard you try, you cannot hide your transgressions from God. Regardless of the steps you take to conceal the offence that shames you, you can be sure that the blinding light of Jesus Christ will uncover it before your all-knowing Father.

Never try to hide from God. Be assured of his love and confess that which you are ashamed of or fear in prayer before Him. Gratefully receive his forgiveness and the peace that goes hand in hand with true contrition.

Lord Jesus, through experience I am assured of your love and forgiveness, and therefore I expose my soul before You time and again. Thank You for your forgiveness and love.

A conscience that is eased by the presence of Jesus Christ in the heart should be the guide of every person.

~ Robert H. Benson ~

Life Partners

"I no longer call you servants, because a servant does not know his master's business. Instead, I have called you friends, for everything that I learned from my Father I have made known to you" (Jn. 15:15).

It is only when you have earnestly requested the risen Chrits to become your life partner that you realise the full impact and implications of your Christian faith. A partnership implies the shared responsibility to achieve a common goal. When Christ is in control, your life undergoes change and transformation as a result of the partnership in which you now find yourself.

The purpose of the ministry of Christ is to unify you with the Father. He asks your co-operation to achieve this, by acknowledging his sovereignty and his redemptive power in your life. If you do, you will experience a growing awareness of his presence in your daily life, because you are following the path that Christ has mapped out for you.

Such a wonderful partnership, which is connected to such a magnificent goal, may sound idealistic and impractical, but it is the pinnacle of wisdom. To live your life in partnership with God and with a focus on spiritual matters, brings an exceptional balance to your life.

With Christ managing and controlling your life, you possess a code of conduct inspired by the Holy Spirit. You will not be a sleeping partner, but will be eager to manifest the partnership in your life at all times. It is your essential part in this wonderful partnership.

My Lord and Master, in partnership with You I will live and work in victory. I thank You for your love and grace.

The Christian has a union with Jesus Christ that is nobler, more intimate and more perfect than the union between the limbs of the human body and the head.

~ John Eudes ~

---

*T*HE PRICE OF DISCIPLESHIP

... "If anyone would come after me, he must deny himself and take up his cross daily and follow me ... " (Lk. 9:23).

---

*P*rompted by today's verse from Scripture, let us use this day for introspection through contemplation and prayer. Let us do so with Christ's sacrifice and love in mind. "Self-denial" is not a word that falls easily on the ears of sinners. Hearing about "taking up the cross" is definitely not music to our ears. But we are called to do so because Jesus has made the incomparable sacrifice for the sake of redeeming us.

Jesus sacrificed his life for us on the cross. His offering was complete and total, because He gave his everything for mankind. While you continue your pilgrimage through life, you should recall and commemorate his sacrifice. Think of his unfathomable love that urged Him to this sacrifice. Then you will realise that you and all of humanity owe the Redeemer infinitely more than we could ever give.

Only complete and unreserved surrender to Jesus Christ can, in a minor way, be compared to his sacrifice. This will call and urge us to a life of relinquishment, cross-bearing and self-denial for every one who calls himself a Christian. If we bear our cross with joy, we will discover that we carry the instrument of our own redemption. And then every act of cross-bearing and self-denial becomes worthwhile over and over again.

Lord Jesus, when I fix my eyes on the cross I realise that my life is still filled with pride and self-interest. I know that nothing could possibly compare to your sacrifice for me, but help me to dedicate myself to You – body, soul and spirit – in answer to your wonderful love.

The world around us will recognise us as Jesus' disciples when they see that our prayers are answered.

~ Colin Urquhart ~

March

It's autumn, Lord and God of creation,

    autumn with its mellowness and abundance of opulent colour.

Thank You for spiritual growth and maturation;

    thank You that it ends in the tranquillity and fulfilment of autumn.

This is also the time of year when we follow You,

    the Man of Sorrows,

    in the spirit on your way of suffering.

You endured suffering for the sake of the world, yes, but also for me.

All your suffering and indignity, all your sorrow and pain;

    every word spoken on the cross – even those of God-forsakenness –

    was on my behalf.

Lord Jesus, You gave your life for me

    even though I am not worthy of the sacrifice.

In profound gratitude I dedicate myself anew to You:

    body, soul and spirit.

Guide me through this month, make me your faithful disciple

    and a fearless witness of your love,

Through the cross, let me realise the wretchedness of sin,

    so that I will flee from it to your grace.

Through the cross, let me see your love

    so that I may take refuge in You.

For your love's sake.

Amen.

The purpose of Christ's mission

... God ... gave us the ministry of reconciliation: that God was reconciling the world to himself in Christ, not counting men's sins against them ... (2 Cor. 5:18-19).

The great separation between God and man took place when man in disobedience declared himself to be independent of God. He thought that through this he would be liberated, but in reality he became the slave of influences stronger than himself. The own I replaced God; love turned into sensuality and self-satisfaction. Man's one-sided declaration of independence from God was disastrous, because subsequent events proved that man cannot control the world in his own wisdom and strength.

Even though man turned away from God, God did not turn away from man. He descended to the level of mankind and was personified in the life and work of Jesus Christ. The purpose of Christ's coming was to bridge the gaping chasm that separated man from God.

Through Christ's worldly ministry God revealed to us what we may become through his strength. We can be liberated from sin, share in the enriching experience of his Spirit living in us, and experience an ever-increasing communion with Him. According to the New Testament it is God's earnest desire to rehabilitate those separated from Him.

God has not changed. His love is eternal and those who accept Christ and his standards find that their relationship with God is fully repaired.

I kneel in gratitude and wonder before your love, o God, because You reconciled us with You through Jesus Christ.

Jesus Christ was the first and greatest missionary of all time.
~ Henry Martyn ~

Rejoice in the Lord!

Then the people of Israel – the priests, the Levites and the rest of the exiles – celebrated the dedication of the house of God with joy (Ezra 6:16).

Unfortunately, there are many people in the world who associate worship with despondency, cheerlessness and even fear. Their attendance of church services is little more than a duty done merely for habit's sake. It is expected of them and they believe that they will be punished if they neglect doing it. The tragedy of an attitude like this is that it deprives people of the greatest of all joys: joy in the Lord.

Through Christ God invites you to find repose in Him and to receive the fullness of life that He offers you. If you turn to Him you become increasingly aware of his life-giving Spirit that works in you. Seemingly unattainable goals are suddenly within your reach; adversity does not overwhelm you because in Him you find the strength to overcome it; a newly found confidence replaces your nervous pessimism and feelings of failure. Day by day your faith grows stronger.

As you open yourself to the Holy Spirit, you will find that your worship, Bible study and prayer life gain new meaning. If you place your trust in the living Christ, you will discover that God is no longer a faraway figure, but an integral part of your life. He will lead you on the path that He has mapped out for you.

Worship ought to be a joyful experience. Open yourself to the Holy Spirit, and He will raise you from despondency to ecstasy in Christ.

O Holy Spirit, come into my life and fill me with the joy of the Lord.

Glorify Jesus Christ! Come, let us bring to Him the great, universal offering of our love and offer Him our most uplifting hymns and prayers. For He has offered Himself to God on the cross as a sacrifice to uplift us all.

~ Efrem of Jerusalem ~

When Jesus comes into your life

"Blessed is the king who comes in the name of the Lord! Peace in heaven and glory in the highest!" (Lk. 19:38).

When we read the account of Jesus' triumphant journey into Jerusalem, we cannot fail sensing the joy and excitement of those who offered Him such a sincere welcome. He was the long-awaited Messiah who would usher in an era of peace, joy, hope and liberation: *"Blessed is the king who comes in the name of the Lord!"*

Throughout the ages this same feeling of wonderment, awe and joy has been experienced by people who welcomed Christ into their lives. Jesus said that He came so that you may experience the fullness of life (see Jn. 10:10). This means that you can live in peace and calm in the certain knowledge that He is with you at all times.

Just as the people of Jerusalem were a captive nation under the hated yoke of the Roman oppressors, so today many people are enslaved by habits that are extremely detrimental to their well-being. The living Christ offers to liberate you from these habits. Similarly, there are many people seeking love, grace and compassion in a world that can be very cruel at times. This is exactly what Jesus still offers today to those who accept Him as their Redeemer and Saviour.

Welcome the Master into your life with the same joy as the people of Jerusalem did and experience the joy that Christ brings.

Redeemer and Friend, in love and compassion You came to claim my heart and soul. I sing a hymn of praise to your glory, because by your grace you raise me from sin and shame, so that I may be your joyful child.

Joyfulness is the unmistakable sign of the presence of God in our lives.
~ Leon Bloy ~

*P*ersevere in prayer

After he had dismissed them, he went up on a mountainside by him-self to pray. When evening came he was there alone (Mt. 14:23).

---

*T*o our Lord and Master prayer was an essential discipline. When He was at the peak of his popularity thousands followed Him to hear Him preach and to learn from Him. But even when He was denied by all his friends and had to endure the humiliation of seeming defeat, He found his strength and inspiration in prayer.

Unfortunately many of his modern disciples only pray when they feel like it, and they forget that prayer does not depend on your emotional state. If you only pray when you feel like it, the time will finally come when you will not pray at all.

At times all Christians experience spiritual drought, when it seems as if God is distant and remote. Consequently, their love for Him cools and their spiritual life loses its lustre. During these times it is difficult to pray, but it is precisely then when prayer is crucial. Even though it might seem as if the heavens are insulated with copper, continue pray-ing, because it is your only channel to God. Job says: *"Though he slay me, yet will I hope in him; I will surely defend my ways to his face"* (Job 13:15). This is what ultimately impelled Job from his sorrow, and guided him to a renewed awareness that God's blessing rested upon him.

Discipline yourself in prayer so that you may triumph over your prayerless times, and so experience the supportive love and strength of the Master in your darkest and most vulnerable hour.

I thank and praise You, Lord my God, that I may experience the sup-portive power of prayer in my darkest hour.

Prayer is the most important thing in my life. Should I neglect to pray for a single day, I would lose a great deal of the fervour of my faith.
~ Martin Luther ~

---

*K*EEP YOUR COMMUNICATION CHANNELS OPEN

And do not forget to do good and to share with others, for with such sacrifices God is pleased (Heb. 13:16).

*T*he cause of the disintegration of many of our relationships is a lack of communication. So many of our relationships lapse into a monotonous rut, and the difference between a rut and a grave is merely a question of depth. We owe it to our fellow human beings to give something of ourselves in every relationship that we become involved in. It is essential that we should take stock of the quality of all our relationships.

In our spiritual life the disintegration of creative communication with the Master is a sure way of detaching ourselves from Him. When prayer becomes the repetition of meaningless phrases piously spoken, true communication dies. Then prayer becomes words without content, and communion with Christ is no longer an enriching experience.

Meaningful communication does not happen easily or as a matter of course. It has to be cherished and developed. The husband has to share his experiences with his wife, because by talking to each other our love and understanding are strengthened.

In prayer and communication with the Master, in our service to our neighbour, in the good deeds that we do in his Name, we are making sacrifices that please God. Talk to your Redeemer as you would to a friend; tell Him of your hopes and fears; tell Him that you love Him. This will keep your communication with others alive and strong.

O Holy Spirit, prevent my communication with God and with others from becoming meaningless. Make the communication of my prayers meaningful, so that my human relationships can also be healthy.

Communication is something so simple and yet so complicated that we can never explain it in words.

~ T. S. Matthews ~

A LESSON IN HUMILITY

While he was in Bethany, reclining at the table in the home of a man known as Simon the Leper ... (Mk. 14:3).

According to the Gospels Jesus was, at this point, on his way to Golgotha, to glory. He was thoroughly aware of everything awaiting Him in the fulfilment of his divine mission. He knew that soon after He would rise from the dead exalted, having conquered the evil one for all time. He would have finally affirmed that He is the Son of God, the Redeemer of the world.

The average person's response to such a situation would in all likelihood have been to revel in all this glory and comfort in the company of those sharing in this glory. But with Jesus it was different. He sought the peace and quiet of a house where He knew that He would be left alone; a house that most people hesitated to enter and that was avoided by the community: the house of Simon the Leper.

If there is any one incident that manifests the humility of Jesus, surely it is this one: the Son of God, on the threshold of exaltation, turns away from the brilliance of popularity to seek out the hospitality and fellowship of a family cast out by society.

This is a quality of sincere humility that is profoudly touching. It is not weak or servile. It is brave and strong without being oppressive or arrogant. It is a characteristic that every Christian should develop through the grace of God.

Lord Jesus, deeply aware of who I am and where I come from, I pray that You will keep me truly humble after your own holy example.

Pride is a cold mountain peak, sterile and bleak; humility is the tranquil valley, fruitful and with an abundance of life, and peace dwells there.

~ Anne Austen ~

YOU ARE A CHILD OF ROYAL BLOOD

You are all sons of God through faith in Christ Jesus, for all of you who were baptized into Christ have clothed yourself with Christ (Gal. 3:26).

You should never feel spiritually inferior. Perhaps you see how others are asked to be involved in congregational activities while you are passed over. It seems as if your friends are bubbling over with the joy of Christ, while your journey with Christ seems drab and uneventful. In prayer and study groups other people speak and pray, but you keep quiet. Others' knowledge of the Bible is so much more comprehensive than yours that it leaves you feeling guilty and inadequate.

You must always remember that when God accepted you as his child He did not do so on the basis of your knowledge, work or worthiness. It depended solely and purely on your faith in Jesus Christ and your acceptance of Him as your Redeemer and Saviour. You will remember that the one criminal on the cross was assured of his acceptance not because of his achievements, but purely because of his surrender and the grace of God.

Jesus accepts you for who and what you are. All He asks of you is that you will believe in Him and accept Him as the Lord of your life. In the Gospel of John Jesus says: *"Do not let your hearts be troubled. Trust in God; trust also in me"* (Jn. 14:1). Joyfully respond to this invitation and experience the grace and love of your divine Father every day.

Holy God and through Jesus Christ my heavenly Father, thank You that I may, through faith, claim the privilege of being called your child.

Our heavenly Father never takes something from his children without giving them something better instead.

~ George Mueller ~

Decisions, Decisions, Decisions

So whether you eat or drink or whatever you do, do it all for the glory of God (1 Cor. 10:31).

To make decisions can be a cumbersome task, because it often goes hand in hand with great responsibility. What you decide can have, and often has, far-reaching consequences for your own life as well as for the lives of other people, especially those who are dependent on you. It is precisely for this reason that so many people try and circumvent their responsibilities. On the other hand, there are also those who make decisions recklessly or with only their own best interests at heart.

To ensure that you do not become ensnared in these traps, you should take all your concerns in prayer to God. Lay your problems, doubts and fears before his feet and talk to Him about your plans and thoughts regarding the future. Leave the matter to Him and ask Him to lead you in every decision that you have to make, so that you may remain within his will.

This may seem very impractical to you, but provided that you are willing to trust the Lord unconditionally, you will find that He will open doors to you in his own wonderful time and way, and will guide you on the path that He has chosen for you.

Remain in the presence of the living Christ and the Holy Spirit, and continually aspire to please God. In so doing you will find that you make the right decisions because God lovingly guides you.

Holy Lord Jesus, I want to lay every decision that I have to make before You in profound dependence. Grant me the guidance of your Holy Spirit so that I may live and make decisions within your will.

Those who insist on seeing with complete clarity before making a decision will never decide.

~ Henri Frederic Amiel ~

*M*AKE SOMETHING OF YOUR LIFE

... But one thing I do ... (Phil. 3:13).

*I*n the human personality there are many forces at work, all of which seek recognition and fulfilment. In every person the characteristics of parent, financier, politician, moralist, religious person, student and many others contribute to the complexities of the human nature. In different phases of your life you move, sometimes reluctantly, from one category to the other, and you fluctuate between those forces that strengthen, co-ordinate and motivate your daily life and those that aim to weaken it.

The people who achieve success are those who realise the importance of specialisation. They choose their goals and strive after them with unremitting zeal. They dedicate themselves to the fulfilment of their ideals. Therefore, ensure that your goals are worthy of the best that is in you. You will never find satisfaction in life if you aim too low.

Some people aspire to excel in the academic world, others in business or the arts. Regardless of the sphere in which you move, you must live life to the fullest. If you are a disciple of Jesus, you want to leave the world a better place than you found it.

The highest goal that you can aspire to is to become like Christ. This may sound too idealistic to be practically possible, but such a goal speaks of true wisdom. Christ calls you to the most exalted life conceivable. However, not only does He call you, He also enables you to achieve heights that you never would have reached in your own strength. Make your life worthwhile through the strength of your Master.

Through your presence in me, Lord Jesus, I will achieve the goals that You have placed in my heart.

Look thoroughly inside yourself; there is a source of strength that will always issue forth should you seek it.

~ Marcus Aurelius ~

How do you handle rejection?

"All that the Father gives me will come to me, and whoever comes to me I will never drive away" (Jn. 6:37).

The experience of rejection is one of the great tragedies of life. The loneliness of being excluded from a community can be extremely painful. Many people undergo the distressing experience of being passed over for promotion or even dismissed from their jobs because of their age. It is difficult to have your sound advice rejected, while knowing that the path followed can only end in disaster. Examples of rejection are rife and can have devastating consequences for your personality and emotions.

When you find yourself in such a situation, turn to Him who knows and understands only too well what it means to be rejected. He was sent by God to bring the message of God's love to humanity. Yet He was despised and forsaken by people. However, despite his physical, mental and emotional suffering, they could never break his spirit or cause his faith in God to falter.

In your loneliness and dejection always remember that the living Christ promised never to forsake or desert you. Whatever you may suffer because of people's changeability, Jesus' love for you remains a constant. Hold on to this immovable truth, and through Jesus Christ you will be able to deal with your feelings of rejection and feel how his love fills your life and your heart.

O Lord, let my soul be quiet, because I know that You watch over me and will never forsake me. Help me to bear all suffering and sorrow with patience and to surrender my entire life to you.

To live in accordance with the laws of Christ and to accept Him in our hearts is to cast a gigantic floodlight of hope on our valley of problems and despair.

~ Charles H. Hembree ~

*W*HICH WAY?

Whether you turn to the right or to the left, your ears will hear a voice behind you, saying, "This is the way; walk in it" (Is. 30:21).

*I*t is not easy to resist the temptation of drifting with the current. It is especially so when you, perhaps for the first time in your life, become part of a group of people with whom you will share your life and time for a shorter or longer period. In the days ahead you may be reliant on them not only for your happiness, but depending on circumstances, even for your life.

If you feel that what others are doing is wrong, you should never be afraid of saying so. There will undoubtedly come times when you will have to decide whether to agree with the majority or to stand up for what you know to be right. Don't compromise your principles. Regardless of how difficult it may be or how unpopular you may be at that moment, hold on to what you are convinced is the right way.

Remember that there was a time when your Master and Example was extremely unpopular, but despite rejection, humiliation and even death He stood firm for his beliefs. If you do the same, you will in time earn the respect of your colleagues, and you will know that you had the privilege of being in the company of Christ – even when you were rejected.

Heavenly Father, through your strength and grace I will choose your way in everything that I do.

The strongest principles of growth are in the choices one makes.
~ George Eliot ~

*F*IND YOUR INSPIRATION IN *C*HRIST

... "Were not our hearts burning within us while he talked with us on the road and opened the Scriptures to us?" (Lk. 24:32).

*J*esus' disciples were devastated. The humiliation and crucifixion of their Master destroyed all their hopes and aspirations. Their lives had become meaningless. Their dreams of a new era being ushered in by the Messiah were dashed to the ground. They were reduced to a small group of uncertian people consumed by fear. Then Jesus appeared once more and their lives gained a new and meaningful dimension.

The hope and inspiration of Easter can be transferred to every negative situation in life. When you are afraid or worried; when your plans fail; when you experience setbacks or disappointments: you can either give up hope and be overwhelmed by despondency, or you can turn to the risen Saviour and receive new inspiration from Him. The choice is yours, as it was for the disciples.

The friends and followers of the Master developed such an intimate relationship with Him during his lifetime that when He rose from death they were newly inspired by his presence, and hope flowed through them once more.

This can be your experience too, despite the disappointments of life, if you open your life and heart to the living Christ. You too will experience his influence and inspiration that will urge you towards a better and more confident life in his Name.

All my hope and trust are anchored in You, risen and glorified Saviour and Lord. Thank You that You inspire me time and again when I find myself in the darkest depths.

Our Lord did not only have the promise of the resurrection written in books, but on every leaf in springtime.

~ Martin Luther ~

*L*ET LOVE INSPIRE YOUR SERVICE

... "Does the Lord delight in burnt offerings and sacrifices as much as in obeying the voice of the Lord? ... " (1 Sam. 15:22).

---

*B*efore Christ came to the world people attached great importance to making sacrifices to God. Over the years these acts gradually became rituals: their significance and meaning were lost in the formalities surrounding them. Sacrifices were no longer acts of worship, but procedures that had to be followed to obey the laws determined by the temple authorities.

Christ clearly and irrefutably showed that obedience to the commandments of God is of cardinal importance in your life as a Christian. No amount of material or financial offerings can ever be an adequate substitute for the love that you should show towards others. You can dedicate a great deal of time to serving the Lord, but unless it is inspired by and linked to his love, it will be of little value in the service of his Kingdom.

The Master set the example for an effective Christian life, and He demands absolute obedience to God's commandment that we should love one another. Whatever you do in the service of God can only be to the glorification of his Name if it is founded on the love of Jesus Christ.

Help me, o Lord, to love You continually more, so that I will also increasingly serve my fellow man in love.

Love is the greatest offering that we can bring God, because God is love!

~ Jeremy Taylor ~

Make time for this

... I looked for sympathy, but there was none, for comforters, but I found none (Ps. 69:20).

*I*t cannot be denied that we live in a fast-paced world. People run around insanely in an attempt to meet an ever-increasing amount of demands. We have less and less time and the pressure on the individual becomes so intense that it becomes increasingly difficult to spend time worrying about the lot of others.

Even the briefest overview of the life of Christ as reflected in the Gospels convinces us of the fact that He too lived under immense pressure. He was in demand as teacher, preacher, comforter and healer. His day was filled with requests to serve others in some way or another. Wherever He went crowds followed Him. He was also aware of the fact that He had limited time at his disposal to complete the work that God had instructed Him to do. Evil forces were perpetually trying to disrupt his ministry of love. Regardless of this, Christ had time for everyone.

There are so many people today who yearn for a sympathetic smile or a comforting word; people who are experiencing a crisis in their lives; people who are lonely, scared and unsure. Always be sensitive to the distress of others and be prepared to lend a helping hand at any time. It doesn't matter how busy you are: make time for this, so that you may carry the joy of Christ into the lives of others.

Help me, o Holy Spirit, to carry the love of Jesus Christ into the lives of other people.

No one can be a friend of Jesus Christ without being a friend of his neighbour.

~ Robert H. Benson ~

You can't serve two masters

... "If you are returning to the Lord with all your hearts, then rid your-selves of the foreign gods and the Ashtoreths and commit yourselves to the Lord and serve him only ... " (1 Sam. 7:3).

Many people claim that they are seeking God and that they are trying to establish a more intimate relationship with Him. Few of them would admit that idols hold sway in their lives and exercise a significant amount of control over them.

In their search for a new life in Christ people stream to gatherings, seminars and retreats; they study the Bible and other Christian litera-ture; they attend Sunday services as well as prayer and study groups. Despite all this, their enthusiasm is often disappointed and their search appears fruitless. Consequently they begin to question the promises of Christ.

If you are seeking a meaningful relationship with the risen Lord, you may be certain that the Redeemer is waiting for you to invite Him into your life so that He may be in charge of it. However, before He will do this, you are expected to banish every non-Christian matter from your life. Jesus has to be the focus of your existence if you expect Him to fill your life with his joy and fullness. You have to give preference to Him above all the habits and ways of life that you have become accus-tomed to. Do this, serve only the Lord, and you will experience his peace and joy in your life.

Lord Jesus, I dedicate my life to You anew, in the knowledge that You will give me life in abundance.

Anything that one seeks, exalts or honours above God is idolatry.
~ William Ullathorne ~

The Joy of Life in Christ

... "Blessed rather are those who hear the word of God and obey it"
(Lk. 11:28).

---

*M*any people's attitude towards their religious principles is one of
reluctant submission to a tiresome yet necessary discipline. Tiresome
because it limits or subdues our pleasure, but necessary for the well-
being of the soul.

This should never be the attitude of the Christian believer, because
Jesus came precisely so that you may have life in all its abundance. He
wants you to have a life of purpose, vigour and joy. The entire Christian experience centres on a caring heavenly Father who wishes only
the best for his children. His love is so incomprehensibly great that He
sacrificed his Son. Jesus offers you forgiveness, redemption and the
hope of eternal life. Through his Holy Spirit He enables you to live in
trust, confidence and victory.

What more could anyone ask of life? Here you have the promise of
the very best that life can offer and all that God expects of you is to
accept his sovereignty in your life. Surely this is little enough to ask in
exchange for a life of fulfilment and joy?

Lord Jesus, I rejoice in the knowledge that you redeemed me and
granted me a life of joy and fulfilment. My heart sings in praise and
gratitude.

It is good if one can manage to have God sing inside one.
                    ~ Rabbi Elimelech ~

What an Amazing Thought!

... But we have the mind of Christ (1 Cor. 2:16).

Even if the Christian faith were no more than a beautiful philosophy, it would still have been applicable to every sphere of life, because it expresses the great human need for love and fellowship. Imperfect people still aspire to perfection and every heart and mind contains the seeds of the quest for God. Until man has found union with the Father, he will feel incomplete and frustrated.

The Christian gospel propounds a unique way of life when it speaks of love for God and surrender to his will. In the gospel this is of much greater value than academic achievement. Such achievements are praiseworthy and those who possess them can offer God a greater spectrum of services, but it is not essential in order to experience the fullness of the Christian faith.

To believe that God is true to his word, that He will do everything He promised, is the greatest stimulus that you can have in your spiritual life. If you have this, you become a channel of his divine love, conveying it to the world in which you live. To allow the world of your mind to be possessed by Christ is not only a religious experience, but also a revolutionary act of faith that brings spiritual forces to the fore in every aspect of your daily life. Through the Spirit of Christ you realise the true splendour of life.

Jesus, my Lord, let your Spirit govern my thoughts and my spirit so that I may gain a new appreciation for life's potential.

He who thinks that he has progressed far on the path of the spiritual life has not yet even made a good start.

~ Jean Pierre Camus ~

Sometimes the Answer is "No"

Answer me when I call to you, O my righteous God. Give me relief from my distress; be merciful to me and hear my prayer (Ps. 4:1).

We often hear people complaining that God does not answer their prayers. They declare that they prayed extensively and earnestly, but nothing happened; they prayed for some or other specific thing, but did not get it; they asked for God's guidance on a particular path, but nothing came of it. The result of these prayer experiences is that many people's faith wanes because they maintain that God does not listen.

However, nothing could be further from the truth, because in the Scriptures we are assured that God hears and answers the prayers of his children. But we err in forgetting that God does, upon occasion, say "no". We focus so much on asking Him for those things that we want that we lose sight of the fact that Jesus assured us that He would provide in all our needs, and no-one knows better than Christ what our true needs are.

True prayer does not consist of telling God what you want or what you are planning to do, and then asking Him to place his stamp of approval on it. Prayer consists of opening up your life to God, laying your needs before Him and trusting Him to lead you on the right path.

Lord Jesus, You are my Guide, my Leader and my Friend. Therefore I submit obediently to your will, even though You sometimes say "no" to me. Lead me according to your will until the end of my pilgrimage.

The purpose of all prayer is to find God's will and to make that will our prayers.

~ Catherine Marshall ~

DEATH IS NOT THE END

Brothers, we do not want you to be ignorant about those who fall asleep, or to grieve like the rest of men, who have no hope (1 Thes. 4:13).

Time and time again we meet individuals or families who have been plunged into the depths of grief by the death of a loved one. To these people it appears as if life has lost its purpose and meaning. They are powerless and inconsolable in their grief. In their state of paralysed shock the future seems empty and meaningless.

On the day after the crucifixion of Jesus Christ his close friends and family must have experienced the same feelings. The Scriptures describe them as a sorrowful, terrified and lost little group of people shocked by the death of their beloved Master. And yet they were at the threshold of a miracle that would change the entire concept of death for all time. Instead of an ending, death suddenly became a beginning. With his resurrection Christ confirmed that He lives eternally and that those who believe in Him will never die.

When a loved one is taken from you by death, don't despair. Christ has gone to prepare a place for us in the Kingdom of the Father. Hold on to his promise that He will come again and take you to Him. In Christ you will be reunited with your loved ones. Do not be afraid and distressed: Christ lives and therefore we too will live.

I rejoice in your triumphant resurrection from death, Lord Jesus. I exult in the knowledge that all of us will be together once more with You.

We understand death for the first time when he has put his hand on someone we love.

~ Anne L. de Stael ~

Washers of Feet

After that, he poured water into a basin and began to wash his disciples' feet, drying them with the towel that was wrapped around him (Jn. 13:5).

Much has been written and said on the topic of love and humility. Many have tried to explain the true meaning of their application in life. Despite all the profound statements, the fact remains that the world still has a desperate need for the demonstration of true love and humility, so that the illnesses of this world may be healed. Everywhere we turn we are faced with examples of behaviour that is in direct contradiction with everything that God expects of his people.

Jesus, in his ordinary and truly earthly way, provided us with a practical demonstration of what is required by God's standards. On the eve of his crucifixion and glorification He took the role of servant upon Himself with the humble task of washing his disciples' feet. He proved that humility can be exalted and that love can conquer all things.

In these days there is a great need throughout the world to let the humility and love of Jesus conquer pride and hatred. Instead of washing each other's feet, we tend to berate each other. Humility and love is the only path to lasting relationships. For this Christ died on the cross. Let us therefore become washers of feet for Christ.

Holy Master, we want to take You at your word and follow your example. Grant that there will be more sunshine in this world because of my humility and love.

The reason why God loves humility so much is because He loves the truth. Humility is nothing but the truth, while pride is a lie.

~ Vincent de Paul ~

*T*HE EXCITEMENT OF NEW IDEAS

The heart of the discerning acquires knowledge; the ears of the wise seek it out (Prov. 18:15).

*D*on't believe it when someone tells you that the world is bankrupt of new ideas or that it is no longer possible to make exciting discoveries. It is said that 80% of our current knowledge has been discovered in the last 80 years. Every day new and exciting discoveries open paths to even greater discoveries. If you can hold on to the truth that the greatest painting is yet to be created; that the most inspiring prose is yet to be written; that music as never heard by the human ear is still waiting to be composed, then you will place your mind and spirit in a state of readiness for the wonders that the future still holds.

God's ideas are not spent, but He is looking for dedicated people through whom He may express Himself, so that his will may be manifested to mankind. To be prepared in all spheres of life for this inspiring service we must cultivate a disposition of unity with God. This is not only a mystical experience, but also a very practical one.

While you are building a uniquely personal intimacy with God, flashes of inspiration will penetrate your mind. Even though some of these may seem foolish to you, follow them and they may lead you into exciting spheres of thought and service.

Heavenly Father, only through complete obedience to You can I share in your divine thoughts for the world in which I live.

The most important reason why God inspired certain books is so that through them He may be present in our midst.

~ Hubert J. Richards ~

The Forgotten Ministry

Joseph took the body, wrapped it in a clean linen cloth, and placed it in his own new tomb that he had cut out of the rock ... (Mt. 27:59-60).

Great emphasis is placed on the special and loving ministry to the ill and dying and their loved ones, and quite rightly so. When a person is seriously ill and his family is surrounded by sympathetic friends offering their assistance and prayers, these tokens of concern are praiseworthy. But what happens when death comes?

The needs of a family who has lost a loved one to death are just as great, if not greater, as during the illness. Now is the time to support them in a variety of ways. There are many things that have to be done and many details that need attention. And these are usually unpleasant, time-consuming matters that are not in the foreground.

To undertake these tasks for the sake of the grieving family calls for special dedication to a ministry that is difficult but also always worthwhile. This is a time when the family is still paralysed with shock, and they need sympathetic, sound advice as well as a strong shoulder to lean on. Never shrink back from this ministry, because through it you will perform a deed of Christian love that is beyond words. You will gain the immeasurable appreciation of those you have ministered to, and through it you will honour your Lord and Master.

Loving and understanding Lord Jesus, grant that when the sorrow of death strikes a family that I know, I will not hesitate to bring the ministry of comfort to those who are grieving, not only in words, but also in practical deeds.

God consoles us not to make us comfortable, but so that we may become comforters.

~ John Henry Jowett ~

Proud Inheritance

... "I am he," Jesus said ... (Jn. 18:5).

Are you proud to be a Christian? Are you at all times ready and willing to stand up and be counted by professing Christ's sovereignty in your life? Or are there times when you keep quiet and are ashamed to profess your religion because you fear that you will not be accepted by a certain group of people?

There are many occasions when a Christian must identify himself with Christ: when the moral behaviour of someone needs to be questioned; when someone's language or jokes turn filthy; when someone airs blasphemous commentary. These are but a few examples of times when it is required that a Christian distance himself from the general inclination, even if it means that he will be unpopular or be ridiculed.

When Jesus was at the point of being arrested and there were people looking for Jesus of Nazareth, He made no attempt to deceive them. His answer to their question bespeaks sincere honesty and surrender and obedience to the will of God. Without hesitation He says: *"I am he."* His answer demonstrates the quality of his courage, because He knew only too well of the humiliation, rejection and suffering that would follow.

Follow his example and draw strength from Him. Be assured that when the time comes, you will also be able to profess with humble pride that you are a Christian.

Crucified Saviour, please keep me from ever being ashamed of professing my Christianity.

A Christian is someone who shares the suffering of Christ in the world.
~ Dietrich Bonhoeffer ~

The honesty that God demands

... "Now then, you Pharisees clean the outside of the cup and dish, but inside you are full of greed and wickedness" (Lk. 11:39).

God must surely often become very tired of all the excuses that we offer Him for the neglect of our spiritual life. Some of the excuses are so clumsy that we would not even offer them to a friend. Social events take preference over worship; laziness is often called relaxation; uselessly running around in the Name of God takes the place of becoming quiet before Him. It is easier to be active for the Master than to become quiet before Him and to learn his will.

When you are involved with God, it is proper and expedient that you will be completely honest with Him. He knows the true reasons for your spiritual neglect; why then would you try to hide anything from Him? When you are honest with God two things happen in your life. You open up the channel between you and Him that had been blocked for so long by hypocrisy, false excuses, laziness and other spiritual obstacles. You ask for forgiveness and experience the feeling of freedom that only God can give to you, a feeling that makes you spiritually sensitive so that you may start growing once again.

A healthy spiritual experience is based on faith and not on feelings. Nevertheless, a feeling of great joy will fill your spirit if you are honest with God. Once you have broken through the obstacle of sin that separates you from Him, you will increasingly experience a sense of unity with Him.

Holy Father, grant me the desire and the courage to be honest with You, so that my relationship with You may be enriched.

Honesty is the first chapter of the book of wisdom.

~ Thomas Jefferson ~

*D*O YOUR MEMORIES NEED HEALING?

... But one thing I do: Forgetting what is behind and straining toward what is ahead (Phil. 3:13).

*M*emories are an extremely important factor in your life. They can create inspiration, despair or peace of mind. Your memories of the past unarguably influence both the present and the future.

Unpleasant and distressing memories have a tendency to persist and to become even more distinct with the passage of the years. You may remember an unkind word or an act of abuse that you fell victim to many years ago. However, continually revisiting this memory will influence and poison your mind to such an extent that a bitter, unforgiving and introspective spirit will take root in you.

The eradication of these disturbing and destructive memories depends on your ability to forgive. This is one of the most difficult aspects of the Christian faith. To hate those who have hurt you is entirely natural. It may be natural, but it is not Christian. The Christian way is the path of reconciliation and healing. To refuse forgiveness is to sow a seed that will eventually destroy your spirit and harm you physically.

You can only forgive others if you yourself have experienced the forgiveness of Jesus. To accept God's forgiveness through Christ enables you to forgive, thus purifying and healing your memories of all damaging influences.

Holy Spirit of God, heavenly Teacher, teach me the ministry of forgiveness so that I can purify my mind and spirit from all destructive influences.

"I will forgive, but I will not forget" is just another way of saying "I don't want to forgive".

~ Henry Ward Beecher ~

Be honest

He who conceals his sins does not prosper, but whoever confesses and renounces them finds mercy (Prov. 28:13).

The proverb that states: "Honesty is the best policy" contains an irrevocable truth. However, there are many people who find it difficult to submit themselves to it. Some of them ignore it on purpose, while others, caught in a web of doubt and fear, suddenly find themselves in a situation where they are unable to handle the consequences of honesty. As a result they try to conceal their shortcomings or failures. In the process they sink deeper into new problems until it eventually seems impossible to disentangle themselves.

Such behaviour inevitably leads to mental anguish and stress, because the emotions and nervous system of the average person cannot cope with the negative influences caused by deception. Consequently you suffer mentally, physically and spiritually, and your life becomes nothing but a torture-chamber.

At one time or another, we all make mistakes in varying degrees. Christ, who lived among flawed people, is aware of and sympathetic to human fallibility. If you did something wrong, don't try and hide it with a lie. Trust in the love, forgiveness and courage that Jesus offers you. Acknowledge and confess your error and try to correct it. This is the only path on which you will find peace for your soul.

Thank You, Holy Spirit of God, that You taught me that I may live in peace by being honest at all times.

No honest person has ever regretted his honesty.
~ German proverb ~

Lonely, but Never Alone

How great is the love the Father has lavished on us, that we should be called children of God! And that is what we are! (1 Jn. 3:1).

The love of family and friends is always a great source of comfort and joy. To have someone to whom you can turn and with whom you can share your life experience is one of God's greatest gifts of grace. It is therefore no wonder that parting with or saying farewell to a loved one always fills us with sorrow and loneliness.

However, you are never alone, because as Paul says, nothing in all of creation can separate us from the love of God in Jesus Christ (see Rom. 8:38-39). The Lord assures us that He will never abandon or forsake us and that He will be with us in all our days (see Heb. 13:5 and Mt. 28:20). These are promises that you can hold on to and draw courage and strength from in all circumstances, especially when tragedy comes into your life and you are at your most vulnerable.

To reaffirm the assurance of God's promises and presence you must often spend time in his presence through prayer and contemplation. Share all your fears and worries with Him, as well as your loneliness and vulnerability. Christ is not only the Lord of your life, but also your Friend, and therefore you must remember that He chose you to belong to Him through his grace.

God of love and grace, those who experience your love can never be lonely. Help me to walk with You and to talk to You as with a friend.

God is not an idea or a definition that we have learnt by rote. He is a presence that we experience in our hearts.

~ Louis Eveley ~

The Test of True Discipleship

"By this all men will know that you are my disciples, if you love one another" (Jn. 13:35).

The majority of Christians are attached to some kind of discipline or credo. This is essential, because without such anchors they become drifters without a safe harbour.

The weakness of these different convictions becomes clear when every association or church believes that it is the only one that is right, and that all the others are wrong. Then an "anti"-spirit becomes prevalent, antagonism reigns supreme and discipleship becomes ineffective.

The Christian faith must centre around and in the living Christ. By accepting Him as your Redeemer, you pledge your faith to Him and submit yourself to his demands. It involves every aspect of your daily life and requires a high quality of dedication. Love is the most important sign of discipleship and without it no one can be his follower. Therefore the litmus test of true discipleship is not which theological conviction you believe in, but whether you lead a life of true Christian love.

This truth may cause some people to hesitate to accept the challenge and responsibility of discipleship, because who can love when surrounded by bitterness and hatred? The demand of love that Christ places on us is impossible for mere humans to obey, but if his Spirit fills your life, the impossible becomes possible. Then love becomes the main ingredient in your life and enables you to become a true disciple.

Loving Lord Jesus, let your Holy Spirit take possession of my life so that I may share in these gifts of the Spirit, and so that love may become the motivating force in my life.

Love heals people; both those who give it and those who receive it.
~ Carl Menninger ~

*T*HE KINGDOM OF GOD

... "The kingdom of God does not come with your careful observation, nor will people say, 'Here it is,' or 'There it is,' because the kingdom of God is within you" (Lk. 17:20-21).

*T*he kingdom of God is to be found in the hearts of those in whose lives Jesus Christ reigns as king. It is the kingdom of good relationships, because you are reconciled with God and live in harmony with Him. This takes place through the power and love of Jesus. As far as possible you then live in peace with your fellow human beings.

Unfortunately political and social digressions have caused many people to end up on a side-track, and they continue trying to reach the kingdom without opening their hearts and lives to the merciful occupancy of Christ's holy presence. Only when the risen Lord reigns supreme in the lives of people can his kingdom be established in their thoughts, spirits and emotions.

Belonging to the kingdom of God demands unconditional obedience to the King. He must be assured of your faithfulness and you must strive to do his will. This faithfulness is not a one-time vow made in a moment of intense emotion, but a daily devotion to Him, regardless of your emotional state.

When the King of this inner kingdom lets his power be felt, you experience his strength, joy, peace and all his other gifts in your daily life. The greatest joy of life is the steadfast knowledge that you belong to Him and He to you, because He lives in you through his Holy Spirit.

Come, Lord Jesus, and reign as supreme King in my heart and life. Grant that the world will know where my citizenship is.

The kingdom of God is a kingdom of love; and love is never a stagnant pond.

~ Henry W. DuBose ~

*W*HO? ME, LORD?

"Will a man rob God? Yet you rob me ... " (Mal. 3:8).

*T*he average person would feel affronted if called a thief. The mere thought that you may be guilty of robbing God is so repulsive that it is almost indescribable. And yet, if we were to be honest with ourselves, there is an element of truth in these words that God directs at us through his prophet.

The commandments of the Old Testament form the foundation of the lifestyle that God expects from his people. Thereafter, with the ministry of Christ, we are shown indisputably and exactly what He requires of us as his children to comply with his demands. Jesus Himself calls all Christians to bear fruit in honour of God the Father (see Jn. 15:8).

When you seriously think about your faith and discipleship you will realise that you are now God's ambassador in the world. It is through the effectiveness of your testimony that souls will be won or lost for the Master's cause. People will keep a close eye on your life and if they see in your lifestyle something that is alien to the principles and example of Christ, they will turn their backs on Him. The church of Christ is judged according to the testimony of his disciples.

If you are guilty of this, you derogate from the glory of God and thus rob Him of souls that you ought to have won for his kingdom by manifesting the love and example of Christ in your life.

Holy Spirit, my Leader and Guide, help me to win and not lose people for God's kingdom through my way of life.

Wherever God reigns as King in the hearts of people, there the kingdom of God is established.

~ Paul W. Harrison ~

Eternal life through Jesus Christ

For this very reason, Christ died and returned to life so that he might be the Lord of both the dead and the living (Rom. 14:9).

Most people fear a lack of security. A child who leaves home for boarding school; a person changing jobs; the loss of a life partner: all these things leave you with feelings of uncertainty and nervousness. You fear what the future holds for you.

Even worse is your fear of death and the uncertainty that goes hand in hand with it. There are many people who brood over this whenever they think of the unknown. In their uncertainty they fall victim to anxiety and tension. They worry about the dark, unknown future that will follow their physical death.

For the Christian believer there is a glorious truth that emanates from the life, death and resurrection of Jesus Christ: in the Spirit He is with you right now to lead you through life with all its problems and fears. He also went to prepare a place for you in God's heavenly kingdom. In this way He assures you that when your earthly life is over, you will be with the Lord eternally (see Jn. 14:1-4).

Instead of being consumed with fear and worry, hold on to the promises of Jesus Christ. Place your faith and trust in Him and rejoice in the fact that because Jesus lives, you too will live eternally.

Risen and glorified Saviour, through faith I know that you live and that therefore I too will live eternally. Praise the Lord! I know that my Redeemer lives!

He who makes provision for this life only is wise for a moment, but a fool for all eternity.

~ John Tillitson ~

April

O Lord, our Lord, how majestic is your name ... (Ps. 8:2).

We worship You in this month as Christ the Conqueror!
You conquered death at Golgotha.
You have broken the power of Satan.
The Lord has truly risen! The tomb is empty!
Let the heavens proclaim his glory!
Thank You, Jesus Triumpher, that You were obedient to death and
    that God has exalted You to the highest glory;
    that You sit at the right hand of God and intervene on my behalf.
Thank You for taking me with on your
    triumphant journey through time and eternity.
I am assured that, because you were resurrected from death
    I too can be resurrected from the death of sin to a life of victory.
Lord Jesus, because you are the resurrection and the life
    I can enter into the eternal home You went to prepare.
Let me never forget your living presence;
    assure me once again that there is nothing and no one
    on earth that can separate me from your love.
Forgive me, merciful Lord Jesus, if I still sometimes live
    as if You were dead.
Let me live every day of this month and all the days of my life
    in the glorious comfort of your promise:
    "And remember, I am with you in all your days!"
In the Name of my risen and glorified Saviour.

Amen.

Live for Christ

His divine power has given us everything we need for life and godliness through our knowledge of him who called us by his own glory and goodness (2 Pet. 1:3).

In this month we once again hear the call to live a Christian life, but some of us are so overwhelmed by the immensity of the task that our faith falters. We tell ourselves that in our human weakness we can impossibly meet the standards that God expects of us. The sad consequences of such an attitude is that you lose courage and refuse to even try. In this way God is robbed of yet another disciple and you deny yourself the joy of serving the Master.

The mistake that you make is to rely on your own abilities to serve Christ, when you should actually from the outset devote yourself to Christ with absolute faith in your heart, and trust Him to enable you to walk his path.

On your Christian pilgrimage you must remember that Christ will not call you to any form of service without equipping you for it. He has set the example, and all that He expects of you is to follow Him. If you dedicate yourself to Him and place your trust in Him completely, He will provide you with everything that you need to truly live.

Heavenly Father, I dedicate myself to your service anew, in the certain knowledge that You will provide everything that I need to live for You.

If we were willing to learn the true meaning of discipleship, the church would be transformed and the resulting impact on society would be astounding.

~ David Watson ~

Let Christ relieve your loneliness

"I will not leave you as orphans; I will come to you" (Jn. 14:18).

The anguish of loneliness is an experience that is difficult to describe or explain; it must be experienced before it can be understood. Of all the forms of loneliness the worst is that which results from the death of a loved one, because the separation is so final, at least in human terms. This profound loneliness may lead to inconsolable sorrow and deep unhappiness, unless you pull yourself together and take positive steps to fight your despair.

On the eve of his own death Jesus promised his disciples that He would not leave his children without a Comforter. Through his Holy Spirit the Saviour undertakes to come to you and be with you at all times, as long as you want Him and invite Him into your life.

When death strikes there is always a tendency to abandon all hope under the burden of sorrow. It is precisely then when you need the help and consolation of the Holy Spirit. In your sorrow turn to Jesus and lay your fears, sorrow and pain before Him. He is always there, ready to share your sorrow with you by giving you his peace or by using someone as instrument to support and comfort you. He will manifest Himself to you in his healing love and in this way take the unbearable pain out of your sorrow.

Be quiet, my soul, the Lord is on your side. Thank You, Lord Jesus, that I may say this from experience and conviction, because You have given me a Comforter.

Where there is sorrow, we move on holy ground.

~ Oscar Wilde ~

*I*T IS PERFECTLY NATURAL TO PRAY

He will respond to the prayer of the destitute; he will not despise their plea (Ps. 102:17).

*M*ost Christians regret the fact that they do not spend more time in prayer. They realise the inadequacy of their prayer life, but when they do try to pray with depth and meaning, their good intentions are defeated by wandering thoughts and a restless spirit.

Prayer is a completely natural act, despite opinions to the contrary. You may set apart little time for God and live without giving Him a single thought, but deep inside you there is a core that cannot be explained without God. In moments of silent contemplation you will think about the meaning and significance of life, and without God there is no answer.

Prayer is the heartbeat of the soul. You may understand nothing of schools of prayer or methods of contemplation, but every time you think of God there is something deep inside you that yearns for a Reality that you cannot always explain. This hunger of your soul and your seeking thoughts are, as a matter of fact, a humble form of prayer.

While prescribed prayers and orthodox methods of prayer may help you to enter into the presence of God, it is the cry of the troubled heart, so often expressed in confusion and despair, that moves the loving heart of God. Every time you invoke his Name, He is there to meet you. Every time you think of Him, you are busy praying. Therefore do not feel discouraged if your prayer life seems inadequate. Every thought that is directed at God is a prayer that connects you to Him.

O, Hearer of prayers, I praise and thank You for the natural prayer that carries me into your holy presence.

In its simplest form prayer is a desire that is turned to God.
~ Phillip Brooks ~

The Truly Abundant Life

He who has the Son has life; he who does not have the Son of God does not have life (1 Jn. 5:12).

One often hears the expression: "This is the life!" Usually it refers to the enjoyment of material things and creature comforts. While we for no moment wish to deny people's right to leisure and even a little bit of self-indulgence, it may, if left uncontrolled, lead to self-centredness and selfishness. Such pleasure in any case leaves one with a feeling of bored dissatisfaction and the need to seek out other forms of sensual gratification. Eventually there is no way left in which you can find joy and life becomes meaningless.

Whatever your methods of relaxation and life enjoyment, you must never lose sight of the fact that Jesus Christ came so that you may have life in all its abundance (see Jn. 10:10). However involved you may feel in your work or relaxation, you will never experience full satisfaction before you have found the living Christ. Don't make the mistake of limiting your life with Christ only to the spiritual aspect. Always remember that He offers to be part of every aspect of your life.

If you open your life to Him completely and allow his Holy Spirit to work in you, your life will take on a completely new dimension. Invite Christ into your heart and allow Him to transform your existence into abundant life.

Redeemer and Master, since I have surrendered my life to You and allowed your Spirit to rule my being, my fetters have fallen away and my heart has been liberated to live in abundance.

Don't be afraid that your life will come to an end, but rather that it will never truly begin.

~ John Henry Newman ~

OLD AGE IS A TIME OF GRACE

"Even to your old age and gray hairs I am he, I am he who will sustain you ... " (Is. 46:4).

As you grow older your attitude towards life also changes. Aspects that you were sure of before are closely scrutinised under the searchlight of experience. Your approach to issues of which you were dogmatically convinced is blessed with a deeper and more sympathetic insight and understanding.

It is unfortunately also true that the progression of age does not necessarily bring with it an increase in wisdom. Sometimes it results in a narrow-minded spirit becoming even more hardened in its views. The subsequent obstinacy can be an obstacle to inspirational ideas.

As a disciple of Christ your mind and spirit must remain receptive to the inspiration and guidance of the Holy Spirit, so that He can lead you deeper into God's protective love. Your faith must continue growing, and it involves the rejection of narrow-mindedness and pettiness.

As someone who lives in the love of God you ought to be liberated from all prejudice and fanaticism. Aware that Christ's love is his special gift to you, you will become increasingly aware that you are one with Him. Whatever changes may take place in your life, you will live in an increasingly deeper and more realistic relationship with God. However, this only happens if you are guided by the Holy Spirit.

God's love will intensify your respect for others who love God, even though they might worship Him differently.

Thank You, Lord my God, that with the passage of the years I also grow in spiritual understanding and thus become liberated from all jealousy and prejudice.

Your life is filled with meaning the moment when Jesus enters it.
~ Stephan Neill ~

When Things Start Going Wrong

I will instruct you and teach you in the way you should go; I will counsel you and watch over you (Ps. 32:8).

Life is very unpredictable. For a while everything may go well and everything you set out to do turns out successfully. And then suddenly, for some inexplicable reason, everything starts going wrong. However hard you try, you cannot manage to achieve your goals; success evades you and it seems as if failure is one step ahead of you the entire time. Such a change in circumstances does not occur without cause. It may be difficult to accept, but its cause lies *within* you.

You may discover that your thoughts have switched from the positive to the negative; your prayer life may have lost its foundation of trust; complaining and grumbling may have become your attitude towards life. Unconsciously you attract every negative influence towards you.

When things start going wrong, it is time for you to isolate yourself with God. Cease all complaining and grumbling and enter the presence of God in humility, in the conviction that nothing is beyond his control. Surrender yourself to Him and He will lead you from this dark country. In Him you will find a divinely inspired path and things will once again start going right.

If your world is threatening to go to pieces, hem it with prayer to prevent it from fraying at the edges. Through Christ and the Holy Spirit God will grant you the courage and guidance in your confusion and uncertainty.

Grant me the wisdom, o Lord, to wait for You in prayer and contemplation when things in my life start going wrong.

He who relies on himself is lost; he who relies on God can accomplish all things.

~ Alphonsus Liguori ~

Reconsider your relationships

"Therefore, if you are offering your gift at the altar and there remember that your brother has something against you, leave your gift there in front of the altar. First go and be reconciled to your brother; then come and offer your gift" (Mt. 5:23-24).

There is always a danger that religious convictions, backed by strong emotion, may overshadow the core of the message of Jesus Christ. When your Christianity becomes so personal and limited that it ignores human relationships, it becomes a mockery. However excited you are in your acts of worship, however enthusiastic you are about the kingdom of God, your worship and enthusiasm become ineffectual if you harbour an unforgiving spirit towards another person in your heart and mind.

It will be impossible for you to know the true freedom of worship inspired by the Spirit, because you cannot appreciate the joy of the living Christ if there is bitterness between you and another person.

Perhaps there is a separation or estrangement not caused by you in your life. If you have done everything in your power to mend the breach and the other person still withholds forgiveness, make sure that you don't cherish any vengeful thoughts. Make sure that you have not only forgiven that person, but that you also still pray for him. When the time comes for your prayers to be answered and the breach to be mended, you will experience great peace and joy because you have proven once more that there is healing power in your Christianity.

Lord my God, through forgiveness and praise I can live in peace with You, my neighbour and myself. I thank You for this through Jesus Christ who has redeemed me from an unforgiving spirit.

Nothing in this unfortunate world bears the sign of the Son of God more than forgiveness.

~ Alice Carey ~

Share your burdens with Christ

Cast all you anxiety on him because he cares for you (1 Pet. 5:7).

Someone in the business world, who was going through a difficult time, was once asked how he managed to sleep with all the worries that he had. His response was that he relinquished all his problems to God, saying, like the psalmist: *(I)ndeed, he who watches over Israel will neither slumber nor sleep* (Ps. 121:4), and therefore he saw no point in the both of them staying awake all night.

Frivolous as this may seem, it nevertheless emphasises our obligation to trust God under all circumstances. Jesus undertook never to abandon or forsake us (see Heb. 13:5). He invited those who are weary and overburdened to come to Him for rest, and He assured us that He would never send away those who came to Him.

This does not necessarily mean that God offers you an instant solution to your problems, or that all your problems will disappear simply because you pray. It *does* mean that if you place your faith and trust in God and confide in Him in prayer, you will experience the peace of mind that will sensitise you to the guidance of the Holy Spirit. He will enable you to think clearly and act positively. In his strength you will be able to handle your problems in accordance with the will of God.

Soothe my restless heart, o Holy Spirit. Calm the tempestuous ocean and the storms that rage. Lead me to waters where there is serenity so that I may experience peace of mind.

Worrying does not empty tomorrow of problems; it only empties today of its power.

~ Corrie ten Boom ~

The Cornerstone of Your Faith

And now these three remain: faith, hope and love. But the greatest of these is love (1 Cor. 13:13).

The Christian faith has many facets because people view and interpret Christ from many perspectives. This is understandable, because your personality and tradition will influence your approach to Him. However, when you refuse to accept the authenticity of someone's Christianity because it differs from yours, serious problems may enter your spiritual life. This refusal causes a fanatic and narrow-minded attitude that will ultimately destroy the beauty of your living faith.

The test of your faith is the amount of love towards your neighbour that it generates – especially towards those who have a different perspective from yours. Such a love finds its roots not in ignoring the teachings and traditions of those who think differently from you, but only in living so close to Christ that his love flows through you. Your love for Christ envelops everyone who loves and serves Him, even though you cannot agree with them on every level.

Love is the most crucial factor in the Christian life. This love isn't always even-tempered, because there are moments when it challenges and admonishes. It makes you humble so that it may exalt you to great spiritual heights; it empties you of yourself so that you may be filled with the life of Christ. Love is an active agent that helps you to grow in the understanding of your heavenly Father, thus also increasing your appreciation of your fellow human beings.

Lord God, I worship you as the Source of all true love. Let your love manifest itself in my life. Grant me an ever greater understanding and appreciation of my fellow human beings.

I have decided to stick with love. Hate is too heavy a burden to carry.
~ Martin Luther King Jr. ~

*P*urify your memories

Why are you downcast, O my soul? Why so disturbed within me? Put your hope in God, for I will yet praise him, my Savior and my God ... (Ps. 42:5-6).

Your memories are of your own making. When you recall times and deeds of which you are ashamed, your conscience will probably be disturbed and uncomfortable. It is at times like these that you wish that you could erase the memories that torture you so. If you sincerely repent of the sin that is the cause of the memory you can be assured of forgiveness through Christ. He forgives and repairs through his redemptive love. Then you will be able to live in peace and harmony with God, yourself and your fellow human beings.

Today you are busy creating memories for tomorrow. Therefore you should be sensible and wise and create happiness for your future through your deeds and thoughts. A sure way of doing this is through a constant awareness of the living Christ. Live a day at a time for Him; trust Him at all times, even when things don't turn out to your liking. In so doing you will not only purify your old memories and create beautiful new memories, but you will also make the fulfilling discovery that you have walked with your Master through pain and tribulation, thus creating precious memories.

Merciful God and Father, my future is in your loving hands and therefore I can live to your glory in the present. Purify my memories through your great love, so that they may honour You.

It is impossible for him who remembers that his Helper is almighty, to despair.

~ Jeremy Taylor ~

Jesus understands because He loves you

Jesus wept. Then the Jews said, "See how he loved him!" (Jn. 11:35-36).

There are people who are sceptical of any suggestion that Jesus understands human problems. Their conception of the Lord is that He is Someone faraway and aloof, removed from our everyday life and only interested in matters of primary importance. Therefore it cannot be expected that He will concern Himself with the apparently inconsequential matters that relate to the personal lives of people.

Such an attitude manifests a complete misconception of God and his loving interest in the world that He created and the human beings for whom his Son died and was resurrected.

It is true that we preach and worship a God who is King of kings and Lord of lords, but we must never lose sight of the fact that Jesus is not only your Master, but also your Friend. Because He lived, suffered and died as a human being, He understands human problems and emotions, since He experienced them Himself. He endured suffering, as well as disappointment, sorrow and joy. The Son of God laughed and cried just as you and I do.

The Saviour is waiting for you to invite Him to share your life with Him. Open your heart to Him so that He may help you in whatever circumstances you may find yourself. Never forget that He is a friend who loves you and therefore understands you.

Lord Jesus, in You I have found a friend who is loving, faithful and understanding. Grant that I will experience your love under all circumstances in my life.

I believe with all my heart that there is no one more beautiful, sympathetic and perfect than Jesus. I tell myself that there can be no one like Him, and never will be.

~ Feodor Dostoyevsky ~

Make Jesus' resurrection a reality

... "Do not be afraid, for I know that you are looking for Jesus, who was crucified. He is not here; he has risen, just as he said ... " (Mt. 28:5-6).

Without the resurrection of Jesus Christ Christianity would have been a long-forgotten religion. His principles touch our hearts, stimulate our thoughts and are an inspiration to innumerable charity organisations. But the same things may be said of other religious leaders. What makes Christ unique is not only the inspiration that may be drawn from his doctrine, but He Himself. He courageously went forth to meet death, and conquered it. He came back from the dead and met his disciples under different circumstances and promised to be with them always.

It is the living Christ that reigns in the lives of a multitude of people in the new millennium. They have dedicated themselves to Christ and their worship of Him is a personal matter to them, not an organisational issue, a religious teaching or a dogma. They meet Him daily in quiet seclusion and are always aware of his living presence.

These people may be unable to give a clearly delineated explanation of their faith. In all likelihood they have no theological training, but deep in their inner being they know that Christ lives, that He loves them and have made them his property. No one will undermine their faith that the risen and glorified Saviour lives and reigns in their hearts and lives.

Risen Lord and Saviour, I thank You that I may exult in your resurrection and glorification. Help me never to live as if You are dead.

Christianity is a religion of miracles, and the miracle of Christ's resurrection is at the centre of the Christian faith.

~ Alan Richardson ~

*G*OD WORKS IN EVERYDAY THINGS

In his heart a man plans his course, but the Lord determines his steps (Prov. 16:9).

*I*t is true that God often works in great and miraculous ways. We see his glory in the changing heavens; his handiwork in the beauty of creation. Despite appearances which seem to indicate otherwise, the earth still belongs to Him and He is still in control of it. When you ponder the greatness of creation, it is impossible to retain a narrow-minded conception of God.

However, you must not lose sight of the fact that God is also the Creator of the small and everyday things: the perfection of the rose; the fragility of the forget-me-not. All these things reflect a creative God who is also the Master of order and detail.

We so easily forget that God is interested in our well-being. If you doubt this, just consider how many times in the past He guided you through difficult circumstances. Looking back, you will realise that you should probably thank Him for prayers that remained unanswered. And sometimes He responded in such an everyday way to your prayers that you hardly recognised it as answers.

Be acutely aware of your circumstances when you pray, because you never know how God will answer. Many people continue praying for things long after God had answered their prayers. Others who see their prayers answered ascribe it to coincidence. God chooses his own way of working in your life and it is often through the everyday and familiar things in life that He chooses to do so.

Thank You, almighty God, that you never cease working in my life and answering my prayers. You speak with a thousand tongues; let me always hear your voice.

Fragrance all your deeds with the live-giving aroma of prayer.
~ Pope John XXIII ~

Accumulate Scriptural Ammunition

He will cover you with his feathers, and under his wings you will find refuge; his faithfulness will be your shield and rampart (Ps. 91:4).

The path of the Christian has its high as well as its low points. There are moments of victory when joy fills your spirit and thoughts and your entire life appears to be full of the Spirit of the living Christ. Then there are times when life is filled with negativity and spiritual matters appear vague and unreal. In such times a heavy depression descends on your spirit and you may even feel that God has forsaken you.

One way to conquer spiritual dejection is to accumulate spiritual ammunition when you are spiritually strong. Don't read the Bible merely as part of a spiritual discipline, but learn to treasure those texts that have a special meaning for you. Learn these texts by heart so that you can call them up in times of weakness and temptation. One thing is sure: a Christian who has a working knowledge of God's Word has a strong defence against the trickery of Satan. Anything that has been inspired by God to strengthen your faith is worth cherishing.

Knowing your Bible as a manual for the Christian life not only strengthens your faith, but also helps you to become more sensitive to the ways in which God wishes to guide you. God often uses the Scriptures to manifest his will to his disciples. Always remember the words of 2 Timothy 3:16: *All Scripture is God-breathed and is useful for teaching, rebuking, correcting and training in righteousness ...*

Jesus my Lord, incarnate Word, through the Scriptures I develop an ever-increasing love for You. Guide me through your Word, thereby strengthening my faith.

The Bible is the inexhaustible source of all truth. The existence of the Bible is the greatest blessing ever experienced by mankind.
~ Immanuel Kant ~

SPIRITUAL HUNGER

My soul yearns, even faints, for the courts of the Lord; my heart and my flesh cry out for the living God (Ps. 84:2).

Spiritual hunger is not that easily recognisable and therefore many people deny its existence. They think that it is a religious term that has no bearing on everyday life. However, its symptoms are apparent to anyone who is willing to look.

Most people experience a profound longing for inner satisfaction. They feel that they would like to reach that point where they no longer have to strive after that which seems unattainable. If they do not experience such a feeling, they embark upon a restless quest for things that are of secondary importance.

This restlessness manifests itself in different ways. Life is lived at a pace and with a passion never intended by God. Time is devoted to and energy wasted on things that are of little or no significance. When this restlessness takes possession of your spirit life becomes a cruel cycle of frustrated ideals and broken dreams.

A person who spends quality time with God is never spiritually hungry and is better able to live a balanced life and to avoid foolish mistakes. Spend time with your heavenly Father and note the effect that it has on your life. Spending time in his presence will fulfil all the desires of your heart and his peace will satisfy all your spiritual hunger.

Living Christ, through my communion with You I experience the deep and peaceful fulfilment of all my needs.

Every person has two journeys to make through life. There is the outer journey with its many incidents and milestones. Then there is also the spiritual journey, the odyssey of the spirit, with its own history.

~ William R. Inge ~

Extract the Most From Your Faith

"Whoever has will be given more ... Whoever does not have, even what he has will be taken from him" (Mt. 13:12).

There are many people who are deeply dissatisfied with their faith. They may not declare their disappointment openly, but their attitude towards the Christian faith is so lackadaisical that their faith in the living Christ has never inspired them to walk more intimately with Him. The inevitable result of this unhappy state of affairs is that their discipleship weakens and becomes ineffectual.

To receive everything that faith offers you, you should regard it as a full-time task and a dedicated way of life, and not as an addendum only to be used whenever convenient. A dedicated Christian must also be a scripturally bound Christian. Refusal to use the Scriptures as a code of moral conduct may cause your faith to become emotionally unbalanced. And then the message of the gospel becomes distorted to suit your own personal conviction and ideology. Eventually all the power of faith disappears in wishful thinking and unscriptural argumentation.

The church and the world currently have a serious need for disciplined Christianity that will affirm and proclaim the ideas of Jesus. The one truth that embraces all others is so simple that people have turned away from it and have called it impractical. Jesus said: " ... As I have loved you, so you must love one another" (Jn. 13:34).

The dedication that is required to live a life of Christian love demands a strength that can only be acquired from the Holy Spirit. This attitude is kept alive through prayer and contemplation and a constant yearning for a more profound experience with God.

I plead with You, o living Jesus, for the gift of your Holy Spirit so that I may experience my faith to its fullest potential.

Faith is the beginning and the end of love, and God is both of these.
~ Ignatius of Antioch ~

BE AN INSPIRATION TO OTHERS

"If someone forces you to go one mile, go with him two miles" (Mt. 5:41).

There are always two ways to carry out a task: you can either do it unwillingly and complainingly while trying to get away with doing as little as possible, or you can do it joyfully and diligently, thereby accomplishing more than could be reasonably expected of you.

If you work according to the first principle you will soon find yourself unpopular with your superiors and colleagues. Even more importantly, you will also be dissatisfied with yourself because you are aware that you are not giving your best. To anyone worth his salt this will be an extremely unsatisfactory state of affairs. However, if the second approach is your life philosophy, you will find that you not only hold the respect of your superiors and colleagues, but also that your task – however humble it may be – has importance. It will provide you with a sense of satisfaction because you have set about a task and completed it joyfully and thoroughly.

You will run into problems if you try to do this on your own and in your own strength, but if you dedicate every aspect of your life to Christ and ask Him to guide everything you do, the strength of the Holy Spirit will soon enable you to undertake your task with a strength and enthusiasm that transcends human limitations.

Master and Saviour, in your strength I am capable of anything. Help me to perform my duty joyfully and thoroughly.

Work is love made visible.
~ Kahlil Gibran ~

Love is the Key

Bless those who persecute you; bless and do not curse (Rom. 12:14).

There are those who find forgiveness extremely difficult. When you or someone that you love suffers as a result of someone else's behaviour, you tend to harbour hatred in your heart towards the person responsible instead of granting complete forgiveness.

True forgiveness requires complete purification. You cannot pretend to forgive while still holding a grudge against the person concerned. Forgiveness demands that the slate be wiped clean so that you can start anew without any anger in your heart.

This is of course humanly impossible, but with God the impossible becomes possible. The first step on the road to forgiveness is inevitably prayer. If someone has wronged you or someone you love, you must pray for the wrongdoer. Ask God to bless that person and to give you the grace to do so. Pray that his love will take away all bitterness so that the healing balm of his peace may flow through your being. Once this has happened, you will find that the obstacle of bitterness has been removed, and the love of God will enable you to grant unconditional forgiveness.

The love of Jesus Christ has achieved victory over evil in its most barbaric forms. Why should you not allow this same love to cure you from your bitterness?

Jesus, my Redeemer, help me to forgive in love as You forgave me in love. You redeem me also from the bitterness of an unforgiving spirit.

He who cannot forgive others destroys the bridge over which he himself has to walk; every person has a need for forgiveness.

~ Thomas Fuller ~

Problems Can Be An Asset

We are hard pressed on every side, but not crushed; perplexed, but not in despair (2 Cor. 4:8).

To be a disciple of Jesus in no way means that your life will be free of problems. Some of his noblest servants struggled with problems from the moment that they swore allegiance to Him. Even Jesus knew what problems his intimate relationship with God the Father would bring over Him.

The important fact is not the problem that confronts you, but the attitude with which you respond to it. Some people regard problems as obstacles or obstructions, while others see them as opportunities to grapple with a challenge, or as ways to deepen their relationship with their heavenly Father.

It is possible to try and solve your problems in your own strength. Many people call this independent thinking, but if your thoughts fail, your problem remains just as insurmountable. It is at this point where those who have adopted Christ as their Lord and Master realise the value of his living presence. They take their problems to Him and in simple faith hand it over to Him.

The solution may appear immediately or it may be delayed, but no one who has ever sought his guidance has ever been disappointed. He guides those who place their faith in Him and turn their problems into an asset for life.

Grant me the faith, o Lord, to regard my problems as opportunities, because in prayer I may invoke your wisdom upon them.

Trust the past to the grace of God, the present to his love and the future to his providence.

~ Augustine of Hippo ~

The Kingdom and the Power and the Glory!

The Lord has established his throne in heaven, and his kingdom rules over all (Ps. 103:19).

In a world where so many people think that evil reigns supreme over truth and justice, we must never lose sight of the fact that the power and the sovereignty and the majesty reside in God. It is this knowledge – and only this – that encourages and strengthens us even in our darkest hour.

History attests to many instances where it appeared as if everything was lost: when anarchy and lawlessness threatened to destroy all good order; when selfishness and lust dominated the thoughts of many people; when powerful nations attempted to destroy weak ones; when innocent people were oppressed and tortured.

Despite all these things history also manifests those times when truth and justice eventually triumphed. There may have been a time of anxiety and concern when fear and suffering were rife, but ultimately the power of evil was destroyed and the righteous prevailed.

However cheerless and hopeless circumstances may seem, never forget that God is almighty and great and that He is still in control. Place your trust in Jesus Christ your Redeemer and find encouragement and peace in the knowledge that our setbacks are merely temporary, because Christ has already conquered the world (see Jn. 16:33).

Almighty God, great wonders are performed by your hand and your mighty deeds are borne out by the history of mankind. From eternity until eternity You are God!

What is impossible for God? Not that which is difficult for his omnipotence, but that which is contrary to his character.

~ Ambrose ~

I IN HIM AND HE IN ME

"Remain in me, and I will remain in you. No branch can bear fruit by itself; it must remain in the vine ... " (Jn. 15:4).

It is a sad truth that many people seek Jesus through inappropriate and ineffective means. They take the inspiration that He offers them and use it in different ways: they become ardent social reformers; they establish political parties; they call themselves Christians and perform many good deeds in his Name. It is possible to be active in Jesus' Name and yet to forget the Source that inspired the service. Attempting to serve the Lord without the strength that He alone can provide inevitably leads to frustration and disappointment.

The glorious truth that Jesus Christ is a living reality is a thought pattern that every faithful person should cultivate until his presence becomes a reality in our everyday lives. To be obsessed with the thought of an immanent Christ does not turn a faithful person into a religious fanatic, but simply creates a new awareness of the meaning of life. By professing his presence you become aware of the problems, challenges, joys and sorrows of your existence as seen from his perspective. In this way Jesus becomes an increasing reality in your life.

The pinnacle of your spiritual life is to know Him as a living reality. This knowledge affects your practical and emotional life. Meeting Christ in the silence of solitude and experiencing the touch of his Spirit upon your spirit can have far-reaching consequences for your existence. It can be a truly enriching experience for your soul, and to separate such an experience from your everyday life may lead to great spiritual damage.

O Hearer of prayers, grant me your Holy Spirit, so that I will persevere in prayer until Christ lives in me and I in Him.

Jesus Christ is everything to man's entire need.
~ Richard Halvorsen ~

What God can accomplish through you

"Remain in me, and I will remain in you. No branch can bear fruit by itself; it must remain in the vine. Neither can you bear fruit unless you remain in me" (Jn. 15:4).

You worship a God that performs miracles. In times of stress and tension you can call upon Him. Experience has proved that He will answer in his chosen way. With God you will always receive what you need, because He is the Giver of every perfect gift and you are the fortunate receiver.

Whenever you wish to respond to the benevolence of God you usually start by looking around you for some or other good deed that you can perform to please the heart of God. You then start doing it with enthusiasm and dedication. But are you sure that this is what He wants you to do?

Discovering God's will for your life can be an exciting adventure. You may try out various directions before you finally discover the path upon which He wishes to lead you. But when you possess the inner conviction that you are within his holy will, you will discover that you are no longer working for Him, but that He is working through you.

When this happens the road ahead opens up miraculously. Problems suddenly become opportunities and your faith becomes practical, alive and dynamic. You realise that by working with God you become an effective instrument in his hand. You will never discover your full potential in the service of Christ until you realise what God can accomplish through you.

Holy Father, help me through your guidance to become an instrument in your hand so that I may work within your will and to your honour.

Enthusiasm, however ardent it may be, is meaningless until it is transformed into action.

~ Thomas Carlyle ~

Share your burden with Jesus

... "I have had enough, Lord," he said. "Take my life; I am no better than my ancestors" (1 Kgs. 19:4).

How often have you felt, like Elijah, that perhaps it was time you gave up? Your plans go awry; your problems seem insurmountable; you have just managed to overcome one crisis when you have to face the next. Your good intentions are misinterpreted: you are misunderstood and blamed for things you are innocent of; you suffer injustice at the hands of others. When this happens you start wondering what precisely the sense and purpose of life is. You are tempted to stop trying to be the person that you intuitively know God expects you to be.

When you find yourself in this unbearable situation all you need to do is think back to the time when Jesus was alive. The Son of God – He who was born from God's love for the world and whose life exemplified the greatest love of all time – was despised and forsaken by people. He was crucified for our sins and to Him belonged the sorrow that brought us peace.

Despite injustice Jesus never hesitated or stumbled. He had a divine mission to complete. By placing his faith in God He completed his mission and as a result the world has learnt to understand the meaning of the words love and forgiveness.

When your spirit is at the low-water mark, turn your heart and mind to Christ who knows and understands your suffering better than even you can. Place your trust in Him and He will lead you from the darkness of your own despondency into his marvellous light.

Light of the world, bright and inextinguishable, dispel all darkness from my life; banish all fear and lead me to your wonderful light.

We can go no deeper into Christ than what we allow Him to come into us.

~ John Henry Jowett ~

You have responsibilities as a Christian

"Now that you know these things, you will be blessed if you do them" (Jn. 13:17).

Where there is fear, there is mistrust, and this in turn leads to confusion. This scenario is clearly evident in national and international state affairs, because fear and mistrust go hand in hand in many countries in the world, thus causing disorder and chaos.

What is happening globally is symptomatic of what is happening in the lives of many people. They become fearful of what other people think and how they act and then become defensive about their own faith and behaviour. In this way the dismal cycle flourishes and spreads its destructive influence until all of humanity is possessed by fear.

It is no exaggeration to claim that a lack of faith in God and one another is what has forced human beings into this dangerous situation. A world that is controlled by fear is not a safe place in which to live. How tragically sad it is that people refuse to proclaim and use the antidote for fear. This antidote was set out by Jesus: " ... *Love one another ... "*(Jn. 13:34). And the apostle of love re-confirmed it: *There is no fear in love. But perfect love drives out fear ...* (1 Jn. 4:18).

Act positively and allow the Holy Spirit to fill you with so much love that you fear no more. Be a proclaimer and example of the peace that only Christ can give. You can influence a terror-stricken world, honour your Christian duties and thereby become part of the solution and not the problem.

Holy Spirit, grant me an infectious faith so that others may share in the love and peace that You bestow upon me.

We never love our neighbour as much as when our love for him is inspired by the love of God.

~ Francois Fenelon ~

A REASON TO LIVE

" ... Because I live, you also will live" (Jn. 14:19).

In these ominous times in which we live there are many people who wonder whether existence is worthwhile. They are possessed by a terrified doubt over an unknown future, and a spirit of pessimism and dejection prevails in their minds. However, life is extremely precious and even the most despairing person realises this when his or her life comes under serious threat.

Despite how cheerless the future may appear, it is of the utmost importance to admit and accept the fact that both your life and the future are in the hands of God. The Christian's life is not ruled by blind fate. God is in control of every situation in which you may find yourself. He knows your needs and is always prepared to provide for you. As your faith grows and you begin to trust Him increasingly, you will also begin to realise the joy of a life in Christ and be comforted by the awareness of the unfailing and immutable God. He is the Rock upon which you can build your entire life and future.

Through his death and resurrection Jesus not only gave you life, but also a reason to live. Through his Holy Spirit He also provides you with the ability to cope with life. Choose life and live it in the abundance of Jesus Christ always honouring Him.

Faithful Leader, in the midst of the change and the corruption that I see around me daily, I am assured that Jesus lives and that He has also made it worthwhile for me to be alive.

He who has no inner life is the slave of his environment.
~ Henri Frederic Amiel ~

From Conversion to Discipleship

But grow in the grace and knowledge of our Lord and Savior Jesus Christ ... (2 Pet. 3:18).

There are people who can very clearly remember the moment when they accepted Jesus as the Lord and Redeemer of their lives. Others cannot remember a time when they did not love Him and did not acknowledge his sovereignty in their life.

The crucial fact of your Christian life is not necessarily the moment of your conversion, but rather how far you have since progressed on the Christian path. Conversion is the beginning of your Christian pilgrimage, but discipleship implies growing trust, increasing love and unconditional obedience to the Master. It is this dynamic discipleship that keeps your faith strong and meaningful.

Always rejoice in the truth that you believe in Christ as your Lord and Redeemer, and be assured that He will lead you in ever more wonderful ways on the path ahead. To begin a new life in Christ is like walking from the darkness into the light. The realisation that Christ wants to live in you and wants to express Himself through you opens up an entirely new world. Discipleship means oneness with the Master and as your love for Him inspires you to greater obedience, his immanent presence will become an ever greater reality to you.

Discipleship implies continuous growth in Christ, until He becomes the greatest motivating force in your life. Then you will discover that you can do nothing without Him, but that with Him you are able to accomplish all things. This is the pure joy of discipleship.

Jesus, I place my love and trust in You and rejoice in the knowledge that I can grow closer to you every day, thus becoming more like your image.

Do not fear growing slowly, only fear inactivity and stagnation.
~ Ralph Waldo Emerson ~

Can the world see that you are a Christian?

... But they rested on the Sabbath in obedience to the commandment (Lk. 23:56).

The cruel deed is done. The Son of God has fallen prey to man's inhumanity to his fellow man. The jeering, screaming, merciless crowds of Good Friday are now the pious people of the Sabbath. The evil deeds of the day are behind them and now they can return to their lives of devoutness and obedience to the law of Moses. They worship and rest as it behoves God-fearing people. It is the Sabbath.

There is a distinct quality of hypocrisy present in this situation, which should serve as a warning to all Christians. Just as you are shocked by the thought of these pious people parading through the temple with the blood of Jesus still on their hands, so you should realise that a Christian's surrender to the Master implies a life of complete obedience, not just an attitude that is displayed on a Sunday.

The authenticity of your faithfulness to Jesus will be judged according to the way you live your life at all times, and not only in the sphere of the church. Your faith and commitment to Christ's cause will be tested precisely when you are most susceptible to irritation, anger, jealousy and pride. It is your responsibility to live every day of the week according to the instructions of Jesus – not only on Sundays. This is what your Lord trusts you to do to show his glory in this world.

Loving Master, I will prove to the world that I am a Christian through the consistency of my love. Enable me to do this through your Spirit.

The serene beauty of a holy life is the most powerful force in the world, after the power of God.

~ Blaise Pascal ~

Spiritual Growth Through Prayer

After Job had prayed for his friends, the Lord made him prosperous again and gave him twice as much as he had before (Job 42:10).

It is by no means difficult to make enemies. You only have to say the wrong thing, or even do absolutely nothing, and you will find that you have somehow managed to make an enemy. Furthermore it isn't necessarily helpful to always hold a post-mortem over a defunct friendship. But some frank talking inspired by a sincere desire to revive a friendship can often be of great benefit. However, if this sincere desire is absent, the air will simply be contaminated even more by attempts at straightforward and candid conversation.

No one enjoys making enemies. Remember that it is possible to turn an enemy into a friend. Granted, this isn't always easy, because forgiveness requires true greatness. Trying to understand the false pride, secret fears and plain foolishness of man is a beginning that may help in this process. Only those who have undergone meaningful spiritual growth can transform enmity into friendship. Those who are spiritually stunted keep the dying embers of bitterness burning in their words, deeds and attitudes.

One sure and practical way of starting to turn enemies into friends is by praying for them. To many of us this may sound absurd and excessively altruistic, but it is a truly wise act if you desire a constructive way of life. Prayer changes your attitude towards people and events, and when this happens, the battle is just about won. With God on your side, you are on the side of ultimate victory.

Dear Lord, help me to grow in You so that I may manifest a forgiving spirit. You have forgiven me through your grace. Help me to follow your example.

It takes two sides to create lasting peace; only one to take the first step.
~ Edward M. Kennedy ~

WE MUST LOVE ONE ANOTHER

Follow the way of love ... (1 Cor. 14:1).

All around the world people are seeking greater knowledge and awareness of our Lord, Jesus Christ. As the Holy Spirit awakens them, people are striving to meet the Master in prayer, worship, communion and study. It is probably true to say that the enthusiasm which people have displayed in this quest is as great now as it has ever been throughout history.

While this diligent approach to one's faith is commendable and should be encouraged, one has to remember not to lose sight of the foundation of the Christian faith in one's eagerness to get to know Jesus better. The birth, death and resurrection of Jesus demonstrate God's unfathomable love for his people. Through Jesus Christ He has made it abundantly clear that of all the things that He has commanded you to do, the willingness to show love stands out from above all other things.

Knowledge of the Master and the blessing of spiritual gifts are much sought after attributes among his modern disciples, but regardless of how scripturally knowledgeable you are or how much you know of God, there is nothing that manifests the glory of God more than the love of Jesus Christ. Concentrate your pilgrimage on continually getting to know Him better. Don't merely learn about Him. Allow his love to fill your being so that you may reflect it in your everyday life.

Jesus, loving Master, let my daily life be an expression of your love.

Loving Christ is something greater than knowing Him.
~ Thomas Aquinas ~

God is with you

"The Lord your God is with you, he is mighty to save. He will take great delight in you, he will quiet you with his love, he will rejoice over you with singing" (Zeph. 3:17).

When things start going wrong in your life it is easy to despair and throw in the towel. It just seems to be such an unfair battle in which you are involved. There are many people who once seemed invincible, but who simply allowed themselves to be overwhelmed by a spirit of helplessness and hopelessness.

If ever there was a situation when everything seemed hopeless it was on the day of Jesus' crucifixion. The hopes and dreams of those who thought that He would be the Saviour of Israel were dashed when He died like a common criminal on the cross.

But then God interceded. The Lord God, who was Christ's hope and strength, miraculously turned apparent defeat into victory. The sorrowful Good Friday was transformed into the triumphant resurrection of Easter Sunday when Christ rose in all majesty from death.

Whatever circumstances you find yourself in; however dismal the future may seem and despite all the problems that confront you, always remember that God is with you and that He is in control of your circumstances. Place your faith and trust in Him and He will grant you victory.

Redeemer and Friend, thank You that I may be sure, through You, that God loves me and is always with me. It makes my heart rejoice in unprecedented exultation.

Keep a stout heart. God is more powerful than Satan. We are on the winning side.

~ John Chapman ~

May

Loving triune God,
   during this month we call to mind the descent of the Holy Spirit.
As always You have kept your covenant:
   You have sent us the other Comforter
   to comfort us in our deepest sorrow;
   to be our Leader when we are unsure of
   the road that we must travel;
   to be our Teacher who reveals your will to us;
   who teaches us how to love You truly and
   how to serve our fellow human beings in love.
Send your Spirit as a flame, to cleanse and purify me of all false
   motives, all envy, all unforgivingness and hate,
   all pride and self-exaltation.
Send your Spirit as a wind, to rush through my life and bring
   new life and growth.
Send your Spirit as a dove, to confer on me the peace of God
   that transcends all human understanding.
Send your Spirit as water, to wash me whiter than snow and to
   allow me to grow spiritually so that I may bear the fruit
   that befits my conversion.
Send your Spirit as the dew, to refresh me and nourish me
   with heavenly strength.
Recreate, o Spirit, let live, o Spirit.
Let the kingdom come in glory.

Amen.

*C*ONFIDENCE FOR THE FUTURE

The way of the Lord is a refuge for the righteous ... (Prov. 10:29).

*T*o be forewarned should mean to be equipped to cope with every life situation. Unfortunately many people disregard warnings and then they are surprised and hurt when they have to bear the consequences of their actions.

The Bible is full of warnings. Some have already been fulfilled, but others refer to prophecies that have not yet been fulfilled. It would seem as if current world events are inexorably moving towards a climax. The times in which we live are unparalleled in human history, and intelligent people justifiably wonder what the future holds.

People who live within God's will because they are faithful, and who believe that mankind is not controlled by fate but by a loving Creator, draw comfort from the knowledge that, despite appearances to the contrary, there is a divine plan at work in man's life.

This faith creates trust and provides hope; it conquers fear and gives the Christian disciple the ability to step into the future with confidence and in the certain conviction that God is still in control. To possess this kind of faith God must stand at the centre of your life. If this is the case you will see world events in the light of the eternal design of God and you will be equipped to meet the future with confidence.

Almighty God, I believe with conviction that You are still completely in control of your creation as well as of the world events of our time. Once more I place my trust fully in You.

The more we trust in God, the trustworthier we find Him.
~ Cliff Richard ~

*F*aith is the answer

... (T)he mystery of godliness is great: He appeared in a body, was vindicated by the Spirit, was seen by angels, was preached among the nations, was believed on in the world, was taken up in glory (1 Tim. 3:16).

*H*owever contradictory this statement may appear to you, it remains an indisputable fact of the Christian faith, in all its simultaneous complexity and simplicity. Where else would you find God assuming a human form or a King living as a simple town cabinet-maker? Kings live in palaces, and yet the Prince of peace had no place to rest his head. Jesus stood his ground against the scholars of his time and overwhelmed them with his knowledge and intellectual abilities. And yet simple people understood Him when He explained profound truths to them in the form of parables.

The circumstances of your life often confuse and trouble you, and sometimes you are simply unable to understand a particular situation. Your peace of mind can be disturbed by fear, illness, death and so many other negative things. Your faith so easily becomes unsettled and then you start questioning God's love and the purpose of your faith.

This is the time for relying on God. He arranges everything for the benefit of those who love Him. For the faithful, good is born from evil. From the evil of Golgotha the victory of the resurrection emerged. God has a sacred purpose with everything that happens in your life, and when the time is right this purpose will be revealed to you.

I praise and thank You, Lord my God, that I may faithfully accept your every act in my life because I know that everything works for the good of those who love You.

Human reason is weak and may be deceived, but faith cannot be deceived.

~ Thomas à Kempis ~

*P*ONDER THE BENEVOLENCE OF GOD

"How I long for the months gone by, for the days when God watched over me, when his lamp shone upon my head and by his light I walked through darkness!" (Job 29:2-3).

*T*here is nothing strange about people occasionally losing their spiritual way. It can easily happen after the ecstasy of a dramatic conversion has abated and you once more start living your life according to your accustomed ways, with old temptations once more cropping up. Or perhaps you are suffering from depression and despondency as a result of sorrow or illness, anxiety or fear, or setbacks and failures. It is in these circumstances that feelings of helplessness and despair may easily overwhelm you.

In times like these you need to hold on to your faith and to place your trust in Christ who has promised never to forsake or abandon you. Think of the goodness of God and constantly remind yourself of the path along which He has guided you up to now; how He has protected you and looked after you in the past.

Jesus never changes. As He has done in the past He now waits for you to turn to Him in your times of crisis. Lay all your fears and worries before Him. True to his promises, his perfect love will drive away all fear and you will be enveloped in his love.

Be still my soul, the Lord is on your side. In this knowledge I will struggle through all my disappointments, sorrow and grief, because You grant me the strength to do so. For this I praise and thank You.

Consider how rapidly people change and how little trust we can place in them. Then hold on to God who never changes.

~ Teresa of Avila ~

Share your problems with Jesus

The troubles of my heart have multiplied; free me from my anguish (Ps. 25:17).

There are few things that can have such a potentially negative effect on your spiritual, physical and emotional well-being as problems and worries. They influence your unconscious to such an extent that your mental abilities may be impaired. In many cases this results in people becoming spiritual and physical wrecks.

When Jesus called those who are weary and overburdened to Him He did not guarantee them complete exemption from problems, nor did He promise that all their problems would disappear instantaneously. Instead, he offered to share your burden and also to teach you how to cope with it so that you may find peace of mind.

You can never predict when you will experience setbacks in life, nor can you foresee how serious these incidents will be. What is of crucial importance is that you prepare yourself to handle these problems when they crop up. To be ill prepared for these eventualities may have devastating results.

To maintain a healthy balance and harmony in your mind, it is essential to develop a healthy personal relationship with the living Christ. Remain near to Jesus through faithful prayer and contemplation. If you do this, you will find that when problems strike, He will be with you to help you conquer them with peace in your heart.

Faithful Lord Jesus, thank You that I may come to You with all my problems and worries in the certainty that I will find peace and repose with You.

God insists that we ask, not because He isn't familiar with our situation, but because we need the spiritual discipline of asking.
~ Catherine Marshall ~

GOD'S WAY

Good and upright is the Lord; therefore he instructs sinners in his ways (Ps. 25:8).

In today's world it is especially easy to lose one's spiritual way. The pressure exerted by the sinful world is felt by young as much as old; temptations are multitudinous and offered on a silver platter; the variety of detours make it extremely difficult to follow the right path. In an era that constantly questions standards and morality there is always a fundamental danger that our principles may be compromised, however innocent and harmless the first step may seem at the time.

There is only one way to live your life and that is to keep to God's ways. In his commandments He set out the basic rules for a pious and devout life. In addition to this Christ became a living example that demonstrated to us how such a life ought to be lived.

Even though centuries have passed, nothing has changed with regard to the way of life that is acceptable and pleasing to God. Christ is still the way, the truth and the life, and the path of righteousness is still that of obedience to God in all things.

If you open your heart and life to the immanent Holy Spirit, you will become increasingly aware of his influence and suggestions. Follow his guidance and you will know that the path you are following is the way of God.

Search me, O God, and know my heart; test me and know my anxious thoughts. See if there is any offensive way in me, and lead me in the way everlasting (Ps. 139:23-24).

If the tenets of Christ were always preached as purely as they came from his lips, the entire world would now have been Christian.

~ Thomas Jefferson ~

When things become unmanageable

... And who is equal to such a task? (2 Cor. 2:16).

We all go through times when things threaten to overwhelm us and our faith appears to be an inadequate defence. It seems as if our circumstances are continually worsening, our relationships suffer grievous blows and everything suddenly appears unmanageable.

What is actually happening is that you have allowed the challenges of the world to exceed your spiritual reserves. The demands of life have proved your faith to be insufficient. When you feel as if you have reached breaking point you need to return to the fundamentals of your faith and assure yourself of the presence of God in your life. This will help you to restore the balance in your life so that you can see people and events in the right perspective.

It is definitely not God's intention to place you under so much pressure that you reach breaking point and collapse under the strain. A living and positive faith is a stabilising influence under the most confusing circumstances. Possessing such a faith is not a spiritual luxury, but an urgent necessity if you wish to deal with the demands of life successfully.

Realising the necessity of faith is the first step to possessing it. If you are unaware of your need, how will you be able to fulfil it? When you tell the Lord that you need his help and trust Him unconditionally you will know that He will carry you through, because you love and trust in Him.

Lord Jesus, through your wisdom and strength I am able to cope with all the demands of life. Keep me close to your heart at all times.

God visits us frequently, but most of the time we are not at home.
~ Blaise Pascal ~

*B*OLSTER YOUR SELF-CONFIDENCE

The Lord is my light and my salvation – whom shall I fear? The Lord is the stronghold of my life – of whom shall I be afraid? (Ps. 27:1).

*T*here are times when everything appears dismal and uncertain. Your thoughts are bewildered, with the result that your life loses its sense of direction. Your confidence in yourself starts fading until it is almost nonexistent. When this happens you inevitably become unsure of God, your faith falters and your life starts losing meaning and significance.

A tried and proven way of restoring your faith in life so that you can live a life free from feelings of inferiority, is to be absolutely sure that God is all-sufficient for you. This all-sufficiency is not something that is forced upon you from an almighty Being, but is rather the effect of the merciful Spirit of God in your own spirit. It is the knowledge that God lives and works in you daily. This tremendous truth gives you the self-confidence to face the demands of every day.

When you invite the Spirit of God into your life all detrimental fear is defeated and eventually vanishes because you know that God is busy actualising his plan with your life. Because his presence is a reality to you, the future will unfold before you in all its joy, peace and self-confidence.

Thank You, almighty God, that destructive fear is removed from my life by the ministry of the Holy Spirit, and instead replaced with quiet confidence.

Trusting in Christ does not make us lazy, irresponsible or reckless; on the contrary, it rouses us, impels us forward and makes us eager to live a pious life and actively serve Him. There is no other kind of self-confidence that can be compared to this.

~ Ulrich Zwingli ~

An Exercise in Prayer

Be joyful in hope, patient in affliction, faithful in prayer (Rom. 12:12).

*I*s your prayer life everything that you would like it to be? And everything that Christ would like it to be? You may regard this as a rather presumptuous question, but you are the only one who needs to know its answer. However, your answer can make the difference between an ineffective prayer life or one that is filled with an awareness of the presence of God.

While you are praying you undoubtedly think of your family and friends. They probably form part of your normal prayer pattern, and it is possible that you seldom think beyond them. And yet the whole world is pleading for prayer. If you doubt this statement, all you need to do is take a look at your newspaper. Every newspaper is a prayer manual in itself. You can pray for the editors and those who are responsible for forming public opinion; you can pray for those who grieve; who are the victims of violence, and if your soul is noble enough, even for those who committed the acts of violence. If you search for it, you may even be able to find something for which to thank God.

When you move out of your everyday world you will find innumerable opportunities for prayer. Give some thought in prayer to those who seem tired and disillusioned or to all the irritable people you encounter. Rejoice together with those who are happy and thank God for their happiness. You never have to search for a reason to pray.

The great advantage of expanding your prayer base is the fact that it intensifies your own quiet time with God. While you are praying for others you will find a more intimate communion with the living Christ.

Lord Jesus, with your disciples I want to plead: Teach me to pray!

Some thoughts are prayers. There are moments, regardless of the posture, when the soul is on its knees.

~ Victor Hugo ~

*B*ₑwₐᵣₑ! Pᵢₜfₐₗₗₛ ₐₕₑₐₒ!

(B)ut they mingled with the nations and adopted their customs. They worshiped their idols, which became a snare to them (Ps. 106:35-36).

*I*t is an overly familiar fact that people attach much value to material things and the pleasures that life offers. This often becomes the dominating factor of everyday life and eventually life in its totality begins to revolve around materialism and pleasure, so that people become completely dependent on it. This dependence may be work or leisure; it may even include some kind of addiction. Whatever it may be, it becomes the controlling factor in the life of the particular person and has preference over everything else.

Regardless of what it may be, when it relegates God to a lesser position in your life it becomes an idol. And whether people like it or not, or whether they are willing to admit it or not, he who makes himself guilty of this becomes an idolater.

Any form of addiction, be it work, pleasure or habit, leads to a road that is riddled with pitfalls. Avarice, obsession, addiction and uncontrolled desires are but a few forms of fixation that, if left unchecked, will inevitably lead to disastrous and grim consequences for those involved, as well as their loved ones and dependants.

Beware of anything in your life that runs counter to your relationship with Jesus. If it clashes with his life, example and principles, abandon it. Follow the living Christ and enjoy a life of peace and fulfilment.

I know, my Redeemer and Saviour, that I will only be happy and prosperous in this world if I follow your example meticulously. Please let your Holy Spirit assist and help me in this.

We first make our habits, then our habits make us.
~ John Dryden ~

Spiritual Maturity

You ... are controlled not by the sinful nature but by the Spirit ... (Rom. 8:9).

To appreciate the greatness of God and to rejoice in the majesty of his creation elevates the human spirit above the pettiness that is the product of a limited view of life.

When you cannot rise above the pain inflicted upon you by the thoughtless tongue of a flippant person; when it seems as if your life is restricted by a lack of opportunities and undesirable circumstances; when you have fallen into a rut from which you just can't escape – these are the times when it becomes necessary to start questioning the basic reason for your existence.

The direction in which you are travelling clearly manifests where you have chosen to place the emphasis in your life. If you seek financial success or social prestige to the exclusion of more important things in life, you may reach your destination but also lose much.

Because God has created you to be a spiritual being, your spiritual life can never be satisfied by purely material matters. You need a dynamic relationship with the Holy Spirit, which is the only thing that will provide you with permanent satisfaction. This personal relationship with God can be achieved only through a steadfast faith in Jesus Christ. This faith is more than an emotional experience. It encompasses your acceptance of Jesus in your life as well as your willingness to allow his Spirit to manifest Himself through you. Together with this acceptance comes spiritual growth that will give your life new meaning.

Holy Father, grant me a profound awareness of the importance of spiritual growth, so that I may possess a meaningful and sensitive spirit.

It is right that you should start every day anew. There is no better way of growing spiritually and never thinking that you have done enough.
~ Francis de Sales ~

Prove to God that you love Him

But if anyone obeys his word, God's love is truly made complete in him ... (1 Jn. 2:5).

There is often a kind of sentimentality present in our spiritual life that detracts from the force and strength of the Christian faith. To resist this, many disciples of the Master refrain completely from any sentiment and propound an unfeeling faith that is often also aggressive.

Telling God how much you love Him may create an impression of cheap sentimentality, and yet it is one of the most inspiring things that you can do. It fortifies your inner spirit, focuses your thoughts on eternal realities and confirms the convictions that you have always held but seldom expressed.

To tell God you love Him is much more than a noble sentiment, because love without constructive action is useless. Love demands deeds that uplift and inspire. James asks: "What good is it if a man claims to have faith but has no deeds?" (see Jas. 2:14). How genuine can your love for God truly be of you are aware of a serious need and do nothing to alleviate it?

When you tell God that you love Him without any intellectual or spiritual reservations, you are offering your very best to Him and expressing your willingness to serve Him in any sphere where He wishes to use you. Love that does not practically manifest itself becomes an emotional gimmick that lacks the essence of dynamic spirituality.

Beloved Father, I want to tell You repeatedly and with complete conviction: I love You with all my heart, o Lord!

Grant me such a love for God and my neighbour that it will erase all hate and bitterness.

~ Dietrich Bonhoeffer ~

Do your thoughts betray the Master?

... "I tell you the truth, one of you is going to betray me" (Jn. 13:21).

The name of Judas Iscariot has a place in the annals of history that will never be erased. His betrayal is known to everyone who has ever heard the Name of Jesus Christ. The world has never given the name of Judas the opportunity to disappear into obscurity.

Nonetheless, is he really the only person to have betrayed Jesus? Whatever the motive for his betrayal, it must already have been developing in his mind while he enjoyed the intimate companionship of Jesus and his fellow disciples. He was one of the chosen twelve. However, the motives that drive people are known only to themselves and God. Judas was probably frequently excited when Jesus spoke of the kingdom of God. Unfortunately his idea of the kingdom of God differed radically from that of Christ. Judas tried to force Jesus' principles into his own thought patterns, with disastrous results.

We must guard against trying to force Christ and his powerful principles into our own preconceived ideas and doctrines. If you are trying to force Christ into your thought patterns you are betraying Him because you are attempting to limit Him. What is of fundamental importance in your relationship with Christ is not what you try to do with Him, but rather what you are willing to allow Him to do with you. Allow Christ to control your thoughts and to expand your spirit. Then you will never betray Him.

Pull me ever closer to You, dear Lord, so that I may better understand your purpose with my life and never betray You for the sake of things that are of lesser importance.

An evil person is worse when he tries to be a saint.
~ Francis Bacon ~

Something to Live For

"Before long, the world will not see me anymore, but you will see me. Because I live, you also will live" (Jn. 14:19).

In these ominous times there are many people who wonder whether it is worthwhile to be alive. They harbour terrified doubt over an unknown future and as a result they lapse into a mood of pessimism and dejection. Regardless of this we have to remember that life is extremely precious, and even the most despairing person realises this when his or her life is threatened.

Despite how cheerless the future may appear, it is of the utmost importance to admit and accept the fact that both your life and your future are in the hands of God. The Christian's life is not ruled by a blind fate. God is in control of every situation in which you find yourself. He knows your needs and is prepared to provide for you through the wealth and abundance of Jesus Christ.

As your faith grows and becomes stronger, and as you start trusting Him continually more, you will also begin to realise how great the joy of a life in Christ is and how trustworthy God is. He is the Rock upon which you can build your entire life and future in the knowledge that his grace is enough to get you through each day.

Through his death and resurrection Jesus not only gave you life, but also a reason to live. Through his Holy Spirit He also provides you with the ability to live life to the fullest. Seize this life and live it in the abundance of Jesus Christ your Lord.

Throughout all the changing circumstances of life, beloved Lord, in joy as well as sorrow, my heart will sing your praise and thank You for the abundant life that You have made possible for me.

The tragedy of life is that which dies in one while one is still alive.
~ Albert Schweitzer ~

A part of God's family

You are all sons of God through faith in Christ Jesus (Gal. 3:26).

No one is alone in this world. This is the gospel of God. There are many people who feel that they have no one to turn to, and there are others who claim that they have no family. Neither they nor you are alone in this world, because through Jesus you are part of the most privileged family on earth: the family of God.

Your surrender to the Lord Jesus opened the door to the love and concern of the almighty God who is also your heavenly Father. Before the coming of Jesus the Almighty was only worshipped and feared, but Jesus came as evidence of God's love for all of humanity. Through Christ you too are invited to become a child of God, and as such to enjoy the ultimate loving relationship that exists between Parent and child. This is a constant relationship, because the Lord has undertaken to be with you always and never to forsake you (see Heb. 23:5).

If you remember to turn to Jesus in all circumstances and place your trust in Him completely, you will experience the protective love of God that will grant you the peace that transcends all understanding. And then you will never again feel as if you are alone in life.

Great and holy God, it is beyond my understanding how You can condescend to be my Father and Friend. My life is too brief to thank You sufficiently for this.

Whatever may happen to you, God is your Father who is concerned about you. This is his attitude towards you.

~ Martyn-Lloyd Jones ~

Worship God

My message and my preaching were not with wise and persuasive words, but with a demonstration of the Spirit's power (1 Cor. 2:4).

There is a great danger present in our churches today, to wit the number of people who attend services to hear the speaker rather than the Word. This kind of attitude may easily lead to church attendance for the sake of entertainment rather than for the sake of worshipping God and sharing communion with the faithful with the purpose of experiencing the living God and fostering a more profound commitment to Jesus.

In the establishment of the first church Christ predominantly used simple and uneducated people. Throughout the ages many of the great pillars of the church possessed little or no learning, and yet hundreds of thousands were converted by their preaching. God has often chosen people who would by conventional standards fail a preaching test to be his instruments.

This serves to prove that it is the Holy Spirit, and not people's competence, which moves people to surrender their lives to Jesus. In all preaching the emphasis should be on the glory of God, and Christ should not be an incidental part of the sermon but its main content.

In your worship you should always seek the guidance of the Holy Spirit. If the message impels you to dedicate your life to Jesus Christ, you will know for sure that you worship God in spirit and in truth.

Help me, o Lord, to worship only You as the triune God: Father, Son and Holy Spirit.

It is only when people start worshipping correctly that they begin growing spiritually.

~ Calvin Coolidge ~

Your invisible support

For who among men knows the thoughts of a man except the man's spirit within him? In the same way no one knows the thoughts of God except the Spirit of God (1 Cor. 2:11).

*T*ramps have no social support structure. These unfortunate people have no money and are dependent on the generosity and charity of their fellow human beings. They live in truly dismal circumstances.

In the spiritual life many people live in similar circumstances. These are the people who manage their pilgrimage towards eternity only by being carried along by the faith of their parents or by a religious tradition. They pride themselves on a religious inheritance, but when tension and pressure start taking their toll and life becomes harsh and merciless, the inadequacy of their faith is revealed and their entire life collapses. They too have no apparent support structure.

As a Christian the inner support of your spirit cannot be calculated in terms that the world would understand or appreciate. Paul writes: *... God has revealed it to us by his Spirit. The Spirit searches all things, even the deep things of God* (1 Cor. 2:10). Only when you have surrendered yourself to the living Christ and have felt his love and strength course through you, can you know the force that supports your inner spirit. Then you no longer need artificial and external support structures.

Without a personal experience of Jesus the qualities that are necessary for a living faith are absent from your inner life. It is Christ in your spirit that is your invisible support structure.

Holy Lord Jesus, I praise and thank You for giving me inner power and strength and sustaining me through your Spirit that is in me.

Spirituality actually means that the Holy Spirit is at work to renew us from the inside.

~ Leon Suenens ~

ASPIRE TO THAT WHICH IS NOBLE

Finally, brothers, whatever is true, whatever is noble, whatever is right, whatever is pure, whatever is lovely, whatever is admirable – if anything is excellent or praiseworthy – think about such things (Phil. 4:8).

Life can be an unpleasant or an exquisite experience, depending on your attitude towards it. It is unfortunately true that when you are confronted with the meanness of life it is all too easy to allow it to become ingrained in your nature and personality. Because we live in a world where the accepted norms are not the standards of God, it is dangerously easy to set your spiritual goals lower in order to conform to popular opinion. When this happens life loses its beauty and you no longer experience the joy and strength of the immanent Christ.

It requires spiritual sensitivity to appreciate the beauty of life consistently. To believe in God as the Origin and Creator of all things that are beautiful and noble you should start by seeing Him in unexpected places: in the smile of a friend, the innocence of a child, the unobtrusive deed of love, the ultimate success of someone who has struggled for a long time ... In ways that are too many to mention you will begin to see the wonder and beauty of life.

However, the greatest gift of all is when through the grace of God you develop the ability to distinguish between that which is base and offensive, and that which is noble and beautiful, and to accept the responsibility for making the right choice. In choosing Christ you open your life to beauty, nobility and truth.

I bring You my humble thanks, o Saviour, that through the awareness of your immanent Spirit I have the ability to appreciate the beauty and grandeur of life.

Though we travel the world in our search for beauty and nobility, we will not find it unless we carry it in ourselves.
~ Ralph Waldo Emerson ~

Conquer Boredom

... And his commands are not burdensome, for everyone born of God overcomes the world ... (1 Jn. 5:3-4).

It is astounding to see how many people are bored with life. Boredom is also not limited to a particular group or class of society. Young people who ought to be enjoying life complain that they have nothing to do, and show little or no interest in the world around them. Many of the elderly who are no longer active find life tedious because they have lost all interest in it. Boredom deprives life of its beauty and creativity. However, those who find life monotonous and boring have no one to blame but themselves.

God has placed you in a wonderful world filled with fascinating people. If you are bored, you have simply become detached from the wonders of God's creation. It is also an indication that your faith is insufficient to satisfy your spiritual needs and therefore you experience a serious deficiency within yourself.

If you are filled with the love of God it will be manifested in your love for people, your appreciation of life and your enthusiasm for everything worthwhile happening around you. True love creates interest and involvement.

When you begin a new day, believe that it will be the best day ever, and live it to the fullest. Resolve to be enthusiastic and joyful. Allow God's purpose with your life to unfold while you live purposefully for Him. Your enthusiasm and joy will flow to others and life will burgeon. There will be no time to be bored.

Heavenly Father, because your Holy Spirit is my inspiration and guide I can never be bored with life. I stand before You in grateful awe.

A sure cure for boredom is to forget yourself through activities that bring you into contact with other people and ideas.
~ Blanche McKeoun ~

True Religion

Now to each one the manifestation of the Spirit is given for the common good (1 Cor. 12:7).

There are many people who refuse to identify themselves with any form of religion. They point out the failings of religion and the hypocritical behaviour of religious people or the apparent conflict between science and religion. Arguments such as these have existed from the earliest days of Christianity and are still with us today. The main objection is not against the Christian faith as such, but against what its followers have made of it and the way in which it is presented. The quality of many of these followers' lives seldom achieves the high standard set by Christ. Their pronouncements and confessions of their faith are not confirmed by their lives, and this causes disappointment and even aggression.

God is closely connected with people. He created us and He supports us with his strength. To those who have broken through the barrier of religious formalism He is a dynamic personality. Because Jesus was the consummate revelation of God to man, and because He still lives today, He manifests Himself in the lives of those disciples who love Him and who discipline themselves to live according to his will. Innumerable numbers of people have reacted to his summons to become vessels that his Holy Spirit may fill and use. True religion is God at work through your life as a dedicated disciple.

Holy Spirit of God, teach me to be a willing instrument in your hands, so that I may reflect your image in my world.

Let your religion be less of a theory and more of a love affair.
~ G. K. Chesterton ~

*L*ᴇᴛ Cʜʀɪsᴛ ʀᴇᴍᴀɪɴ ᴄᴇɴᴛʀᴀʟ

... (T)hey were furious and began to discuss with one another what they might do to Jesus (Lk. 6:11).

*I*t is so easy to allow your values to become jumbled. When this happens unimportant things become extremely important and essential matters are treated as trifling. This confusion of priorities happens in all spheres of life, but when it occurs on the spiritual level the consequences can be disastrous.

Confessions and dogmas are important because they strive to express the deepest feelings of a group of dedicated people. But if these take the place of Christ the result is pettiness, bitterness and hate. Whatever your Christian convictions may be – and there are many – nothing should detract from the sovereignty of Christ in your life. Christ is the centre of your religion; He is your inspiration and the strength that enables you to live and act in the awareness of his presence.

These spiritual privileges are not your due because of your personal moral or spiritual achievements, but rather because of the grace and mercy of Christ. If his Spirit takes possession of your spirit and you experience a sense of unity with Him, all pettiness, bitterness and hate will disappear from your life and spirit. If Christ's life fills your entire being, all disparaging and disobedient characteristics are eliminated from your personality and replaced by a constructive attitude towards life and a desire for God's will to be done in your life.

Come and fill my life with your Spirit, Lord Jesus, so that there will be no room in my life for bitterness, jealousy and hate.

Experience through the ages has proved that people are willing to fight to the death and to persecute others mercilessly for the sake of a religion of which they do not understand the credo, while nevertheless following its instructions meticulously.

~ Thomas B. Macaulay ~

God is with you everywhere

When Jacob awoke from his sleep, he thought, "Surely the Lord is in this place, and I was not aware of it" (Gen. 28:16).

Through the ages the practice or convention developed for people to attend services of worship to enter into communion with God. It is true that many search for Him in their quiet time through private prayer, Biblestudy and contemplation. But in many cases there is still the feeling that you can only really encounter God during the communal worship of a church service.

However, God is omnipresent. While it is undoubtedly true that you are in the presence of God during church worship, you should remember that He is present in *every* situation in life.

When you stand in awe before the beauty of a sunset or are astonished by the wonder of a sunrise; when birdsong fills you with excitement or the laughter of playing children gladdens your heart; when you look with reverence at the grandeur of the mountains or the splendour of the restless ocean; when you admire nature's wealth of flowers: be assured of God's presence!

When you enter a sick-room or provide help to an aged person; when you assist someone in need or offer loving sympathy to someone who is grieving; when you rejoice with someone who is happy or help carry someone else's burden: then too will you become aware of the presence of God. Look around you and you will see God everywhere.

Omnipresent God, when I put myself in your service, I realise once again the wonder of your love and I know that You are with me.

The remarkable thing about the way in which people speak of God, or their relationship with God, is that it seems as if it completely escapes them that God hears what they say.

~ Søren Kierkegaard ~

*P*REPARE YOURSELF FOR ETERNITY

"Do not work for food that spoils, but for food that endures to eternal life, which the Son of Man will give you ... " (Jn. 6:27).

---

*I*t is amazing how many people have limited patterns of thought. Some live from day to day without any thought of tomorrow. Others, who carry certain responsibilities, plan their financial matters carefully, but refuse to think about the certainty of death.

It is astonishing that intelligent people seriously consider the development of their earthly plans, but pay no attention to the time when they will leave this world and step into eternity. Only a fool ignores this certainty. To plan for greater profits and to neglect planning for death is to be spiritually short-sighted; to try and avoid something that you have to face at some point or another.

To say that one cannot plan for something that you cannot know or determine is also not an appropriate response, because the Scriptures teach us the truth about the spiritual world. Jesus spoke of the life after death in realistic terms and his words ought to be sufficient for anyone thinking seriously about the matter.

To survey life with a sense of eternity is to give new perspective to your daily life. You ought to perform your daily task to the honour of God and should live your entire life so that it is acceptable to Him. To stand in the doorway of the spiritual life and place your hands with love in the hands of God, is the soul-enriching culmination of this life.

Risen Saviour, I place my life and welfare in your faithful care and step into the unknown future with confidence.

For the Christian the final heartbeat is not the conclusion of a meaningless existence. Rather, it is the glorious beginning of a life that will never end.

~ James Dobson ~

Jesus: Truly Human

Many deceivers, who do not acknowledge Jesus Christ as coming in the flesh, have gone out into the world. Any such person is the deceiver and the antichrist (2 Jn. 1:7).

It is fundamental to the Christian faith that Jesus Christ was born as a human being and lived, died and was buried as such, and that He was resurrected from death and ascended into heaven. If this was not the case the Lord that we worship would have remained a supernatural being – completely inaccessible to ordinary people. He would have been revered as a faraway, remote God to be feared and obeyed.

It was precisely to destroy this conception that God, in his infinite wisdom and love for the world, assumed human form and came to live amongst humans. He shared in their joy and sorrow and suffered the same pain and emotions as they did. Therefore, this Jesus understands people and life – the good as well as the bad. This places an extremely strong emphasis on the importance of Christian love. If God had not assumed human form we would never have known the dynamic impact of Jesus Christ on mankind, and man would still be walking in darkness.

It is now your duty as a disciple to show Jesus to the world in the way that you live your life. His Holy Spirit enables you to be a follower of Jesus and your task is made easier by the knowledge that Jesus understands because He has walked along this path as you are doing now.

Lord Jesus, You left the glory of heaven and laid down your royal crown to come to this world for the sake of people like me. For this I thank and praise You.

If Jesus Christ were not truly God, how could He have helped us? If He were not truly human, how could He have helped us?
~ Dietrich Bonhoeffer ~

The Danger of Spiritual Lethargy

"Wake up, O sleeper, rise from the dead, and Christ will shine on you" (Eph. 5:14).

Abnormal sleepiness is also called lethargy. The dictionary defines this word as "apathy; lack of interest and energy." This drowsiness can sneak up on you unexpectedly and when it takes hold of your spiritual life it spells disaster for you as well as your church.

No one deliberately wishes to be a lukewarm or weak Christian, but when your Christian standards are compromised your spiritual life will inevitably be adversely affected. It is simply a matter of time before these second-class standards drive out the dynamic principles of the Master. And then they become a pleasant, gentle-sounding philosophy that no longer challenges you to a life of quality and excellence.

To keep your faith alive you need to work at it constantly. It is fatal to rest on your spiritual laurels, because in the love to which God has called you there can be no vanity. How does one then sustain a living and dynamic faith? A continually deeper prayer life, an inspired and intelligent study of the Bible and participation in the fellowship of the faithful are essential factors for spiritual growth. You know all these things; the question is whether you apply them.

If every believer would wake up spiritually, the world would be on fire for Christ. It would mean the end of violence, racial tension, bitterness and avarice, and Jesus Christ would reign as King.

Holy Master, through the inspiration of your immanent Holy Spirit I plan to be a resolute and alert Christian, all to your honour.

If God sends us down rocky paths He will provide us with strong shoes.

~ Alexander Maclaren ~

CAN PEOPLE SEE JESUS IN YOU?

If Timothy comes, see to it that he has nothing to fear while he is with you, for he is carrying on the work of the Lord ... (1 Cor. 16:10).

So many of people's problems originate from their inability to communicate. Interpersonal relationships are of the utmost importance for our social well-being, and yet it is a sad fact that we often pay little attention to this important aspect of our behaviour.

This is especially true of the relationship between employer and employee, because it is a relationship in which social status and rank play an important role. In the same way someone who asks a favour of us may become the victim of a curt refusal, and this can wound deeply and inflict severe emotional scars.

Jesus commanded us to love one another, and Christian love may be basically defined as doing good and doing it in a nice way. It follows necessarily that when we do something for someone else we should do it in such a way that the presence of Jesus is evident. Treating someone with contempt or creating the impression that they are a nuisance is in direct conflict with everything that the Master taught and did, and everything that He expects of you and me.

In order to create good relationships among people it is essential to follow Jesus' example. Seek the help of the Holy Spirit and ask Him to take control of your life so that you may act with love, peace, joy, patience, benevolence, compassion, faithfulness, tolerance and self-control. This will be your contribution to making the world a better place.

Holy Spirit, please help me to act towards all people in the spirit of Jesus Christ.

Christianity is not a religion, it is a relationship.
~ Dr. Thieme ~

*I*N THE SERVICE OF *G*OD

Do your best to present yourself to God as one approved, a workman who does not need to be ashamed and who correctly handles the word of truth (2 Tim. 2:15).

---

*G*od has many workers who are active in his service. Their involvement becomes apparent in various ways. They often attend church meetings, persevere in the doing of good deeds, and seldom have idle time on their hands. Some of them tend to move in a clique that forbids interaction with anyone whose feelings and beliefs are different from theirs. The sad result is that their mental and spiritual views are very limited.

This can have dismal consequences. You can become so involved in God's work that you lose your vision of what God wants you to do. Then you are diligently working *for* God without working *with* Him. You may nevertheless be industriously busy and other Christians may be impressed with what you are doing for the kingdom of God. You may even delude yourself into thinking that you are doing extremely important work. And one day, when it is too late, something suddenly just dries up in your soul, you become tense, and you simply snap. You cease your Christian activities because of a nervous breakdown, and a life that may have been of great importance to God is lost.

The most important duty of any Christian worker is to maintain and strengthen his relationship with God every day. If you are too busy to spend time with Him in daily prayer, you are simply too busy to be an effective servant to Him.

Loving Master, I humbly ask that You will inspire and strengthen me for the service that I offer to You in gratitude for my redemption.

Service is God's way of liberating man from himself; slavery is man's way of destroying himself.

~ Michael Harper ~

LIGHT IN THE DARKNESS

... To those who have been called, who are loved by God the Father and kept by Jesus Christ: Mercy, peace and love be yours in abundance (Jude v. 1-2).

For as long as one can recall it has seemed as if the world were in a state of chaos. Apart from dozens of lesser confrontations between nations and people, humanity has also experienced two world wars in the past century. Lawlessness and violence have lately been increasing steadily. The cost of living continues to climb and people live lives of fear and insecurity. What is the solution to this sad state of affairs?

There can be only one answer and this is fearlessly to place your faith and trust in Jesus Christ. He has conquered a dark and hostile world and replaced fear with love. He has restored hope where circumstances appeared to be hopeless. To those who believe in Him He has given the blessing of his peace that transcends all understanding.

This is your answer to the dismal confusion and fear of our time. Believe in Jesus Christ and his promises; place your trust in Him unconditionally and He will lead you from the darkness into the light of his unfathomable love for mankind. If you do this you will no longer worry about the future because you will always be protected by the peace of God.

Thank You, Lord my God, that You grant perfect peace to your children in this dark world. Thank You that I may experience this inner peace because I trust in You.

Peace is not achieved in council chambers or through political agreements, but in the hearts of people.

~ Edward Hoover ~

What do we owe one another?

Bear with each other and forgive whatever grievances you may have ... Forgive as the Lord forgave you. And over all these virtues put on love, which binds them all together ... (Col. 3:13-14).

Courtesy is not so much an outward act as the expression of an inner spiritual experience. If Christ lives in you, you will be kind and patient towards your neighbour. This is what courtesy is all about: to take others and their feelings into consideration.

In some social circles courtesy is cultivated only to impress those gullible people who are easily deceived by appearances. A person who is truly courteous is humble and never tries to impress others. His attitude is the same regardless of whether he is talking to his equals or his subordinates. He treats everyone alike, regardless of race, colour or religious creed. He rejoices in making his neighbour's path easier to travel. This attitude is the consequence of regular contact with God.

It is impossible to say that you love and serve God while at the same time treating your neighbour with contempt and disrespect. If you *choose* the people you want to treat with respect you expose the superficiality of your spiritual experience. Courtesy is not something that you can switch on and off. It is either an inherent part of you, or an act of hypocrisy that is despised by your fellow human beings.

When the Holy Spirit lives in you, you reflect the qualities of Christ in your life. Love and courtesy are basic characteristics of the Christian life, and good manners are the product of true Christianity.

Favour me, Lord Jesus, with the gift of courtesy that springs from a heart that is in harmony with You.

There is a courtesy of the heart that is linked to love. It creates a joyful outward demeanour at all times.
~ Johann Wolfgang von Goethe ~

*T*HE SCOURGE OF DISCOURAGEMENT

(T)hough he stumble, he will not fall, for the Lord upholds him with his hand (Ps. 37:24).

---

*F*eeling discouraged is an experience that is all too familiar to most people. It usually occurs when disappointment or failure destroys a long-cherished dream, or when lofty ideals and plans collapse like a house of cards. If discouragement takes hold of your spirit your life becomes bitter and you may find it difficult to recover your vision or ideals.

If you are discouraged by the rejection of an idea of yours, carefully scrutinise the idea in its relation to your discouragement. If you are convinced that the idea is bigger, you can reject the discouragement as the nonsense that it really is. Always keep the vision of what you are trying to attain clearly in your mind, and do not allow it to be suppressed by thoughts of failure.

Apart from always focusing on positive thoughts, it is also important to retain an inner strength that enables you to control those thoughts. When your spirit is sound and healthy, it will be able to limit negative thoughts. Therefore it is important to cultivate a positive spirit.

The application of Christ's teachings and the guidance of his immanent Spirit form the foundation upon which rests your decision to fight discouragement as something fleeting, so that you may achieve the goal that burns brightly in your heart.

I praise you, Lord my God and Father, that I am able to combat discouragement successfully with your help.

I have fathomed the depths of discouragement and found that they are not bottomless.

~ Thomas Hardy ~

*G*OD CALLS EACH OF US INDIVIDUALLY

Let us examine our ways and test them, and let us return to the Lord (Lam. 3:40).

*O*ne of the wonderful facts of the Christian life is that the Lord knows our backgrounds and personalities, and yet still loves us. Sometimes his challenges to us are so direct that we want to avoid them if we can, but at other times He calls us to Him with a tenderness from which we cannot turn away, because we know of his eternal love for us.

No one can say how God will work within a particular person, or in which way He will choose to call someone to his service. He has his own methods of doing this, and a wise disciple will never try to enforce his own will on another person. Instead, he will always be sensitive to how the Master directs other people's lives.

To know that the living Christ works in different ways with different people deepens our understanding, expands our view, improves our sympathy and enriches our communion with the Master. If your heart is filled with love towards your neighbour, there can be no space for the meanness that embitters your spirit and deprives it of the wealth and beauty of God's grace. By realising that God uses different methods for different people you will intensify your understanding of the Master and add to your love for Him in a marvellous manner.

Be continually mindful of the way in which the Lord handles people. This will not only strengthen your faith, but also make life interesting and exciting.

Lord Jesus, grant me an immeasurable love for my fellows and their unique personalities so that I may serve them more effectively.

It is often our own individuality that prevents us from fully respecting the individuality of others.

~ Johann Wolfgang von Goethe ~

*T*HE JOY OF OBEDIENCE

Moses did as the Lord commanded him. He took Joshua and had him stand before Eleazar the priest and the whole assembly. Then he laid his hands on him and commissioned him, as the Lord instructed through Moses (Num. 27:22-23).

---

*F*aith and obedience are essential ingredients of a Christian life of maturity and fulfilment. When a Christian complains that his life is at a spiritual low-water mark, or that it seems as if the spark that used to bring him so much joy has lost its radiance, you may be sure that he is trying to live his life in his own strength or in his own way. When this happens, and you refuse to place your trust in God or obey his will for your life, you are on your way to a dismal spiritual existence that will cause your life to become unhappy and purposeless.

Among the heroes of faith that we encounter in the Old Testament Moses stands out as one who placed his faith in God despite the opposition of both the Egyptians and the Israelites. He obeyed the Word of God and as a result he played a leading role in the establishment of the Jewish nation, acting as mediator between them and the Almighty.

You too have an important role to play in your modern life. You must guide others towards a deeper and more meaningful relationship with the living Christ. The only way in which you can hope to achieve success is to trust that He will give you the ability to accomplish your goal, and – just as importantly – to obey his will unconditionally. Do this and He will use you for great deeds among the people of your time.

Loving Father, through the strength of the Holy Spirit I will try to remain within your will and to trust and obey You without any protest.

How will you find what is good? It is not a question of choices; it is a river that flows at the foot of the invisible throne and moves along the path of obedience.

~ George Eliot ~

June

Eternal God and Creator-Father,

the winter brings its own enchantments and its own apprehensions.

Thank You for blossoms in the winter – even though they are freak
blossoms – they remind us of how almost impossible your love for us,
sinners, appears to be.

Thank You for rain and cold and time to read and contemplate;
for nature that waits slumbering for new growth.

Master, teach me throughout this winter to make time for You and
to become tranquil in your presence;
to sometimes slow down to ponder the
essential matters of life;
to gather strength for a new time of growth.

The winter's cold also brings deep concerns, O Lord:
the poor and the elderly who are dying of hardship while I
sit snug and warm before the hearth;
the unemployed who do not know where
tomorrow's bread will come from;
the hungry who walk past me with beseeching eyes;
the homeless who must endure the cold outside and feel the chill
of heartless people in their bones.

Help me to care with love and to lend a helping hand.

Warm our wintry world with the glow of your love.

Let it be Christmas amidst June's cold.

In the Name of the Great Merciful One, Jesus Christ.

Amen.

*W*HEN YOU PRAY

One of them ... came back, praising God in a loud voice (Lk. 17:15).

*I*t is probably accurate to state that a large percentage of people's prayers consist of requests. We are always asking things of God: we pray for healing, for guidance, for deliverance from our distress, for peace and for God to provide in our needs. Prayer encompasses matters as diverse as journeys, the weather, family life and business ventures. We seek God's help in matters pertaining to the church as well as the state. Ponder this matter for a moment, analyse your own prayers and you may find that the above description is fairly accurate.

There is nothing wrong with this, because our Lord Himself invited us to come to Him with our needs. However, what is our response when God answers our prayers? How do we react when He, in his infinite wisdom, does not give us what we ask for? Or when He gives us something different from what we asked?

Paul encourages us to present our requests to God in thanksgiving, so that we may experience the peace that surpasses understanding (see Phil. 4:6). This is the key to true prayer and a life of fulfilment.

When you lay your prayers before the Lord, leave it to Him and his will. Be grateful that He hears and understands you. Know that in his own perfect time and in his own unique way He will answer in a way that is best for you. Gratefully accept everything that God bestows upon you from his house of treasures and be content with his will.

I praise and thank You, o God, for all the gifts of grace that I receive undeservedly from your hand. Even when You say no to me, I know that it is for my own good.

He who has learnt to pray has learnt the greatest secret of a blessed and happy life.

~ William Law ~

CAN YOU COPE WITH CHANGE?

Since you are my rock and my fortress, for the sake of your name lead and guide me (Ps. 31:3).

*A*s you grow older you become increasingly aware of the changes that are taking place around you. "Things are not what they used to be," is a phrase that escapes our lips all too easily. This constant change can become a problem if you have fallen into a rut. If you are constantly criticising new ideas and innovative actions it is time to reassess your approach to life.

Although it is true that God has existed for all eternity, He is also just as modern as this precise moment, and what is more, He also encompasses the future. There is nothing old-fashioned about the eternal God, and even though theories and ideas about Him come and go, He remains the eternal God. His everlastingness is the foundation upon which those who love and serve Him build their lives.

As a child of God you will be confronted with change in every sphere of life. Some changes you will reject and others you will accept. Some will threaten your faith, but if you hold on to the scriptural promise of Malachi 3:6 (*"I the Lord do not change"* ...) you will survive and even be enriched by new and stimulating ideas.

In the steadfast knowledge of the unfailing truth that the eternal God is also eternally present in your life, you can scrutinise and evaluate every change in light of the knowledge that He gives to you. Then you can be assured that He will guide you on the path of truth in the midst of an ever-changing world.

O Lord that never changes, stay with me!

In the Higher World it is different, but here where we are you must change to stay alive, and to be perfect is to have changed often.
~ John Henry Newman ~

SLOW DOWN

But I trust in you, O Lord; I say, "You are my God." My times are in your hands ... (Ps. 31:14-15).

There are people who are so busy that they have no time to *really* live. Every minute of every day is jam-packed and the mere thought of slowing down fills them with aversion. However, these people do not always achieve more than people who have learnt to live at a slower pace and with a greater balance.

It is really a question of determining your values. That which some people regard as a waste of time others gratefully view as a time of rest and rejuvenation. There are people who believe with conviction that they have no time to develop a meaningful prayer life. They are so busy working – even working for God – that they regard it as unimportant to spend quiet time in his holy presence.

Only a spiritually immature person will write off time spent in prayer, Bible study, contemplation with God, spiritual relaxation and other spiritual disciplines as time wasted or lost. If you use your quiet time with God to plan your life, the world may speed on, but you will achieve more in eternal value than those who anxiously drive themselves on from minute to minute.

Never make the mistake of regarding the time you spend with God as squandered time. To be still in his presence can be the most constructive and productive moments of your life.

Holy Spirit of God, make me aware that the most precious moments of my life are those that I spend in your presence.

Life's problems overwhelm us only because we refuse to be still in our rooms for a while every day.

~ Blaise Pascal ~

The reduction of God's Word

The law was added so that the trespass might increase. But where sin increased, grace increased all the more (Rom. 5:20).

Many new Christians tend to disregard the principles of the Old Testament in their zeal to get to know Jesus better. As a result they limit their study of the Bible to the Gospels and the letters of the New Testament. While any form of Bible study is commendable, it needs to be pointed out that knowledge of the New Testament only is insufficient, because it lacks the disciplined foundation of the Old Testament.

Many claim that the love of Jesus Christ is all-absorbing, and this may blind you to the basic duties of the true Christian. While it is completely true that Jesus came to bring the love of God to his people, Christ never intended that we should do away with the law of God. Indeed, Jesus said that He came to fulfil the law.

If you scrutinise the Ten Commandments in depth, you will discover that they provide an infallible blueprint for the one all-encompassing commandment: love.

The importance of the commandments of the Old Testament live in the fact that they leave little space for speculation or interpretation by the human mind. They are distinct and clear, and indispensable if you wish to live a truly Christian life.

In my zeal to get to know You better, Lord Jesus, let me never lose sight of the fact that You are the Word of God made flesh.

People do not reject the Bible because the Bible contradicts itself, but because the Bible contradicts their way of life.

~ E. Paul Hovey ~

Look around you

Then the disciple whom Jesus loved said to Peter, "It is the Lord!" ... (Jn. 21:7).

There are innumerable people who yearn for a personal experience of Jesus Christ. Some are new converts to the Christian faith while others have been Christians for many years, but have lost their way and are struggling through a spiritual desert. Whatever the reason, these people are constantly seeking something, and in some cases they risk becoming discouraged and damaging their faith. This is especially true when they see other Christians around them who rejoice in an intimate and personal relationship with the living Christ.

One of the mistakes made by people who seek the Lord is to limit their search to the time that they spend in a place of worship, or the hours spent in prayer and contemplation. While these things are essential to your Christian conduct, and while God will certainly manifest Himself to you in these circumstances, prayer and Bible study should equip you to move out into the world so that you can serve God among his people.

The Scriptures show how Jesus manifested Himself to people in their everyday lives. He asks a publican to follow Him; in a crowd He sees Zacchaeus sitting in a fig tree; He asks a Samaritan woman for water to drink. He breaks through the ranks of status, and through these deeds give new hope and life to people.

Seek the Lord in the everyday, simple things of life, because this is where you will find Him.

Teach me, Lord my God, to see You in all things, and to do everything I do for others as if for You.

Jesus became what we are so that He could make us what He is.
~ Atanasius ~

Be patient and sympathetic

Be merciful to those who doubt (Jude v. 22).

The story of the torment in the mind of Thomas the Doubter is well known to all Christians. While the other disciples rejoiced in the knowledge that Jesus rose from death and was alive, Thomas flatly refused to believe it before having sufficient proof. Ultimately it was Jesus Himself who proved to Thomas beyond all doubt that He is the living Christ, and the Bible confirms Thomas' poignant acceptance of this fact (see Jn. 20:26-31).

There are many people today whose thoughts are filled with doubt about their Christian pilgrimage. The most general and destructive doubt is caused by a feeling of unworthiness or rejection, or the inability to find God regardless of how hard they try. Some people are constantly filled with doubt and it seems to be an impossible task to try and help them because they reject every suggestion you make. They live in a state of self-inflicted despondency.

However difficult and appealing the temptation to abandon your efforts to help them, you must persevere in the Name of Christ. Try to understand the torment in their minds and hearts and show them patience, understanding, and above all, the love of Jesus. When you finally notice the signs of their acceptance of Jesus into their lives it will be more than sufficient reward for your perseverance.

Loving and patient Lord Jesus, grant me the patience, love and understanding to assist those who are doubting through your strength, and to bring them to You to be healed.

Every step closer to Jesus means the death of a doubt.
~ Theodore Cuyler ~

*M*ANAGE ANGER CAREFULLY

... Do not let the sun go down while you are still angry (Eph. 4:26).

There are times in life when anger can correct social and moral evils. And our society would be all the poorer if those who were moved to indignation did not act according to the instructions of their hearts. This kind of anger can be creative if the person experiencing it always keeps his ultimate goal in sight.

One of the disastrous consequences of unchanneled anger is that it easily rages out of control. When this happens, reason is supplanted by panic; planning by confusion. The vision of the greatness of life is reduced to the meanness and pettiness of the moment. The greatest tragedy of self-centred anger is that it separates you from God. If you feel insulted and hurt, or if you have allowed anger to saturate your spirit, it is certain that God will feel far away from you.

The answer to this sad state of affairs is to restore God to his rightful position at the centre of your life. It is surprising how easily anger abates and balance returns to your life if He is at the centre of your life. If anger erupts once again it will not be over a personal matter, but rather because God's Name has been dishonoured or because a fellow human being has been wronged. Uncontrolled anger can destroy your life, but the force of anger can become a righteous power if it is controlled by the Holy Spirit.

Holy Father, allow all the energy aroused by emotion in my life to be controlled by the Holy Spirit.

He who wants to be angry without sinning should become angry over nothing but sin.

~ Thomas Secker ~

Live in the Love of the Father

For you did not receive a spirit that makes you a slave again to fear, but you received the Spirit of sonship. And by Him we cry, *"Abba*, Father" (Rom. 8:15).

*O*ne of the fundamental differences between the Christian faith and paganism is that the pagans' idols are feared, while we as Christians know that God is love. The pagan is focused on pleasing his gods because he fears that they will be angered and that he will become the object of their terrible wrath. The Christian desires to please his God because of his love for One that he may call Father.

Nevertheless, the spiritual growth of many Christians is stunted because fear penetrates their hearts. This may sound somewhat paradoxical, but even in the life of a Christian there is a great temptation to yield to feelings of guilt, shame and unworthiness at times. The devil uses all his cunning to discourage the disciples of Christ and lure them away from the path upon which Christ wishes to lead them.

While we do not for a moment allege that Christians cannot commit sin or be overwhelmed by feelings of guilt the important thing is the way in which we handle such situations. Be fully aware of the love that God possesses for you, confess your shortcomings in prayer to Him, be sincerely repentant and gratefully accept the assurance of his loving forgiveness. And then continue with your life: victorious and with complete trust in the love of your heavenly Father.

Heavenly Father, I rejoice in the fact that You have called me to be your child.

The Father is the fountainhead and the origin of our life and our being.
~ John Ruysbroeck ~

Talk things through with the Master

Be joyful always; pray continually (1 Thes. 5:16-17).

There are many ways to pray. Some people find liturgical prayers dignified and valuable. Prayers that are spoken in deep distress possess an urgency that does not take style and composition into consideration. The silence of contemplative prayer is another way to move into the presence of God. Prayer in whatever form is a way of reaching out to a God that cares. The steadfast belief that God does answer your prayers is of cardinal importance, regardless of the form of prayer that you use.

In prayer the attitude of the heart and mind is of essential importance. No fixed and predetermined method should have preference over the cry of the yearning heart that craves communication with God. At any given time or place this cry has priority over all other forms of prayer. When you are confronted with overwhelming temptation; when the heavy burdens of life threaten to crush you; when life is comfortable and attractive ... These are all occasions that may be shared with Him. Whatever your circumstances or your needs, learn to turn to God and share them with Him.

As you talk things through with God you will discover that you become sensitive to his guidance and leadership. You will also become aware of a newly found strength that inwardly fortifies you. Eventually everything that you think or do will come under the influence of your conversation with God. And then your prayers become meaningful and significant.

Loving Master, I entreat You to grant me the gift of your Holy Spirit so that I can pray meaningfully in any place and in all circumstances.

Prayer is essentially a conversation with the almighty God.
~ Clement of Alexandria ~

Faith requires trust

... "Master, we've worked hard all night and haven't caught anything. But because you say so, I will let down the nets" (Lk. 5:5).

To many people true faith is nothing more than an unattainable dream. They will sometimes admit with reservation that other people's faith is rewarded, but they seriously doubt whether faith will work in their own lives.

The Bible provides us with ample proof of the reality and the rewards of faith in the lives of ordinary people. One of the great misconceptions about true faith is that you can simply ask what you want from God and then sit back and wait for it to realise.

The disciples once laboured hard throughout the night without catching any fish. They were experienced fishermen and knew that under the circumstances that prevailed there would be no fish to catch. Regardless of this, as well as the risk of appearing foolish in front of their colleagues, they let down the nets once more. According to the Scriptures they caught so much fish that the nets threatened to tear. In this way their faith was rewarded.

When you lay a matter before God you should trust Him so much that you will be willing to accept his will and be obedient to the suggestions of his Spirit. Forget about what others will think or say. Trust God unconditionally and He will reward your faith.

I place my trust in You completely, Lord Jesus, in the knowledge that You will never disappoint me. Help me not to disappoint You through disbelief.

True prayer is to stand to attention in the presence of God and to be willing to accept orders from Him.
~ Donald Coggan ~

The simplicity of Jesus Christ

Yet I am writing you a new command; its truth is seen in him and you, because the darkness is passing and the true light is already shining (1 Jn. 2:8).

Religion has always been a controversial subject. Since the beginning of time people have argued about doctrinal issues and much blood has been shed in the Name of the Prince of Peace. The thought of this is distressing and confusing to ordinary people whose only desire is to experience the reality and the abundance of Christ in their lives.

Too many dedicated Christians are dogmatically oriented instead of being Christ-centred. They argue so seriously about a dogmatic detail that they become isolated from their fellow Christians. Their love for Christ is not big enough to include someone who differs from them theologically. Unknowingly they become trapped in a haze of religious narrow-mindedness.

If you are experiencing a phase of mental and spiritual confusion and feel inclined to abandon all faith, briefly take a step back from all your doubts and uncertainties and again experience a vision of the holy simplicity of the living Saviour.

Despite his greatness and uniqueness Jesus lived a simple life. He was at home among people and they were able to identify with Him. He reduced a complicated religious code to a simple, practical proposition that was intelligible to everyone. His commandment of love for God and for one's neighbour was all-important. Let this command be the motivating force for a more effective faith.

Beloved Saviour and Redeemer, my faith in You is strong and simple because it is focused on You alone.

All great things are simple and many can be expressed in a single word: freedom, justice, honour, duty, grace and hope.

~ Winston Churchill ~

Use tribulations to your advantage

Consider it pure joy, my brothers, whenever you face trials of many kinds, because you know that the testing of your faith develops perseverance (Jas. 1:2-3).

We are easily inclined to become discouraged when problems and trials come across our way. Depending on the circumstances there is always the danger that you may lose all hope and surrender to despair. Anyone who has experienced prolonged illness, or who has had to carry heavy financial burdens will know the destructive effect that these things can have on your life perspective.

If you tend to become discouraged, try to accept the situation as a challenge and a discipline of your faith. Try to extract the best from the circumstances of your tribulation. Instead of giving up, earnestly try to understand the reason for it and decide how to best limit its damage.

If you persistently maintain an intimate relationship with the Master and remain open and sensitive to the influence of his Holy Spirit, you will find that you possess the strength and wisdom that enable you to look beyond the present moment. Then you will realise that God is in control of your life. Despite your immediate problems and tribulations He will enable you to surrender all of them to Him in the joyful knowledge that He desires only the best for his children.

Master of love and grace, I will continue to trust You unconditionally, and so continue on the path to spiritual maturity.

If I constantly walk in sunshine, I surely live in a desert.
~ Gustav White ~

God is in control

He is before all things, and in him all things hold together (Col. 1:17).

Whether in matters pertaining to the state, or the world of commerce, or your personal life, there are always times when it seems as if everything is going wrong. The future appears dark and uncertain and the present is unstable and leaves much to be desired. It is in these circumstances that we tend to look back with a feeling of nostalgia and yearn for "the good old days".

Whatever problems you may experience in the world, why don't you for once look back to the very beginning? If you do this you will find that people and nations have lived through dismal times that are comparable to our own situation. In the past people have experienced disaster, suffering and danger. People have had to struggle with sorrow, adversity and pain equal to anything that we experience today. Regardless of this they, and the world, have managed to survive.

Before you yield to a mood of intense despondency, acknowledge the greatness and glory of God. He who created the world and mankind will not simply let go of the work of his hands. He has watched over us for centuries and has kept us from all evil. In his unfathomable love He gave his Son to the world so that those who believe in Him will not be lost, but will be redeemed for all eternity. Through Him we will be able to overcome every tribulation. God is in control!

Almighty God, You are my powerful Redeemer, and therefore I will not fear. In the darkest night You are my light and my strength. Therefore I will not despair.

God is called almighty because He can do all things possible and impossible perfectly.

~ Thomas Aquinas ~

Cultivate Time for Waiting

(B)ut those who hope in the Lord will renew their strength. They will soar on wings like eagles; they will run and not grow weary, they will walk and not be faint (Is. 40:31).

The results of waiting for the Lord are truly astounding. You find strength to sustain you in days of frailty; enthusiasm that never wanes; and you can walk through life in faith.

You may rejoice in the truth of this wonderful promise, but the problem is to know how to wait for the Lord. There is a world of difference between knowing the truth and practically applying it. The average disciple does not find it easy to trust in the Lord and wait for Him. Impatience, lack of time, thoughts that wander, an unforgiving spirit and the desire to satisfy yourself instead of God are all contributing factors that make the art of waiting for the Lord a difficult one.

You must first realise that the spirit inside of you governs your mind. If you convince yourself that you cannot control your wandering thoughts, you will never manage to control them. But Christ's Spirit inside you can help to subdue your thoughts. It may require patience and perseverance, but if you allow the Spirit of God to control your spirit and mind, your quiet wait for the Lord will not be a time of tribulation, but a blessing filled with hope and expectation.

When you have developed the art of waiting for the Lord, a sacred quality will fill your life and be reflected in everything that you do, because then you have discovered the secret of allowing the Lord to work through you.

Empowering Master, under the guidance of your Spirit and in your strength I will develop a patiently waiting spirit.

In prayer it is better to have a heart without words than words without a heart.

~ John Bunyan ~

*W*ITH WHOM DO YOU IDENTIFY?

... Does not he who guards your life know it? Will he not repay each person according to what he has done? (Prov. 24:12).

You cannot go through life without certain influences having an effect on you. If you were born in circumstances dominated by hate your character and your perspective on life will constantly be threatened by hatred. If you grew up in a family where every penny had to be counted, you will feel its influence in some way or another. These are influences over which you have little or no control.

While growing up you also willingly identified yourself with certain forces that had a formational influence on your life. Many of these influences would have been positive and progressive, while others would have had a destructive effect on your character and life.

It is unquestionably true that you eventually become like the company you keep. There are many young Christians who try to maintain connections with their former friends after their conversion, and then find that the influence of the past is too strong. Consequently they start straying from their faith. Where circumstances exist that may favour the re-forging of old friendships, the situation must be prevented by cultivating strong Christian friendships. It is true that the love in your heart is that which you identify with.

If you identify yourself with the living Christ his influence will rapidly become visible in your life. Your perspective, attitude, hope and ambition all fall under his control and you continually grow in his image. Then your life will assume a purposeful course.

Come live in my heart, Lord Jesus, and make me what You are.

Jesus Christ will be Lord of everything, or not be Lord at all.
~ Augustine of Hippo ~

Resist the Temptation

... "Bad company corrupts good character" (1 Cor. 15:33).

There are those unhappy individuals who find it immensely difficult to follow Jesus. They want to receive Jesus into their lives, but they find it difficult to break with old habits that run counter to his ordinances. They want to be his disciples, but on their own conditions. This is simply impossible, because Jesus Himself said: *"He who is not with me is against me ... "* (Mt. 12:30).

If you are sincere in your desire to be a follower of Jesus you should be prepared to make sacrifices. Habits or a way of life that is contrary to his will must be discarded. If the company you keep is dubious, you will have to avoid it, unless the persons involved are willing to accept your dedication to the Master. There is simply no space to compromise your Christian principles, or to allow anything that could possibly negatively influence your commitment to the Master.

It requires great strength of character and faith to be able to resist these temptations, because the temptation to compromise is great. However, Jesus Himself was no stranger to the subtle tactics of Satan, and He is prepared and willing to give you his strength to resist temptation. Place your trust in Jesus and faithfully walk the path that He has mapped out for you. He will not disappoint you and you will certainly experience success.

Help me, almighty God, to resolutely resist temptations that will impede my Christian pilgrimage.

The realisation of the presence of God is the one sure antidote to temptation.

~ Francois Fenelon ~

*A*VOID LIMITED KNOWLEDGE

And the peace of God, which transcends all understanding, will guard your hearts and your minds in Christ Jesus (Phil. 4:7).

*I*f you have trust in your Christian faith, thank God for the certainty that you have about the reality of the living Christ. In this fortunate state of being you should just be wary of your steadfast conviction degenerating into fanaticism. It is easy to convince yourself that you know everything and then to walk with hobnailed boots right over things that were of great help to other pilgrims on their journey.

Many dedicated disciples speak proudly of the number of times that they have read right through the Bible from Genesis to Revelation, as if this is a qualification for a superior species of Christian. Yet others declare that they read only the Bible and no other reading matter, without realising that in this way they isolate themselves from an understanding of the historical and social background and customs of biblical times. By refusing to study the accounts of the struggles, sorrows, victories and tribulations of those people God used in generations past, you are denying yourself a source of immense encouragement and inspiration.

When your heart is filled with Christ and the Holy Spirit, and your mind is focused on seeking God's will in your life, you will not hesitate to explore other channels of truth that have enriched the lives of fellow disciples, even though they might have been of a different Christian conviction. A closed mind is no tribute to God.

Beloved Lord Jesus, as I grow in your grace, grant that I will gather knowledge that will continue to broaden my spiritual perspective.

Fanaticism may roughly be described as the rage of people who have no opinion of their own.

~ G. K. Chesterton ~

BEYOND THE SCRIPTURES

... but Christ is all, and is in all (Col. 3:11).

Christianity is divided into innumerable factions. Many claim to be the sole possessors of the Christian truth and regard those who differ from them as being outside of God's plan of redemption.

The vast majority of churches and sects base their faith on an intellectual exegesis of the Scriptures. Unfortunately there are as many interpretations of the Scriptures as there are organisations that claim to be inspired by the Scriptures. What should one believe and accept?

The purpose of the Word of God is to lead people towards an understanding of the merciful God and to manifest his will to them. Unless your Bible study leads you beyond the written Word to a personal experience of Jesus your studies are worthless. Jesus Himself said: *"You diligently study the Scriptures because you think that by them you possess eternal life. These are the Scriptures that testify about me, yet you refuse to come to me to have life"* (Jn. 5:39-40).

It is deplorable that so many people know their Bible but do not know Him of whom the Bible speaks. If every student of the Bible possessed the Spirit of Christ, there would still have been dogmatic differences, but the spirit of love and compassion would transcend all intellectual differences, and love for Christ would be the unifying force.

You get to know Jesus in the Bible through an act of surrender and dedication. Then you will also be able to love those who differ from you in the interpretation of God's Word.

O Holy Spirit, lead me beyond the Scriptures into the holy presence of the living Christ.

We should not only become still to ponder passages from the Bible, but also matters from practical life. We must be able to reconcile them with each other and with the will of the risen Saviour.

~ Michel Quoist ~

BE PRODUCTIVE

The Lord said to Satan, "Where have you come from?" Satan answered the Lord, "From roaming through the earth and going back and forth in it" (Job 1:7).

There are people who are exceptionally active and yet seem to achieve little. They seldom have time to become still and ponder the beauty and love of God. They live at such an accelerated pace that they have no time for the bonds of friendship or any of the ordinary small pleasures of life. Their lives are busy but unproductive.

To live a constructive and therefore productive life it is essential to plan wisely. A life without a plan is like a ship without a map or compass. The plan doesn't have to be fully detailed, but it is crucial to know your purpose and aspiration. Without a sense of direction your life will become meaningless and frustrating.

How is it possible to plan your life? It depends on the stage of life in which you find yourself. Young people will have different goals from a more mature person, but in all cases judicious planning is required. It is God who guides us. To understand and execute God's plan for your life requires faith, patience and courage. Faith to believe that God has a plan for your life; patience to wait until He unfolds his plan to you; courage to obey his commands.

If you carry out God's will in your life, you will be constructively busy, and as you work with God, you will get to know Him ever more intimately.

Heavenly Father, when I am busy, may it be to carry out your holy will for my life.

One person who has learnt to master life is better than a thousand who have learnt to do it only through the content of books, but no one can derive something truly worthwhile from life without God.

~ Juniester Eckhart ~

Self-respect through dedication

... Who will rescue me from this body of death? Thanks be to God — through Jesus Christ our Lord! (Rom. 7:24-25).

If we could see ourselves as others see us, we would probably hold an entirely different opinion of ourselves. In our own estimation we are probably fairly virtuous people with a few flaws — we hesitate to call them sins. All in all we are able to maintain completely normal and average relationships with the people we live and work with. True goodness should not make anyone feel uncomfortable. Jesus, who was the personification of virtue, attracted large crowds of ordinary people to Him and they liked to listen to Him.

Maybe it is because we know ourselves so well that we hold such a low opinion of ourselves. Hidden in our minds there are thoughts and deeds that we would rather forget. Our spirits have often been damaged by narrow-mindedness, zealotry and laziness. We realise what we ought to be and know what we are, and therefore we become discouraged.

The strength that Jesus grants to all people who acknowledge his sovereignty and who open their lives to his Holy Spirit enables ordinary people to live extraordinary lives. A life that was morally weak is strengthened; through his redeeming grace and love life is liberated from guilt feelings, and a broken life is made new and strong.

Although the experience of renewal is often a moving one, it also surpasses all emotion. It is the dedication of every aspect of your life to the service of the risen Christ.

I praise and thank You, my Lord and my God, that through dedication I may achieve spiritual and mental maturity.

It is the greatest conceivable disaster to struggle with God and not to be conquered.

~ Simone Weil ~

*G*OD AND HIS MESSENGERS

In the sixth month, God sent the angel Gabriel to Nazareth, a town in Galilee, to a virgin ... (Lk. 1:26-27).

*F*rom Genesis right through to Revelation references to angels are common. Some appear in their heavenly glory while others show themselves as ordinary people. All of them, except for the rebellious ones, are in the service of God. Because God's messengers often appear in ordinary, human guise, the writer of the book of Hebrews admonishes us: *Do not forget to entertain strangers, for by so doing some people have entertained angels without knowing it* (Heb. 13:2).

Perhaps there have been occasions in your life when someone, whom you would never have classified as an angel, brought God's comfort to you in times of sorrow. Sometimes the message was conveyed to you through an ordinary conversation, or maybe through an act that reminded you of Jesus' life. Some of God's messengers wear ordinary work clothes, or the apron of a housewife or even a servant. But they have one thing in common with the angel Gabriel: they have stood in the presence of God and declared themselves willing to be his servants.

Let us thank God for these people, for our lives are enriched because they move among us. Let our gratitude also lead us to commit and dedicate ourselves sincerely to the service of God, so that we too may become messengers of God, conveying the message of his will and his love to those we live with.

Holy Father, may I be your dedicated messenger in whatever place You choose to place me.

Millions of spiritual beings walk the earth without us noticing them, both when we are awake and when we are asleep.
~ John Milton ~

Death brings hope

Brothers, we do not want you to be ignorant about those who fall asleep, or to grieve like the rest of men ... (1 Thes. 4:13).

*U*p until fairly recently the colour black has always been associated with death: black clothes, black drapery, black armbands, black-bordered writing paper. This sombre and morbid colour contributed to the sorrow that hung like a dark cloud over those touched directly by death, and added to the sadness and grief they experienced.

While it is both natural and understandable that we should feel sorrowful when we are separated from a loved one, the death and resurrection of Christ should bring an end to inconsolable grief.

Jesus Christ has conquered death and has taken our sins upon Him through his crucifixion. He has given us the assurance of redemption, and his triumphant resurrection offers us the certainty of eternal life and his kingdom. The brightly lit gateway to this kingdom is death.

Eternal life in Jesus Christ is offered to anyone who dies as a believer in the Christian faith. In addition we have the steadfast knowledge that we will also be reunited with our loved ones. Death should be accepted as a friend, because only through death can we inherit the ultimate glory of eternal life.

Risen Lord Jesus, when the darkness recedes and the new day dawns, we welcome the luminous rays of sunlight because they illuminate everything. Let us perceive death in the same way.

Death is the great adventure, besides which lunar landings and space travel are mere trifles.

~ Joseph Bayley ~

So much depends on you

In the same way, faith by itself, if it is not accompanied by action, is dead (Jas. 2:17).

To be a Christian means to accept responsibility for your own life. You may argue that, because you belong to God, He is in control and therefore everything depends on Him. Nevertheless, if God is to do anything with your life He needs to have your co-operation.

The Creator has equipped you with a mind, not only to enable you to excel academically, but also so that you will manifest the right attitude towards Him and towards life. A sound and positive mentality is the product of a life lived in harmony with God

The vast majority of people yearn for happiness. They work and strive to achieve it. They often pray to God to make them happy, but in spite of their prayers still maintain unhealthy patterns of thought.

If you lead a self-centred life and only live for the things that concern you personally; if you are blind to the distress of your neighbour, you are ignoring the great truth that helping others is a prerequisite for happiness. You cannot be truly happy without trying to alleviate the unhappiness of others. This is done by prayer and creative deeds.

Whatever your prayer requests may be, offer yourself to the Father so that He may work through you. In that way you contribute to your own prayer being answered. Become an active partner of God, and experience how He works in your life and expands your spiritual understanding.

Heavenly Father, grant me the earnest desire to become your working partner in my daily life.

He alone loves his Creator who manifests a pure love towards his neighbour.

~ The Venerable Bede ~

*B*E POSITIVE

Do everything without complaining or arguing, so that you may become blameless and pure, children of God without fault in a crooked and depraved generation ... (Phil. 2:14-15).

*C*ircumstances in large parts of the world leave much to be desired. There are wars and rumours of wars, bitterness, poverty, famine and disasters, corruption and scandals. If one takes stock of the situation, one can't help but feel that the world has veered far from what God meant for it to be, and that humans are abusing that which God has entrusted to their care. Consequently humankind has become unhappy, discontented and unsafe. People have developed the tendency to assume a critical and pessimistic attitude towards life in general.

Even if we accept that there is much that is wrong with the world, the fact remains that we as Christians are Christ's ambassadors, with the duty and the privilege to preserve the Christian faith in even the most negative and difficult circumstances.

If you open your life to the influence of the Holy Spirit and allow Him to strengthen your faith so that your life may bear witness to the power and glory of God's love, you cannot be anything but positive. In so doing you will uplift the spirits of those around you and once again find meaning and significance in life.

Lord, You have always been the mighty Redeemer. Use me through your Holy Spirit to be your witness in a negative world.

No one can do the work of God before he has been equipped with the strength of the Holy Spirit. It is impossible to be positive, except in this strength.

~ G. Campbell Morgan ~

Are you a Christian?

Follow my example, as I follow the example of Christ (1 Cor. 11:1).

How do you recognise a Christian? More to the point: how can others recognise Christianity in you? There is much to ponder in these questions, and we should consider them thoughtfully. If we try to answer these questions in all honesty and sincerity, it will invariably lead to earnest self-scrutiny.

If you profess to being a Christian, it is your responsibility to manifest the characteristics of Christ in your life. No amount of biblical knowledge or church attendance can ever substitute for the reflection of the Master in your life. However laudable good works may be, unless they are based on and performed to the honour and glory of Jesus Christ, they lose their impact and meaning.

Your entire life will have to reflect the sacrificing love, grace and forgiveness of Jesus so that people may know that you are a true Christian. You should be tolerant and understanding; without being overly pious you should lead a life of integrity that in no way compromises your Christian standards.

When you manifest Christ-like qualities in your life, nothing more will be required to confirm that you are a Christian.

O Holy Spirit, I plead that You will grant me the ability to live like Christ more and more each day.

To be a Christian is much more than a momentary conversion. It is a daily process in which you grow to become more and more like Christ.

~ Billy Graham ~

Do not resist authority

Now we ask you, brothers, to respect those who work hard among you, who are over you in the Lord and who admonish you. Hold them in the highest regard in love because of their work ... (1 Thes. 5:12).

Throughout the ages the Christian church has suffered as a result of internal strife and arguments. You will find examples of this even in the letters of the apostles. In some cases the differences were about important dogmatic and theological matters. However, in most cases they were of a more personal nature, originating from conflicting personalities, antagonism between people, and other similar causes of quarrels.

Healthy leadership is essential if a community is to function successfully and in an orderly manner. This is evident even in the animal world. Someone has to be given the authority to make decisions for the good of others, so that the entire group may lead an orderly and peaceful life as far as possible.

In this respect the church is no different from any other group, except that the responsibility that rests upon church leaders and members is much greater, because they are working for the kingdom of God. To ensure that a harmonious and effective testimony exists in your denomination, church leaders should be elected in strict accordance with the will of God as revealed through prayer. If it is certain that they have been chosen according to this principle, you should continuously pray for them, so that the heavy burden of their responsibilities may be eased by Jesus. His will and pleasure should be the principal matter at all times.

Holy God, and in Jesus my heavenly Father, help me to rise above pettiness and personality differences so that I can praise your Name.

I am convinced that people are open to the Christian message if it is leavened with authority and explained as God's own word.

~ Billy Graham ~

*T*HE VALUE OF MEMORIES

I remember the days of long ago; I meditate on all your works and consider what your hands have done (Ps. 143:5).

---

*E*very one of us has memories. Depending on their nature, they may cause either joy or intense remorse. It is a wise person who realises that today creates tomorrow's memories, and that their future happiness is therefore in their own hands.

Memories of the past play an important role in your everyday life. If you have clung to an unhappy incident for more than twenty years, so that it ultimately became a hidden obsession, you will find that all your thoughts are tinged with bitterness and negativity. The grace of forgiveness is essential, and so is the blessing of being able to forget.

Recalling happy memories is a source of inspiration and joy and can often provide guidance for future behaviour. Such memories are strengthened and ennobled by sincere deeds of gratitude. To say to the Father: "I thank You for happy memories and the ability to recall them," is in itself a way to enrich your relationship with Him. Consequently life will possess a deeper meaning and happiness for you.

Because you have a choice regarding the memories that you create, you should be extremely careful. Look ahead and try to imagine how they will appear in the distant future.

Merciful God and Father, let nothing that I do today cause me sorrow and remorse when I look back upon it.

We should spend just as much time thanking God for blessings as we do requesting them from Him.

~ Vincent de Paul ~

What makes a Christian different?

Therefore, as God's chosen people, holy and dearly loved, clothe yourselves with compassion, kindness, humility, gentleness and patience (Col. 3:12).

Because you are a Christian, people expect an honourable code of conduct of you. This is a challenge, and yet also a disturbing thought. It is a challenge in that it calls you to be Christ-like, but also disturbing because it invariably brings with it the realisation that you have failed to achieve the spiritual goals that Christ has set for you.

Whatever your reaction to the world's expectations of you the fact remains that you have to be different because you are a Christian. Your value system is determined by the Master; your code of conduct gives precedence to others above yourself; you have a constructive approach to life and therefore you are slow to judge and quick to forgive. When you are confronted with destructive antagonism, you have the ability to demonstrate love in the face of hatred. Above all, because you are a disciple of Jesus Christ, you possess his Spirit. Make no mistake: you are different and it is his immanent Spirit that makes you different.

If this truth overwhelms you and causes you to feel inadequate in your spiritual experience, thank God that his Word gives you this guarantee: ... *"My grace is sufficient for you, for my power is made perfect in weakness"* (2 Cor. 12:9). It is precisely your inadequacy that may be transformed into constructive purposefulness if you relinquish it to the Master. As a Christian you possess something very special, because the Spirit of Christ lives in you.

In your strength, Master, I can become what You meant for me to be.

To be Christ-like is to be a Christian.

~ William Penn ~

GOD WILL SHOW YOU THE WAY

After the death of Joshua, the Israelites asked the Lord ... (Judg. 1:1).

Joshua was well known as a loyal and dedicated servant of God, and also as a wise and respected leader of his people. The Israelites relied very heavily on this man who has been described as a soldier-saint. He became their leader who safely led them to take possession of the long-awaited Promised Land.

It then follows as a matter of course that with the death of Joshua his people would feel confused and lost. This is what happens when we have to bid farewell to someone in whom we have placed a considerable amount of trust. Usually the first question that we ask is: "What are we to do now? To whom can we turn? Whom can we trust?"

A similar situation can crop up in basically any of life's circumstances. Few people can say that they have never experienced something like it and that they have always been in control of all circumstances.

If you find yourself in such a situation do not suffer through the frustrations, sadness and anxiety of trying to continue in your own strength. Follow the example of the Israelites and seek the help and guidance of the Saviour. He alone wants to and can lead you in his path of righteousness, and as He leads you, He will grant you the ability to handle every situation so that you may have the peace of mind that banishes all fear and anxiety.

Mighty Redeemer, in all the circumstances of my life I will seek comfort and guidance from You alone.

God wants us to take on life in the full expectation that He will be with us in all circumstances if we place our faith and trust in Him.

~ Colin Urquhart ~

The Friendship of Jesus

"You are my friends if you do what I command" (Jn. 15:1).

The risen Christ gives abundant blessings to those who love and serve Him: liberation from the bondage of sin; a new life in Christ; a deeper and richer communion with the heavenly Father; the awareness of the practical feasibility of his precepts. For these and many other gifts we praise and love Him.

One gift that is highly valued by Christian disciples is the gift of friendship that Jesus offers to everyone who acknowledges his sovereignty. It is a gift of grace, because it is one that you can never earn, but only accept. Christ very simply says: "I am your Friend. Will you accept this and treat Me as a friend that you love?"

If you accept this invitation, you submit yourself to his loving discipline, because it is only in doing so that you can grow in the generous friendship that He offers you. True friendship with Jesus can be strengthened only by persevering in communion with Him and by a continually purer understanding of his love. Such a communion and understanding is the result of a meaningful prayer life that is developed through complete obedience to your Lord.

The friendship that Jesus offers you can only become a reality if you submit yourself to his will. He knows what is best for you, and only by obeying Him, will you realise that your Friend is your Guide through life.

Thank You, loving Lord Jesus, for the merciful gift of your love, which I accept in thanksgiving together with the demands associated with it.

God's only Son embraces humankind with his love.
~ Edward Taylor ~

July

Eternal God, You who hold our times and fortunes in your hand:
 July is the holiday month and everyone is travelling –
 inland to go hunting; to visit family;
 to game reserves or the coast.
And death mercilessly takes its toll on our roads.
So much unnecessary loss and so much raw grief!
You gave us life, our most precious possession.
Help us to travel responsibly.
Thank You for a time of rest with our families.
Once more bind us to each other and to You, our Father.
Thank You for friends with whom we can share the holidays
 and for the beautiful memories that are stored in our hearts.
We pray for them who work while we rest.
Thank You for the beauty of winter's landscapes.
Renew our spirit while our bodies are resting.
Let us not forget You while we are on holiday:
 our Bible study, our prayer life, and our interaction with You.
Make us salt for the earth and light for the world.
We pray this in the powerful Name of Jesus Christ, our Saviour.

Amen.

Know God and live in abundance

This is what the Lord says to the house of Israel: "Seek me and live" (Amos 5:4).

However dismal it may sound, there are innumerable people in today's world who have little or no desire to live. Perhaps death has taken a loved one from them; maybe illness or tribulation has drained the dynamism from their lives. Loneliness may have deprived them of their will to live, or scandal and financial disaster may have caused them to lose their ability to face life. Whatever the reason, to them life has lost its meaning and in their sorry state they can find no reason to live.

If you are seeking a reason to live in your own life or in the circumstances in which you find yourself, you will be disappointed. The only true life comes from Jesus Christ alone, who came to the world so that you can have life in all its abundance (see Jn. 10:10). This is what the Son of God, who is the true source of life, is offering you. He is the bread of life and He invites everyone who is hungry to come to Him.

When you are experiencing those human emotions that spring from the misfortune in which you find yourself, turn to the living Christ. Seek Him in prayer and contemplation, hold on to his promises, and, however dark the road ahead may seem, cling to Him. He will grant you life in all its abundance!

In You alone, Lord Jesus, do I find true life and a reason to live.

To live a good, decent Christian life, that is the gist of the matter. Live this life and the rest will follow of its own accord.

~ Spike Mulligan ~

The Power of Positive Prayer

"Therefore I tell you, whatever you ask for in prayer, believe that you have received it, and it will be yours" (Mk. 11:24).

All things are grounded in our thoughts. When a thought is empowered by dynamic enthusiasm, nothing can thwart its realisation. When you pray you use the pictures in your mind to give substance to that which is already a mental reality. It is a simple and established truth that whatever you desire with intensity and visualise with clarity will realise in your life.

This fact means that you are responsible for choosing your prayer needs with great circumspection. Because you love God, your requests will be related to what you believe his will for your life to be. You should accept the assistance of the Holy Spirit in the development of your thought patterns. This is the only way to have prayers that can inspire, heal, empower and guide your step on a path of no regrets. Open your mind to the influence of the Holy Spirit and form strong thought patterns under his guidance. Keep them simple at first, but always remain strong in the faith that – because they are divinely inspired and firmly rooted in your mind – they will ultimately be realised.

God does answer prayers and therefore we should choose our thought patterns with great responsibility.

My Example in prayer, Lord Jesus, help me so that the thoughts inspired by the Holy Spirit will become the prayers of my heart.

Prayer is and always remains an innate and profound impulse of the human soul.

~ Thomas Carlyle ~

Grace Indescribably Vast

... "My grace is sufficient for you, for my power is made perfect in weakness" (2 Cor. 12:9).

People often find themselves in situations that make them feel incompetent and inadequate. You may have a mission to carry out, a task to perform, a decision to make; and you feel that you are simply not up to it. The immense magnitude of the situation or the responsibility attached to it; its possible consequences in your own life or in the lives of others: all these factors weigh heavily upon you and so you tend to avoid the responsibility as much as possible.

When you find yourself in such circumstances and are required to take action, you should never rely on your own abilities. Jesus made it very clear that we are capable of nothing without Him, but that with Him we can accomplish anything. In this truth lies the answer to all your fears, doubts and feelings of inadequacy.

Whatever you undertake in your life, first take it to God in prayer and confess all your expectations, fears and worries to Him. Jesus is your Friend, and in the same way that you would consult with another person, first seek Christ's help in prayer and in the serenity of contemplation. His Holy Spirit will stimulate you to move forward in faith. By allowing Him to work through you, you will achieve the kind of success that would be unattainable in your own strength. His grace will be sufficient to sustain you in all circumstances.

Loving Father, I praise and thank You for the joyous assurance that I can achieve anything through Christ who gives me the strength.

A state of mind that sees God in everything testifies to growth in grace and a grateful heart.

~ Charles G. Finney ~

Your responsibility as a Christian

Instead, speaking the truth in love, we will in all things grow up into him who is the Head, that is, Christ (Eph. 4:15).

The moment you accept Christ as the Lord of your life, you also accept certain responsibilities. Refusing these responsibilities creates a weak spot in your dedication and commitment, and it means that your spiritual life becomes crippled and your relationship with the Master weakened.

When you become a Christian you step into a new life with new values and fresh goals. You no longer live to please yourself, but your goal is Christ, and therefore you attempt to forget yourself in your service to others. The good works that you do for others are the expression of your faith. However, it is not faith itself, because a person who does not believe in Christ can also do good works. Your good works will earn you nothing, but are proof of your gratitude for your redemption.

The new life in Christ has certain requirements if you wish to grow spiritually. It is your responsibility to stimulate this growth. As a disciple of Christ your have the responsibility of honouring your Lord and pleasing Him. You dare not live only to please yourself. You must be completely obedient to God's will for your life. You are responsible for confessing your sins before God.

Paul continually urges us to be filled with the fullness of God. Christ should become visible in you, and it is the sacred responsibility of every Christian to constantly grow spiritually, so to reach maturity in faith.

Help me, Lord Jesus, to strengthen my bond with You so that I will never fail to experience your sacred presence.

Because of Christ many Christs arose in the world, who loved justice and hated injustice as He did.

~ Origen of Alexandria ~

ACHIEVE YOUR GOALS THROUGH THE STRENGTH OF CHRIST

Be on your guard; stand firm in the faith; be men of courage; be strong. Do everything in love (1 Cor. 16:13-14).

As the years pass it seems as if life is becoming more and more rushed. There is so much to be done that we often complain of just not having enough time to pay attention to everything. In addition there are so many confusions and diversions that we easily neglect the things we should do.

There is really only one way to achieve those truly worthwhile objectives, and that is through the strength of the living Christ. If this sounds like too much of a simplistic approach to you, especially considering the busy life that you lead, just think of everything that Jesus achieved in the three short years of his ministry on earth. Think of all the achievements that He accomplished regardless of the strenuous demands placed upon Him and the threats that He had to endure.

Jesus now offers you his Holy Spirit to enable you to meet the demands of modern life – and to do so with love. Trust Him to lead you on the paths of service in his Name. He will grant you the ability to accomplish everything that you undertake in his strength and love.

Keep me, o Holy Spirit, from becoming so involved in my personal goals that I fail to see God's great goal for my life.

The test of an ideal, or rather of an idealist, is the strength to hold onto the ideal and to draw inspiration from it under difficult circumstances.
~ Oliver Wendell Holmes ~

The Gift of Grace: To Give Yourself

... but they gave themselves first to the Lord and then to us in keeping with God's will (2 Cor. 8:5).

You can only lead a rich and satisfying existence if you are willing to give yourself completely to life. You have a personal contribution to make to ensure yourself of a life that will be happy and beneficial to yourself as well as other people. You may initially question the truth of this statement, possibly because you think that you have nothing worthwhile to contribute. If your idea of giving is limited only to money, prestige and social status, this may be the case, but the old saying that the best things in life are free still holds true.

When someone has to endure fierce opposition for the sake of a just cause and you make it clear that you support them, they will be much encouraged. Maybe some of your family feel that you are taking them for granted, and if you display some love and affection towards them, you will bring joy and inspiration to their lives. It is within your ability to freely share true love, profound understanding, faithful friendship and other forces of healing and blessing with other people.

The glorious truth is that when you give these precious things to others, your own life is enriched far beyond comprehension, because it is impossible to be a source of blessings for others without receiving blessings yourself. Your own life will begin to flourish and bear fruit because you give yourself joyfully to the Lord, to life and to your fellow human beings.

Lord Jesus, You who have given Yourself to me, make my life a blessing to others.

We should not only give what we *have*, but also what we *are*.
~ Joseph Mercier ~

WHEN FEAR OVERWHELMS YOU

But Jesus immediately said to them: "Take courage! It is I. Don't be afraid" (Mt. 14:27).

Fear is an ugly reality of contemporary society. It dominates the council chambers of the world. It destroys the peace and harmony of innumerable lives. The vast majority of people live in the shadow of fear from morning to night, and even when they are asleep fear still remains active in their subconscious.

The fruits of fear emerge in all spheres of human life. For example, irritation easily leads to strained and broken human relationships. When you are afraid, you are not pervious to reason and consequently you become aggressive. Fear also manifests in illness and a desire to avoid life's responsibilities.

Fear has a thousand faces. However, Jesus knows all of them, and He tells you not to be afraid. Remember that He commands his disciples to banish all destructive fear, regardless of external circumstances and pressures, and to be happy in the surroundings of their lives.

You and this world still belong to God, even though it might not always seem so. Your heavenly Father has not abandoned or forsaken you or his world. He promised the Holy Spirit to those who love Him. If this Spirit takes possession of your life, destructive fears will no longer have any hold on you. And then you will begin to know the joy of a fearless life.

When your Holy Spirit fills my life, Lord my God, there is no space for destructive fear.

Fear is never a good adviser, and victory over fear is the first spiritual duty of a Christian.

~ Nicolai Berdyaev ~

God is with you wherever you go

... "You are the God who sees me," for she said, "I have now seen the One who sees me" (Gen 16:13).

The question on everybody's lips is: "Who is God? What is He really like?" In their imaginations people conjure up images of Him in an attempt to visualise the Almighty. Some people claim to have seen Him in visions. However, others feel that they are unable to see Him, and consequently start to doubt or even deny his existance.

Jesus Christ told his followers that no one has seen the Father except for the Son. On another occasion He told them that no one will come to the Father except through the Son, who is the Way to God. It therefore follows as a matter of course that you should first seek Jesus before you can find the Father.

In your search you will quickly realise that your relationship with Jesus requires you to fully surrender and commit your life to Him. And as you become more and more involved in his service, you will become increasingly aware of his presence. When you visit ill, lonely and sorrowful people you will find Him there. In your acts of compassion you will experience the living Christ. Through your ministry of love to those in need you will see Him looking at you through the eyes of those you are helping.

Because Jesus is in the Father and the Father in Him, you ought to remember that in every act of grace, every little bit of compassion, every fraction of love that you show to others in the Name of Jesus, you will meet God in Jesus Christ.

Holy God and Father, I rejoice in the knowledge that I encounter You in every deed that I perform in your Name.

A sentence of the Deity is written on every human heart.
~ John Calvin ~

*H*UMILITY IS NOT A WEAKNESS

Be completely humble and gentle; be patient, bearing with one another in love (Eph. 4:2).

---

*I*n the demanding world in which we live there are many people, especially in the business world, who look upon humility, patience and a loving, caring spirit as signs of weakness. They tend to regard people with these traits as ineffectual failures in the business world, and as such they are supposedly not worthy of respect. When it comes to promotions, people who have this attitude and who occupy positions of power often overlook many competent people for the sake of others who are aggressive and even reckless. Ultimately the business world is all the poorer for it.

The greatest Leader ever known to mankind is Jesus. His entire being reflected humility, meekness, patience and love. People paid attention to what He said and did. They obeyed and followed Him. Even his enemies respected and admired Him.

To achieve success in life you don't always have to prove that you are better than others are. You don't continually have to try to outdo your adversaries, or assume a domineering and aggressive attitude. Be firm, definitely; be sincere in all your negotiations; but temper everything that you do with the spirit of the Master. Then you will undoubtedly gain the respect of those with whom you interact.

Lord Jesus, help me to reflect your love and compassion in all my interactions. Protect me from the monster of pride.

The humble man accepts praise as a clean window accepts the light of the sun. The more pure and intense the light is, the less you see of the glass.

~ Thomas Merton ~

---

*I*T'S IMPOSSIBLE!

Where can I go from your Spirit? Where can I flee from your presence? (Ps. 139:7).

*I*t is a comforting and encouraging thought that however far away you may feel from God, God is never far away from you. This feeling of isolation lies within you; it is of your own making, not of His. It is worthwhile to remember this fact when your spirits are low and you feel powerless, or when your love for the Master is not as ardent as it used to be. If your faith has lost its spark and you are feeling that it no longer benefits, but rather obstructs your attainment of a creative life, it is definitely time to take stock of your life and to discover what exactly it is that has replaced your burning love for the Father.

When your faith starts to degenerate, it is inevitably because you are trying to eliminate God from your mind and life. You are deluding yourself if you claim that it is because you have outgrown religious superstition. You will not get rid of God that easily. Even though you are dishonouring Him by refusing to acknowledge his presence in your life, He will still be with you always. It is impossible to escape from God and his unfathomable love for you.

Because He only desires what is best for you, it is wise to accept his love and grace, and to enjoy the life that He wants to give to you.

I have surrendered myself to your love, o God, and therefore I enjoy the goodness and grace that flow from your throne. For this I thank You, o Father.

We have to admit that God is attendant everywhere through his sacred presence, but not everywhere through the residence of his Spirit of grace.

~ Augustine of Hippo ~

Grow to Maturity

When I was a child, I talked like a child, I thought like a child, I reasoned like a child. When I became a man, I put childish ways behind me (1 Cor. 13:11).

Sadly, there are some people who never become spiritually mature. With every passing year their bodies grow older, but they continue to cling to childish and immature thought patterns. The hurts of their past are consistently transferred into the present to poison their spirits and impede their future plans.

You should forgive and forget the injuries and insults that you have nursed over the years. To say that an injury was so serious that it could never be forgiven or forgotten is to allow its effect to continue and become even worse. Harbouring such an attitude can cause you irreparable harm.

The quality of your Christian experience should enable you to unequivocally overcome all injuries and irritations that are impeding your spiritual growth. Now is the time to grow in grace.

God has granted us the gift of the Holy Spirit to be our Leader to spiritual maturity. If you open your spirit to the grace of his Spirit and allow Him to reveal Himself through you, a new phase will open up in your life. One aspect of this new life is that it enables you to forgive and forget and to commit yourself to everything that is good, loving and noble.

Holy Spirit of God, please grant me a fervid desire to grow towards spiritual maturity every day.

The only true forgiveness is that which is offered even before the culprit has apologised and asked for forgiveness.

~ Søren Kierkegaard ~

Place yourself in the other person's position

"Do not judge, or you too will be judged" (Mt. 7:1).

It is easy to criticise others and therefore it happens all too often. Businessmen criticise each other's behaviour and plans; sportsmen and referees endure criticism; neighbours are critical of each other's houses and gardens; parents find fault with other people's children; professional colleagues are highly critical of each other's work. The fact of the matter is that criticism is the order of the day, and it is truly refreshing to meet someone who reveals a measure of tolerance.

Constructive criticism that is a sincere attempt to help someone is commendable and should always be accepted in the spirit in which it is offered. However, unfortunately most criticism is negative and is aimed at ridiculing and humiliating its victim. It is also sad that the majority of people are only too eager to listen to this kind of criticism, while few are interested in hearing of the other attributes of the person in question.

Before you add your voice to the crowd of critics, become still for a moment and place yourself in the other person's position. Try to understand the reason for his behaviour. There may be worthy and honourable reasons for his behaviour. We don't always understand the tension and stress in other people's lives. Look at your neighbour through Jesus' eyes. Then you will not only be reluctant to criticise, but by following his example you will compel the critic to silence.

Loving heavenly Father, make me ever tolerant, sympathetic and understanding in my interaction with other people.

To escape criticism you should say nothing, do nothing and be nothing!

~ Elbert Hubbard ~

IN PARTNERSHIP WITH GOD

"Now let the fear of the Lord be upon you. Judge carefully, for with the Lord our God there is no injustice or partiality or bribery" (2 Chr. 19:7).

There are those who believe that religion and business should be kept separate. Some people accept this idea on the basis that the two matters simply do not mix, while others become uncomfortable when they consider their business practices in the light of Christian principles.

God unequivocally has a place in your business practices and in your social life, just as He does in your spiritual life, and you cannot eliminate Him from one of these spheres without inflicting damage on yourself. Your entire life is ruled by Christian principles and you should bear witness to your Christianity, regardless of the sphere of life that you are moving in: both in your worship and in your activities outside of the church.

Integrity is one of the most important qualities in this respect. The surest way to reflect integrity in all your interactions is to make the living Christ your business partner. Whatever you do, scrutinise it through the eyes of Jesus; ask yourself how He would have reacted and what He would have done in your circumstances.

Follow Christ's example and you will be assured of a virtuous life that will earn you the respect of everyone you interact with.

Lord Jesus, I am not ashamed to acknowledge You as the Lord of my life, or to profess your Name under any circumstances.

I hope that I possess the firmness and the virtue to be worthy of what I regard as the greatest title: the character of an honest man.
~ George Washington ~

Be continually grateful

(C)ontinue to live in him, rooted and built up in him, strengthened in the faith as you were taught, and overflowing with thankfulness (Col. 2:7).

---

*I*t is extremely easy to be unhappy and ungrateful. This is especially true in these ominous times in which we live, in which there are so many people who restlessly pursue empty dreams of a better world and a better life. It so often causes a negative perspective on life as well as a limited and purposeless lifestyle that finds fault with everything. People focus so much on the flaws and faults around them that they fail to see the wonders of God and his grace.

Every detail of your life, from the cradle to the grave, is known to God. In his design for eternity He plans what is best for you. It is true that things sometimes go wrong, but you can't always attribute it to God. However, He can, at any given moment, change your life situation to such an extent that light radiates from the darkness and hope is born from despair.

If you feel dejected, maybe it is time to think back to all the good things that have happened in your life. Recall those times when Christ's presence was an undeniable reality to you and his love filled your entire being.

Thank the Lord for his grace and blessings. Then the Holy Spirit will start his healing work in your life and you will once again see life in a positive light. Praise and gratitude uplift the heart and honours God who is the giver of all that is good.

We praise and thank You, o Lord, with our hearts, our mouths and our hands, for all the wonders that You have done.

You have granted me so much already! Please grant me only one more thing: a grateful heart!

~ George Herbert ~

*T*HE REWARDS OF PATIENCE

I waited patiently for the Lord; he turned to me and heard my cry (Ps. 40:1).

---

*W*e often feel that our prayers are ineffectual; that our cries of distress go unheard and that He takes no heed of them. We pray earnestly and sincerely, but it seems as if there is no answer. Then we begin to doubt our faith, or even worse, we begin to question the purpose and value of prayer. As a result, many people end up in a spiritual wilderness.

We have to realise that God is all-knowing, and consequently He views life from the perspective of eternity. You, on the other hand, cannot see beyond the present with any measure of certainty. He knows everything that awaits you, today as well as in the distant future. Consequently God's answers to your prayers take into consideration what will be best for you – today, tomorrow *and* all the days after. Therefore God also sometimes needs to lay a restraining hand on your impulsive spirit.

He often does this by withholding the answers to your prayers until the time is right. Never become impatient with God or try to anticipate his answers. Seek his presence in prayer and contemplation and become still before Him. In his own perfect time He will reveal Himself to you. He will answer your yearning cries for Him.

O Hearer of prayers, everyone has to draw near unto You. As our succour in troubled times You are tried to the extreme, and yet You have always proved Yourself to be faithful.

The extent of our faith is the extent of our prayer. The strength of our hope is the strength of our prayer. The warmth of our love is the warmth of our prayer.

~ Carlo Caretto ~

---

*U*NITED IN JESUS CHRIST

Make every effort to keep the unity of the Spirit through the bond of peace (Eph. 4:3).

*S*ince the time of its inception the church of Jesus Christ has been subject to the onslaught of the forces of evil, which have threatened to undermine Jesus' work. This is just as much the case today as it has been throughout the ages, as is evident in all spheres of life.

Unfortunately, it is true that at a time when all churches ought to stand united in keeping the principles of faith extant, conflict and intolerance seems to be the order of the day. Denominations differ from each other regarding issues of dogma, theology and the interpretation of the Bible. All too often these differences escalate into bitterness and anger, which are in contradiction with the principles of the love of Christ upon which the church is founded.

No one has the right to deny anyone else his own opinion and your Christian testimony should be founded on the kind of tolerant love that is evident in all your interactions and deeds. It may be true that you disagree with others' approach to the Christian faith, or their understanding and exegesis of the Holy Scriptures, but you should be able to exercise restraint, so that you will not allow anger to cloud your judgment or to alienate you from your fellow believers.

When you surrender yourself to the living Christ and open yourself to the influence of his Holy Spirit, you will find that He grants you the ability to cope with all situations in the love of Christ.

Holy Lord Jesus, as your body on earth we dare not be divided against ourselves. Make us one in mind, spirit and love through the strength of the Holy Spirit.

The church of Jesus Christ is not an institution; it is a new life with and in Jesus Christ, guided by the Holy Spirit.

~ Sergius Bulgakov ~

*H*OW TO LIVE

How can a young man keep his way pure? By living according to your word (Ps. 119:9).

*O*ne of the most prevalent questions of our time is: "How is it possible to live a virtuous life in today's world?" When one considers all the temptations and enticements that are associated with contemporary life; the pressure under which people live and work; the high expectations that young people are required to meet in their studies; you simply can not forbear having sympathy with those in such situations. You sense a feeling of helplessness in the demeanour of those asking this question in the midst of their desperation.

There are no instant solutions to the problem. Our Saviour made this abundantly clear during his earthly ministry. Obedience to his commandments is essential, and this means that you should submit yourself to his dominion in every sphere of your life.

Many people feel that they simply cannot satisfy all the demands that Jesus places on them. Just think of the rich young man in the Bible. Consequently they turn away from Him. This reveals their lack of faith, because they are not willing to trust Jesus in their surrender.

Jesus Christ will never expect something of you without assisting and supporting you. Therefore walk the path of the Lord in this assurance, and enjoy the peace and fulfilment that is experienced only by those who serve Him with sincerity.

Lord my God, let your will and not mine be done in all spheres of my life. Help me through the Holy Spirit to live according to the instructions of your Word.

No one gives himself freely and willingly to the service of God, unless he has tasted his Fatherly love and is compelled by it to serve and love Him.

~ John Calvin ~

EXCESSIVE EMOTION IN SPIRITUAL MATTERS

From the ends of the earth I call to you, I call as my heart grow faint;
lead me to the rock that is higher than I (Ps. 61:2).

*E*motion plays an important role in the Christian faith. When the
mind is tranquil and the spirit still, the awareness of God's presence is
an acute reality. His Spirit permeates your spirit and you feel that you
are at one with Him. These moments may be laden with nourishing
emotion that refreshes and invigorates your entire life. Ecstatic religious emotion may provide you with a sense of contentment, but if it is
not founded on and controlled by the infrastructure of reality, it will
never lead to effective service to the Master.

The pure Christian experience is a combination of emotions inspired
by the Holy Spirit and their daily practical application. If you found
your faith purely on emotion it is only a matter of time before it collapses under the pressure of ever-changing moods. On the other hand,
if you advocate a "practical" religion and try to avoid all forms of religious emotion, you deny yourself a spiritual power that should be an
inspiration to you. To be a well-balanced Christian you need to be
empowered by the Holy Spirit, to be spiritually enthusiastic, and to
manifest your deepest spiritual experience in a practical way in your
everyday life.

Master and Leader, I continually seek the inspiration of the Holy Spirit
to temper my emotions, so that I may lead a practical Christian life.

Emotions should be servants and not masters, and especially not ty-
rants.

~ Robert H. Benson ~

Look for the Goodness in Others

Finally, brothers, whatever is true, whatever is noble, whatever is right, whatever is pure, whatever is lovely, whatever is admirable – if anything is excellent or praiseworthy – think about such things (Phil. 4:8).

There are Christians who unconsciously usurp the functions of the Holy Spirit for themselves. They are constantly busy trying to convince others of their sinful nature, and therefore continually point out others' mistakes. It is the prerogative of the Holy Spirit to convince people of their sinfulness and to guide them to a real experience of the living Christ. When a Christian constantly condemns other people, he becomes blind to an important dynamic element of the Christian gospel: that all people may become new creations in Jesus Christ.

Someone who has been renewed in Christ has been forgiven, and though he is still prey to temptation, he is able to deal with it through the strength of Christ, his Saviour. A true Christian sees the newly reborn disciple in a new light. He no longer only sees the weakness, irascibility and sin of the human personality, but starts to comprehend the hidden potential for good that is always present. He sees good even in those who are unfaithful to Christ, and he appreciates everything that is true, noble, just, beautiful and praiseworthy.

When a Christian expects to find virtue in people, he will observe that people gradually start reacting in a way similar to what is expected of them. It may take time, but if you use the intuition granted to you by the Holy Spirit to seek only the best in others, you will often find that people accept the challenge of Christ.

Loving Master, through the enlightenment granted to me by the Holy Spirit, I always see the good in my neighbour.

It is ridiculous for any person to criticise the deeds of another unless he has proved himself through his own behaviour.

~ Joseph Addison ~

THE STRENGTH OF THE HOLY SPIRIT

So I say, live by the Spirit, and you will not gratify the desires of the sinful nature (Gal. 5:16).

Much has been said and written about the necessity of putting Christ first in your life. The summons to submit yourself to his will and to be obedient to his commands is often emphasised. Christians are urged to turn away from the demands of society so that they may joyfully follow Christ. Countless sincere believers have tried to measure up to the demands imposed on Christians. If they were to be honest, they would have to confess that it is much easier said than done.

If we take into account all the temptations and enticements that come across our paths, it is understandable why it is so difficult to live a life that complies with the demands of Jesus Christ. It requires a measure of willpower and a strength of character that are far beyond the capacity of the average person. The pace and tension of contemporary life places you under enormous pressure. This pressure only increases when you are called to testify for Him in circumstances that are in direct contradiction to a Christian lifestyle.

It is precisely in these circumstances that you have to open your life to the influence of the Holy Spirit. Invite Him to take control of your entire being and you will experience the power of Jesus that enables you to overcome all obstacles while you live for, through, and in Him.

Come, o Holy Spirit, and permeate my life so that the strength of Jesus may be revealed in my life and I may become a powerful witness for You.

The future of the entire human race depends upon whether we can bring the individual soul more completely and perfectly under the dominion of the Holy Spirit.

~ Isaac T. Hecker ~

TO IDENTIFY WITH CHRIST

" ... The life I live in the body, I live by faith in the Son of God, who loved me and gave himself for me" (Gal. 2:20).

This is one of the most inspiring and yet also challenging texts in the entire New Testament. It transcends theological argument and penetrates into the sphere of true spiritual experience where the fullness of God saturates one's life in so far as it is allowed to. The love, peace, strength and other attributes of the living Christ become a glorious reality to those who accept Him and who are obedient to his will.

However, no human being can, in himself, accomplish such an intimate identification with the living Christ. It is only through God's goodness and grace that we can experience the reality of Christ's Spirit. Identifying with Christ means to walk as close to Him as is possible for a mortal man.

This privilege also encompasses weighty responsibilities. To be one with Christ implies an involvement with his redeeming purpose for the world. It means experiencing some of the pain that He suffers as a result of the depravity of mankind. It means to be compassionate and generous, to love others in his Spirit and his love.

To identify with Christ you need to surrender and commit yourself completely to Him. You need to have the same disposition as Jesus Christ did. Your attitudes, behaviour, motives and lifestyle should be the expression of the Spirit of Christ in you. Identification with Christ means to grow towards being increasingly more like the Master.

Thank You, heavenly Teacher, that I may grow in the grace and wisdom of my Redeemer, Jesus Christ. For this I thank and praise You.

I know Jesus Christ and He, as the crucified one, is my life philosophy. There is no higher aspiration in life.

~ Bernard of Clairvaux ~

*J*EALOUSY AND CHRISTIAN SERVICE

And let us consider how we may spur one another on toward love and good deeds (Heb. 10:24).

*U*nfortunately jealousy is a common sin among Christian workers. It is often concealed in religious semantics and clever phrasings, but where competition exists in a church or Christian organisation the results quickly become evident. And once these results become apparent in church organisations, the testimony of the body of Christ is weakened and undermined.

Jealousy is the consequence of self-centredness. When you are interested solely in your own little world of service while simultaneously envying the success of others, your vision becomes limited and restricted. Your service is no longer a source of satisfaction to you. And if you persist in your jealousy, it eventually corrodes your spiritual life until you no longer experience God as a reality.

The most basic way of conquering jealousy in your Christian service is to allow the Holy Spirit to take possession of your life. The practical manifestation of this experience will encourage you to serve others in sincerity. To overcome jealousy you should take control of your thoughts and allow the Holy Spirit to renew your mind. Be sincere in your delight over the successes and achievements of others. It may not be easy initially, and you may even feel like a hypocrite, but as your awareness of the presence of the Holy Spirit in your life increases, you will experience a wonderful feeling of liberation. Then you will be able to inspire others to achieve their full potential in Christ.

Holy Jesus, through your immanent Holy Spirit I am gloriously liberated from all forms of jealousy. For this I sincerely thank You.

In jealousy there is more self-love than neighbourly love.
~ Francois de la Rochefoucauld ~

*S*ɪɴ ᴡɪʟʟ ᴄᴏsᴛ ʏᴏᴜ ᴅᴇᴀʀʟʏ

" ... The soul who sins is the one who will die" (Ezek. 18:4).

---

*I*n contemporary society sin has lost its sting. It is derogated with psychological terms and referred to as weaknesses or illnesses. But the consequences of sin still remain the same. Sin separates us from God, creates feelings of guilt, inferiority and frustration, and deprives the sinner of inner calm and peace of mind.

You cannot sin without eventually being caught. This is a fact that many people try to ignore with all their might. They believe that they are the exception to the divine law that one reaps as one has sown – with interest. People commit sin without giving any thought to the consequences. Sin has its own price, and it can be extremely costly, if we calculate how much sadness, scandal and sorrow is inflicted upon loved ones when sins are disclosed.

God does not tempt anyone; you commit sin by your own free choice. You isolate yourself from Him by walking your own path and deviating from God's path. To deliberately continue sinning is to commit spiritual suicide.

To accept Jesus Christ as the Redeemer and Saviour of your life, and to consciously live in the presence of God, are the only ways to preserve yourself from sin. In doing so you will experience freedom and be liberated from your guilt. The Holy Spirit grants you the strength to live victoriously.

Through your immanent Spirit, holy Lord Jesus, I obtain the strength to live in triumph over sin.

Sin is a force in our lives: let us clearly understand that it can only be conquered by a greater Power.

~ Henry Drummond ~

CHRISTIAN FANATICISM

Some of the Pharisees said, "This man is not from God, for he does not keep the Sabbath" ... (Jn. 9:16).

The dictionary defines a fanatic or zealot as someone who admires and worships something in an excessive manner, or someone who is stubborn and intolerant. Unfortunately these traits are often found in religious people. Their misplaced values cause unimportant things to become crucially important.

Jesus restores a blind man's sight on the Sabbath, and yet the Pharisees fail to notice the miracle because they are unable to see beyond the violation of the law of the Sabbath. They couldn't share in the man's joy at being able to see, because they classified his cure as "work". They condemn both the man and his Healer.

In the Christian life it is easy to become so entangled in matters of lesser importance that you start confining the living Christ to your intellectual limits. Because you cannot understand how the Master did some of his miracles, you refuse to accept that they were done at all. You ignore the fact that there are depths that are as yet unexplored by your intellect.

No disciple of Christ should be so unwise as to close his mind to new ideas about his faith. There are many facets to the life, teachings and personality of our Lord Jesus, but the common factor among all his disciples is an overwhelming love for the Master and for one another. Love is the death-knell of fanaticism and the origin of understanding. Fanaticism will prevent the love of Christ from flowing through you.

Beloved Master, your love for me and my love for You rescues me from blind fanaticism. For this I praise and exalt your holy Name.

Fanaticism may roughly be described as the rage of people who have no opinion of their own.

~ G. K. Chesterton ~

Receive God's forgiveness

I prayed to the Lord my God and confessed ... (Dan. 9:4).

*I*t is one of the great privileges and joys of the Christian faith that regardless of what you have done God is always waiting for you to come to Him in prayer. His love for you is so vast that you are assured of his forgiveness even before you enter into his presence. This assurance was given once and for all on Golgotha. All that you have to do is to turn in repentance to Christ and confess all your sins to Him.

Maybe it is precisely because it seems so simple and easy that so many people do not make use of this glorious offer of grace from Christ. Or maybe they are too ashamed to confess their failures. However, one thing is sure: the longer you postpone matters and bottle up your guilt, the more difficult it will become to make your confession, and the more unhappy you will become.

There are two important matters that you need to consider. One is that God knows everything about you, including your weaknesses and shortcomings. The other is that despite of it all He still loves you and always will. He gave his life in Christ to prove it.

Why would you continue to torture yourself and deny yourself the inner calm and peace of mind that Jesus offers you? Open your heart to Him and lay your guilt and fear before his throne of grace. Here you will experience the purifying balm of his unfathomable love.

By confessing my sins to You, gracious God, I experience your merciful forgiveness and can therefore live in joyful abundance.

For him who confesses his guilt the pretence is past and the reality has begun.

~ William James ~

*G*OD CHOOSES HIS WORKERS

... being confident of this, that he who began a good work in you will carry it on to completion until the day of Christ Jesus (Phil. 1:6).

In every generation God has had followers to proclaim his truth and do his will. Sometimes they have been held in high esteem by the community. Others have remained unknown and have modestly performed the task that He assigned them to the best of their ability. Regardless of their status, all of them loved God with a fervour that inspired and challenged their fellows human beings.

The spiritual giants of the Christian faith have always had a uniquely personal experience of the living Christ. Paul never forgot his meeting with the Master on the road to Damascus; brother Lawrence met Christ in his kitchen; John Wesley felt his heart becoming strangely warm in a room in Aldersgate Street in London; many other disciples experienced the reality of the Lord in a unique way.

Every child of the Lord should realise that Christ comes to each of us in a personal and unique way, so to meet us on our own level. The ordinary disciple need not necessarily expect a Damascus road experience, because the Saviour will prepare a special experience that is uniquely suited to the individual person.

As your experience of Jesus deepens and expands into constructive service, you will become aware of a divine plan that is in the process of unfolding in your life. This plan may not be particularly dramatic or impressive by the standards of the world, but it will be God's plan for your life. In accomplishing it you will experience immense joy and profound satisfaction.

Leader and Redeemer, I pray that I will be a faithful worker in your service, and that I will never be ashamed when You judge my work.

God does not call the qualified, He qualifies those He calls.
~ Charles H. Spurgeon ~

The Important Role of Women

Early on the first day of the week, while it was still dark, Mary Magdalene went to the tomb ... (Jn. 20:1).

Throughout the Scriptures women play an important role, and their influence on the Christendom should never be underestimated. They were the last ones present at Jesus' cross and the first at his tomb; they were the first to announce his resurrection and they were undoubtedly present at the first domestic devotions. While Jesus ministered to the crowds of Galilee, He was served by a group of women who used their own possessions to support Him and his disciples. When the apostles first arrived in Europe they were welcomed by women.

The church is greatly indebted to devout women who love Christ with so much dedication that they are willing to sacrifice anything. When cynical people declare that most congregations consist almost entirely of women, they are merely confirming a scriptural truth. Why is this so? One reason may be that women are more sensitive and spiritually aware than men. Some men would have been much wiser and richer if they had followed the advice of a devout mother or a dedicated spouse. Others are where they are today only because of the prayers and support of a loving wife.

Paul tells us that there are no differences between men and women, Jews and Gentiles, slaves and free people: in Jesus Christ we are all one. This unity in Christ makes Christians dependent on each other, and men and women draw their inspiration from the same Source. Therefore we should show respect and appreciation for the service that every person offers.

Thank You, heavenly Father, for the noble and enriching service that devout women have offered to You and your church.

There are no limits to the influence of a devout and noble woman.
~ Robert H. Benson ~

Guard Against Double Standards

... But you – who are you to judge your neighbor? (Jas. 4:12).

It is inevitable that you will form opinions about things that you approve of and things that you condemn. However, we have to ensure that our condemnation is always tempered with forgiveness, because we must also be perpetually aware of our own weaknesses and the failures in our pasts.

Many people have a condemnatory attitude towards their fellow human beings. They scrutinise every deed as if under a magnifying glass, and are quick to emphasise others' mistakes. In addition, they also like to insinuate that *they* would never be associated with such deviant behaviour. People who are constantly passing judgment on others usually have a limited spiritual outlook, and inevitably only manage to make life miserable for themselves as well as others.

People with a condemnatory attitude seldom use the same standards to judge themselves as they would to judge others. They expect a high standard of behaviour from others, but not of themselves, and, what is more, they are quick to make excuses when their behaviour falls short of this standard.

In the Christian life there is only one standard that applies to everyone. What is applicable to one is applicable to all. Therefore, if you see someone doing something that contravenes God's laws, you should ensure that you are not also guilty of transgressing a law before you pass judgment. The law that you are transgressing may not be as blatant as the one you are condemning, but the awareness of your own sin should humble you and make you more careful in your judgments.

Merciful Lord Jesus, because I am so aware of my own weaknesses, I should be slow to condemn others and quick to forgive them.

The more one knows of oneself, the easier it is to forgive others.
~ Catherine Marshall ~

---

*P*RAY FOR YOUR NEEDS, NOT YOUR WANTS

"Every word of God is flawless; he is a shield to those who take refuge in him" (Prov. 30:5).

*W*e often hear people complaining that God has disappointed them by not answering their prayers. All too often these are also the people who blame God for their circumstances. When misfortune or disappointment strikes, God is blamed for the predicament in which they find themselves.

To find an answer to these accusations it is necessary to ask this question: How many of these people have entrusted their requests in prayer to the throne of grace and have completely submitted themselves to the will of God?

Jesus invited us to ask anything of the Father in his Name, and promised that we would receive it. However, this by no means implies that God will give you everything you ask for. What it *does* mean is that He will provide for all your needs through Jesus Christ. You should pray for God's guidance before making your requests, so that you will ensure that what you are asking for are truly your needs, and not only things that you desire to have.

God never disappoints, but you have to completely surrender yourself and your will to Him and open yourself to the influence of the Holy Spirit, who will guide your thoughts and deeds. In this way you will live in harmony with God's will and experience the abundance of true life.

O Holy Spirit, help me to grow in faith through fervid prayer. I know that my heavenly Father will provide for every legitimate need that I have.

Prayer enlarges the heart so that it eventually becomes big enough to contain God Himself.

~ Mother Teresa ~

Your reputation is of inestimable worth

... for they loved praise from men more than praise from God (Jn. 12:43).

Your good reputation is of inestimable worth. Your worthiness depends on society's opinion of you. It cannot be gained overnight, nor can it be bought by favours with hidden agendas. It can only be earned by living a noble life.

Standards that are founded on essential values ought not to be influenced by the opinions of other people. Your standards should not be of the world, but rather of God. If you allow your reputation to be shaped by other people's opinions and expectations of you, your life will be governed by ever-changing values. People have differing value systems, and you cannot comply with all of them.

When you live to please God alone, you accept principles that create a strong character and a good reputation. Your word becomes your bond; your candour is tempered with love; honesty becomes an integral part of your being; and, because you are aware of your own vulnerability, you refrain from harsh criticism.

Living to please God has a powerful formative influence on your life. If you honour God and allow Him to govern your life, you will have the respect of those who maintain God's standards.

Holy Lord Jesus, help me to live to please You alone. May your values always be manifested in my life.

Many people's reputations would not recognise their characters if the two were to meet in the street.

~ Elbert Hubbard ~

*T*HE SECOND COMING OF CHRIST

The end of all things is near. Therefore be clear minded and self-controlled so that you can pray (1 Pet. 4:7).

---

*F*or centuries people have been trying to determine the exact date on which the world will end. Despite the fact that Jesus expressly told us that it is not for us to know the time, and that God alone knows it, the prophecies just seem to continue.

The actual date of the end of our conjuncture is of little importance if you are equipped and ready to meet it. The most important aspect of the second coming of Christ is not when it will take place, but rather whether you will be prepared to meet your Lord and to account for your life and deeds.

People go to much trouble to prepare themselves for special occasions; they make ample provision for their retirement; they ensure that their affairs are in order should they suddenly pass away. When a storm looms the doors and windows are locked; farmers protect their livestock from the cold of winter; insurance is taken out to provide in the event of theft, loss and accidents.

How much more important is it then to prepare yourself spiritually and mentally, so that you may joyfully anticipate the second coming of Christ? Discipline yourself to spend time in prayer and contemplation in the presence of the Master; surrender yourself to the influence of the Holy Spirit, so that you will be ready whenever He comes.

Come, Lord Jesus, come soon!

God has ordained that the day of his second coming will remain a secret to us, so that we will be suspensefully on the lookout for it, as it were.

~ Martin Luther ~

UGUST

*H*eavenly Guide, I so much want to begin this month with
faith, hope and love in my heart.
I so much want to believe unconditionally:
like Abraham and Enoch and Moses and all those in the
gallery of heroes in Hebrews 11.
But so often I am more like Thomas; I first want to feel and see;
my faith is often limited to my senses.
I so much want to believe the unseen and quietly profess:
"My Lord and my God!"
I so much want to experience perfect hope,
hope that all the ardent and noble ideals of my heart
will be realised;
that my spiritual life will grow in knowledge, love and truth,
so that I will be able to distinguish what is truly important.
Keep the spirit of optimism burning in my heart.
I so much want to love, God of love.
I want to say to You with the honesty of dying words:
"Lord, You know everything. You know that I love You!"
I want to love my neighbour with a sincere, unselfish love
that breaks down all the walls that divide us
and make reconciliation a glorious reality.
In this month, guide me to a true understanding of
faith and hope and love!
In the glorious Name of Jesus.

*A*men.

Respect the Scriptures

All Scripture is God-breathed and is useful for teaching, rebuking, correcting and training in righteousness (2 Tim. 3:16).

The Bible is an essential manual for the Christian. From it he draws guidance, admonition, hope and everything else that is necessary for his spiritual development. However, it is also often abused, not only by its enemies, but also by those who acknowledge it as the Word of God. This happens especially when texts are used out of context to construct religious theories. Inevitably, these theories are divested of any true meaning. For many dedicated Christians the letter of the Scriptures is much more important than the spirit behind the words. It is disturbing to hear the Word of God loudly quoted without the presence of the Spirit of God.

For centuries people have explained the prophecies of the Scriptures in the light of their own times, forgetting that the Master expressly told his followers that it is not for us to know these things. Many believe that the times in which we are now living are the "last days". This knowledge belongs to God alone. Never try to answer divine questions in human terms. You are not expected to strive after the possession of knowledge about matters that God keeps secret. Rather, you are expected to trust the Master to bring all things to their God-determined end, while living in harmony with Him.

The Bible encompasses the whole world, but it also speaks deeply to the individual human soul. It is especially for the latter purpose that the Scriptures may be most useful to you.

Incarnate Word, I thank You for revealing Yourself in the Word that God has made available to us in our own language.

The Bible is alive, it speaks to me; it has feet, it follows me; it has hands, it takes possession of me.

~ Martin Luther ~

Jesus Illuminates the Darkness

... Let him who walks in the dark, who has no light, trust in the name of the Lord and rely on his God (Is. 50:10).

There comes a time in everyone's life when the path ahead seems dark; when difficulties overwhelm you and you become despondent because of the darkness and despair that seem to surround you. Often your circumstances are so desperate that you feel completely helpless and simply cannot free yourself from the darkness. In these circumstances you are at your most vulnerable and pressurised.

Despite how far from God you feel in times like these, you must remember the glorious truth that He is actually closer to you than ever before. Your heavenly Father has assured you that He will never abandon or forsake you. He is constantly at your side, waiting for you to turn to Him for help, which He is always ready and willing to provide.

Regardless of what is happening in your life, yes, even when you are unable to pray, never neglect turning to Christ and laying your fears and concerns before Him. Because He lived among people He is all too aware of the difficulties and problems that you experience. Allow Him to lead you and you will experience the blessing and joy of his love and peace.

O Lord, please send your light and your truth to me; let it guide me to your holy mountain so that I may enter and go to the altars of God.

For the church Pentecost brought light, strength and joy. It wasn't necessary for anyone to ask whether they had received the Holy Spirit. Light and strength are self-revealing.

~ Samuel Chadwick ~

---

*H*ow great Thou art!

Since ancient times no one has heard, no ear has perceived, no eye has seen any God besides you, who acts on behalf of those who wait for him (Is. 64:4).

---

*T*hroughout history Christianity has come under fire from all quarters. The validity of our faith and even the existence of God have been challenged and questioned. Many have suffered torment and persecution for the sake of their faith and thousands have chosen death rather than to deny their God. This surely indicates the greatness and strength of God's love for the Christian and the Christian's love for God.

As you live your life faithfully in Jesus Christ, you will become more and more aware of his presence with you. When you place your trust in God and dedicate your life to Him, you become increasingly aware of the fact that his hand rests upon you and guides you through the maze of life. The healthier your relationship with the Master, the more aware you will be of the Holy Spirit who speaks to you and leads you through each day.

A life that is lived in, with and for the living Christ will strengthen your faith and allow you to seize each day joyfully. Nothing else can provide you with this joy and peace. And then you can do nothing but whisper in grateful prayer: "How great Thou art!"

Saviour and Redeemer, I kneel in helpless wonder before your greatness and majesty. I truly love You, o Lord!

There is only one thing in life that is worthwhile pursuing, and that is knowledge of God.

~ Robert H. Benson ~

The inspiration of the Holy Spirit

"And I will ask the Father, and he will give you another Counselor to be with you forever – the Spirit of truth ... " (Jn. 14:16).

If one considers all the demands and expectations exacted by modern life, it is not surprising that there are so many people who collapse under the pressure and fail to comply with the standards prescribed to them. Sadly, this often causes people to turn away from the Christian faith in despair, and consequently they experience the torment of wandering around in the wilderness of uncertainty.

Jesus knows human fallibility and fragility all too well. That is why He prepared his disciples for a life without his physical presence. He granted them the gift of the Holy Spirit to enable them to cope with the demands of life. And they undoubtedly needed it, because they experienced such virulent opposition to their preaching of the gospel.

The gift of the Spirit is yours too, because God has said: " ... *I will pour out my Spirit on all people* ... "(Joel 2:28). Jesus confirms this in the words of today's verse from Scripture.

To enable you to cope with life in all its many facets in accordance with the instructions of the Master, it is essential to allow the living Jesus into your life. Do it, and allow his Spirit to direct your life according to the will of God. Then you will be able to handle any situation, however difficult.

O Holy Spirit, come and fill my life. Inspire me to live according to the will and instructions of God the Father and my Saviour, Jesus Christ.

The Holy Spirit is the living immanence of God.
~ Romano Guardini ~

CHOOSE GOD'S WAY

Surely the arm of the Lord is not too short to save, nor his ear too dull to hear (Is. 59:1).

We so often live as if God did not exist. We make our own plans and work hard to accomplish them. We develop ambitions and devise ventures without any thought to what God expects of us.

And usually, when we decide to follow our own way instead of God's way, things start going awry. We run into the proverbial brick walls and start thinking that we are being pursued by bad luck. We become despondent and feel that it is useless to attempt anything, because it will just be a failure anyway.

The truth of the matter is that our problem is not bad luck, but rather our deliberate disobedience to God's summons to live a nobler life. If things seem to be going wrong for you all the time, pause and consider why they are going awry. Are you choosing your own way instead of God's way? However desperate your circumstances may appear, it can always be reversed if you abandon your own selfish way and choose God's perfect way. But this is a demanding process, and few people are willing to pay the price exacted by it. However, it remains a fact that being obedient to God and walking in his way will bring deliverance from even the most wretched circumstances.

Holy Master, your way for my life may seem demanding and difficult, but it is the only and the best way for my life. I want to follow You every day of my life.

There are two kinds of freedom: the false kind, where man is free to do what he wants; and the true kind, where man is free to do what he must.

~ Charles Kingsley ~

Together with God

I can do everything through him who gives me strength (Phil. 4:13).

When you think of God in all his divine glory and of yourself as an insignificant little speck on the planet earth, it becomes incredibly difficult to identify yourself with Him. Despite this, the Holy Spirit of God, who inhabits God's entire creation, can also inhabit your spirit. Accepting this truth releases a hitherto unknown force in your life. It is God's will that you should have a vigorous and living relationship with Him.

When you think of yourself as a part of God's revelation of Himself, you share an empathy with Him that will bring strength, balance and dynamism into your life. It will also provide you with a strong sense of responsibility. If you realise that you have been created by God and that you are possessed by his Spirit, you also realise that your life should live up to his expectations. You no longer live to please yourself, but rather to do his will. Through the grace of God you can attain this kind of life in the strength of the Lord Jesus Christ.

Before our Saviour ascended to heaven He promised that his Spirit would be with those who have accepted him as Saviour and Lord and who are willing to allow his Spirit to work through them. It is the Holy Spirit who makes God reality in the life of the Christian and who enables him to live in harmony with and in the strength of God.

Merciful Lord Jesus, I accept the gift of the Holy Spirit and therefore enjoy intimate communion with You, my Lord and my God.

Nothing that the human soul can do brings more joy to God than for it to have communion with Him through his grace.

~ Alphonsus Liguori ~

The will of God alone

"By myself I can do nothing; I judge only as I hear, and my judgment is just, for I seek not to please myself but him who sent me" (Jn. 5:30).

There are few people who have not at some point experienced the frustration of plans that go awry or expectations that are disappointed. In many cases it goes much further than mere disappointment because of failure. The consequences of failure can take on immeasurable proportions. When this happens, many people ascribe it to fate, or economic circumstances beyond their control, or chance, or bad luck, or any of a host of other reasons. Few people will admit that the fault lies within them, because they refuse to live according to the will of God.

God's sacred plan with your life is one of perfection. Because you are his child and He loves you, He wishes only the very best for you. For this reason everything that happens in your life is intended to ultimately give you the very best, even though it may not appear so to you at the time.

To achieve this goal with as little trouble as possible, it is your responsibility to live and work within God's will. Submit your ideas and plans to Him and faithfully seek his guidance. The closer you live to your Master, the easier you will find it to know his will for your life. Never embark on any endeavour that falls outside the will of God, and you will experience peace of mind and tranquillity, as well as the assurance that Jesus will be with you in all your endeavours.

Eternal and loving God, I surrender myself to You completely. Lead me according to your will from day to day.

Blessed are those who obey God's will, because He will never let them go astray.

~ Francis de Sales ~

*I*NTEGRITY BEFORE *G*OD

"I know, my God, that you test the heart and are pleased with integrity ... " (1 Chr. 29:17).

---

*I*f you sincerely try to cultivate a positive and meaningful prayer life, you will at some time or another have experienced the problem of wandering thoughts. In the time you have set aside to be alone with your heavenly Father you may read a passage from the Bible or from an inspirational spiritual book. Then you start praying, only to discover that instead of being focused on God, your thoughts run amok and start focusing on the most irrelevant or even profane things.

If this has happened to you, take comfort in the thought that it happens to everyone who takes prayer time seriously. However, those who have persevered have ultimately succeeded in making their prayers a delightful reality and powerful force in their lives.

When your thoughts wander, don't become upset or frustrated, because then you are playing right into the hands of the evil one. Gently turn your thoughts back towards God, and ask the Holy Spirit to take control of your mind. You may rest assured that the problem of your wandering thoughts can be conquered, so don't allow it to spoil your relationship with the living Christ.

The wonder of Christian prayer is that when you turn to Jesus you will find that He is already awaiting you. Prayer is not a one-way communication, because in this sacred practice Jesus is just as eager to meet you, his child, as you are to meet Him.

Thank You, heavenly Master, that I may experience the reality of your living presence through prayer. For this I praise your Name.

Talk to Him in prayer about all your needs, your problems, even the fatigue that you experience in his service. You can never talk too freely or candidly to Him.

~ Francois Fenelon ~

*D*OES YOUR RELIGION LEAD YOU TO *G*OD?

Taste and see that the Lord is good ... (Ps. 34:8).

*I*t is commendable to accept the doctrine of your church, because it provides you with a foundation upon which to build your faith. In a traditional church environment you may become familiar with certain liturgical forms of worship from which you can draw hope, courage and strength. Or perhaps you are profoundly touched by the warmth, enthusiasm and spiritual intensity of the charismatic movement. Between these two extremes there is a host of lukewarm Christians who fail to experience the satisfaction of a living faith.

The litmus test of your way of worship is whether it leads you into the presence of God. If the living Christ is at the centre of your faith you will know the deep hunger of the soul that yearns to know Him more intimately. You will discipline your prayer life and organise your reading of the Scriptures to facilitate a more profound understanding of the Master and his way of life.

Whatever your theological position or church affiliation, the crucial aspect of your spiritual pilgrimage ultimately remains your personal relationship with Christ Jesus. Knowing Him through faith, prayer and contemplation will elevate your faith beyond differences in theology and dogma. It will engender in you a love for all people and transcend all differences. When this happens you will be overwhelmed by the greatness and benevolence of your living Lord.

Merciful Lord, grant me a spiritual temper that will enable me to transcend all religious differences, so that I may meet You in all your glory.

Truths become dogmas as soon as they are debated.
~ G. K. Chesterton ~

Listen to God

Listen to what the Lord says ... (Mic. 6:1).

Most people have an opinion on virtually every matter under the sun. Should you pose some or other abstract question to them, their response would probably be: "I don't really know because I haven't considered the matter, but I think that ... " If a great number of people start enthusiastically expressing immature and unconsidered thoughts, the situation can easily become chaotic. However, if you are sensible you will remember that behind this veritable Babel of tongues the immutable truths of God stand steadfastly. In the heat of the argument these truths are seldom evident, and are also usually not expressed in devout theological terms.

God reveals his truths to those who invite Him to share in their lives; who gladly give up time to be with Him; who ponder his Word so that they can understand his will more thoroughly. Make sure that you always spend more time in the awareness of God's presence than in argumentation – regardless of how interesting the argument may be.

The art of listening to God is an enriching and inspirational experience. It imparts tranquillity and balance to your spirit and mind in the midst of disquiet and endless arguments. The art of listening to God is usually practised in a private but sacred place, but this discipline yields its abundant results when you have to venture into our tumultuous world.

Holy God, in listening to You I receive wisdom, peace, balance and stability in my daily life.

God is a tranquil Being and lives in a peaceful eternity. In the same way your spirit should become a tranquil, peaceful and limpid pool in which the serene light of God may be reflected.

~ Gerhard Tersteegen ~

Establish Trust Through Partnership

So we say with confidence, "The Lord is my helper; I will not be afraid. What can man do to me?" (Heb. 13:6).

If you are trying to take on life's difficulties and problems in your own strength and wisdom, it is likely that you are fighting a losing battle. This does not necessarily mean that you are grumbling or complaining, or that you are constantly asking for the sympathy of others, but if you were honest with yourself and others, you would have to admit that there are moments when you long for your burden to be lifted by some positive guidance.

In such moments it is advisable to grow quiet before God, and to realise that He is closer to you than your breathing, or your hands and your feet. The only reason why He did not come to your rescue was because you did not ask Him to. You cannot take God's help for granted. When you seek his help, you place what you are and what you have at his disposal. You become God's partner in your everyday life. This partnership means that you should constantly do the will of your heavenly Partner, and do it in such a devoted and enthusiastic manner that destructive fear will have no place in your life.

When you have conquered fear through constructive service, you can face anyone with a peaceful confidence that is the direct consequence of your union with God. Because God is your Helper, and because you serve Him joyfully, you can step fearlessly and confidently into the future.

Good Shepherd, because You are my Helper and I serve you with sincerity, my life is filled with trust that is born from my relationship with You.

God's grace is abundant and He never disappoints those who are afflicted or tormented, if they fully trust in Him.
~ Teresa of Avila ~

Jesus will lead you safely

"When you pass through the waters, I will be with you; and when you pass through the rivers, they will not sweep over you ... " (Is. 43:2).

Anyone who is a poor swimmer will know the fear of finding yourself in a pool, a river or the sea, and knowing that you are out of your depth. It causes a feeling of uncertainty, danger and anxiety, because you have nothing to hold on to and no fixed foundation to stand on. The thought of sinking and drowning only contributes to the fear and can easily be converted into panic.

Your pilgrimage through life can be a similar experience. There are so many situations in which you feel incompetent, vulnerable and uncertain. In the business world you are constantly expected to act quickly and decisively, but a wrong decision or move can mean the difference between success and dismal failure. In your personal life you constantly have to make decisions and these decisions often have far-reaching consequences for yourself and for others.

The question is how you are supposed to act logically and calmly in these circumstances. There is only one way, and that is to cultivate an awareness of the living Christ in your life. Let Him be the deciding factor in all your ventures and first seek his will before you make any decisions or take any steps. Do so in faith and in the knowledge that He is the only Way to success.

Lord Jesus, I worship You as the Way, the Truth and the Life. Not my will, Lord, and not my way, but your will and your way for me.

A true Christian can almost be defined as someone who experiences a constant controlling feeling of God's presence.

~ John Henry Newman ~

Is your concept of God broad enough?

"How great is God – beyond our understanding! ... " (Job 36:26).

One of the obstacles to our spiritual development is our limited concept of God. You may believe that God loves and cares for you. You freely accept that He is all-powerful, all-knowing and omnipresent. But as soon as disaster starts to threaten, you relegate God to the back seat. Your fail to use the wisdom, calmness and strength that He has placed at your disposal. In these trying moments you find that you do not live up to that which is expected of you. Your problems appear to be bigger than your concept of God.

You ought to broaden your vision of God while things are going well. This may be accomplished by intensifying your quiet time with Him, and expanding your interest in the world around you. Be determined to increase your awareness of the greatness of God and use all the agents of his grace that He puts at your disposal to get to know Him more intimately. When the inevitable storms start looming you will find that you possess spiritual reserves that will enable you to be strong, regardless of how difficult your circumstances are.

The greater God becomes to you, the more strength you will draw from Him in moments of temptation. Your faith will no longer be an emotional matter, but rather a lasting experience of God Himself. He will give you the assurance of his presence at all times. Know that your God is great, and you will possess a lasting faith!

Great and wonderful God, grant me a spirit and attitude of appreciation for your greatness, so that my spirit and perspective may be broadened.

People who claim that there is no God are like a six-year-old boy who claims that there is no such thing as passionate love; they simply haven't experienced it yet.

~ William Alfred ~

The reality of the living Christ

The Spirit himself testifies with our spirit that we are God's children (Rom. 8:16).

Whichever Christian dogma you ascribe to or whichever church you belong to, your ultimate goal should be to know and experience the living Christ in your life. Without Him your faith may maintain a high moral standard, but it will lack the spiritual dynamism and force that are essential elements of a living faith.

Jesus Christ is much more than a historical figure who can be conceptualised in religious terms. He is the inspiration and driving force of innumerable lives in our modern age. It is insufficient to recognise only the Christ of history: what you really need is an awareness of his living presence at this moment in your life.

The yearning for this awareness should be the first priority in your life. It will never become a reality before you have been possessed by a passionate longing to make Him your own. A half-hearted desire will simply not be spiritually good enough.

When your greatest passion is to experience the immanent presence of Christ, you should act as if you are always in his presence – which you are, in reality. Speak to Him from the silence of your heart; share with Him the things that are happening to you; and if there have been moments when you excluded Him from your life, don't waste time in self-reproach. Tell Him that you are sorry, and you will find that his grace enables you to renew your relationship with Him. Then He will become an ever greater reality in your life.

Merciful and loving Master, I praise and thank You for your presence at all times in my life.

Golgotha is the key to a Presence that works only and always through a love that is willing to sacrifice all.

~ Michael Ramsey ~

BE PATIENT WITH OTHERS

Now when he saw the crowds, he went up on a mountainside and sat down ... (Mt. 5:1).

The wonder of Jesus' ministry lies in the fact that He had time for everyone. Despite the immense pressure that heavily burdened Him, He was able to accomplish more in three short years than what we accomplish in a lifetime. And yet He was never hurried, impatient or tense. When reading the Gospels you can share in that feeling of peace and calm that He radiated to everyone who came into contact with Him.

There are many occasions when we are approached to provide some advice, support or companionship, and so often we respond only by showing our impatience. We are pressed for time; we have very busy schedules; we are working to beat the clock. We show it in the hurried way in which we try to get rid of people in distress, so that we can rush on to whatever is demanding our attention. This inevitably leaves the other person with the feeling that he is nothing more than an annoying intruder who has to be pushed aside.

If you are faithful to your calling as a follower of Jesus, you should never show impatience or irritation when you are dealing with the distress of other people. Despite your busy life, Christ will always give you the time to do his work. Trust Him unconditionally and you too will be able to treat people with the same patience, compassion and empathy that He did. In this way you will become a source of encouragement, calmness and peace for others.

Lord Jesus, I open myself to your Spirit of peace, patience and encouragement in my interaction with other people.

Patience and diligence, like faith, can move mountains.
~ William Penn ~

---

*L*asting Glory

And if what was fading away came with glory, how much greater is the glory of that which lasts! (2 Cor. 3:11).

*S*ome things are made to last, while others are created only to fulfil in a passing need. Both kinds of things may appear attractive and enduring. Only time and use will show how one differs from the other. This is true of every aspect of life, and our spiritual life is no exception.

There are many forms of the Christian faith that appeal to people because they emphasise material assets, which people usually desire. Prosperity, luxury and happiness are promised and guaranteed to those who follow Christ's precepts. Unfortunately many people are drawn to following Jesus because of what they can get from Him, rather than for the sake of Jesus Himself. If their expectations do not materialise, the glory of their faith fades along with their expectations.

The true glory of the Christian faith intensifies as the years pass. A young disciple may be extremely enthusiastic about his faith and his zeal for the Lord may be a joy to see. But all the beauty of youth cannot compare with the fullness of character that is part of someone who has followed Christ through decades.

The eternal Christ brings lasting glory and enrichment to every aspect of the personality that He possesses. This glory develops slowly, like an oak tree rather than like a mushroom, but it always reflects the lasting glory of the living Christ.

I pray, Lord my God, that my life will reflect your lasting glory, for the sake of your exaltation and my spiritual growth.

Grace is only the beginning of glory, and glory is grace perfected.
~ Jonathan Edwards ~

The Big Mystery

I ... present to you the word of God in its fullness – the mystery that has been kept hidden for ages and generations, but is now disclosed to the saints. To them God has chosen to make known ... the glorious riches of this mystery, which is Christ in you, the hope of glory (Col. 1:25-27).

There is a certain quality of mysticism that is inherent to all religions, and Christianity is no exception. Since the early days of the church there have been schools of mysticism whose doctrine was known only to the initiated. This exclusivity often creates the false impression that God only reveals his mysteries to a select group of individuals.

The Scriptures reveal the amazing truth that God has no favourites and that He is willing to share his truths with everyone who is willing to live up to his demands. Paul tells us that God wants to reveal his mysteries to his people, and that this secret is the fact that Christ is present in us. This secret is the basis of a dynamic Christian lifestyle. If you accept the principle that Christ can live in you, you have discovered the greatest mystery ever to have been revealed to mankind.

If you trust that Christ controls your thoughts and emotions, and believe that He seeks to manifest Himself in your deeds, you will be carried to new spiritual heights. The things you used to fear attempting now become possible, and the things you used to shy away from no longer scare you. If you possess God's secret of the immanent Christ you are able to face life with self-confidence and expectation.

Holy Jesus, open my life to your immanent presence. I humbly plead that You will make me a channel of your love to the world.

The great truth of Easter is not that we will live anew after death, but that we will live anew now and here through the power of the resurrection.

~ Phillip Brooks ~

Source of Inexhaustible Power

(B)ut those who hope in the Lord will renew their strength. They will soar on wings like eagles; they will run and not grow weary, they will walk and not grow faint (Is. 40:31).

Familiarity is a great threat to our spiritual lives. It is possible to become so familiar with religious clichés and phrases that they lose their deeper meaning. The spiritual discipline that once fortified your faith may have become an obstacle that prevents you from growing spiritually. You may have addressed God as "Father" for so long that you have come to think of Him as a grey old Lord who closes his eyes to your sins, thus forgetting that He is also a God who punishes sin. If you have lost your sense of wonder and awe for the greatness of God, you have lost something for which there is no substitute.

To regard God with respect and awe moves your to true worship. It once again creates a moral and spiritual basis for you worship. It is unlikely that you will spend time contemplating the wonder of God and his truths revealed through Jesus Christ, and still remain spiritually weak and ineffectual. There is an essential power in praising and worshipping Him.

To praise God not only means that you become involved in an act of communal worship. It implies an attitude towards life that is constantly on the lookout for opportunities to praise and thank God. Let the thought of praising Him dominate your thoughts, and you will feel the power of the almighty God flowing through your life.

Through praise and worship, heavenly Father, my strength is renewed so that I can grow spiritually to be equal to the example of your Son, Jesus my Lord!

You should not be afraid to praise God too much; unlike people it will not give Him a swollen head.

~ Paul Dibble ~

Freedom Has Its Own Responsibilities

Live as free men, but do not use your freedom as a cover-up for evil; live as servants of God (1 Pet. 2:16).

The word freedom is a much-abused word. It is used to muster rebellious people together, and heinous crimes are committed in the name of freedom. Those who follow false leaders promising freedom, usually find themselves trapped in a new form of slavery.

True freedom can only be experienced if the human spirit is liberated from hate, meanness and envy, because true freedom possesses a spiritual quality that is known and experienced by everyone who loves and serves God.

The vast majority of people live in slavery. However, they may be unaware of the fetters that constrain them because they have grown so accustomed to it that it has become a habit. Their preconceived ideas and false thought patterns are reflected in their negative attitudes. Their irascible tempers, their hate and their bitterness all reveal the slavery that constrains them.

The message of the Christian gospel brings freedom for everyone who is held captive by the destructive influences that control their inner being. The living Christ forgives our sins and frees us from the shackles of the evil one. This is a gift, part of God's perfect love, if it is accepted in faith. As you experience the blessing of God's deliverance, you will be transformed into a new, free being who lives in harmony, peace and love with God and your fellow human beings.

Perfect Jesus, through your Spirit I am freed of all sin and unacceptable habits. Because I know You, I have become truly free.

Freedom! No word has ever been spoken that has contained greater hope, demanded greater sacrifices, needed more care, bestowed more blessing on the recipient, or come closer to the will of God.

~ Omar Bradley ~

Love is the answer

And this is my prayer: that your love may abound more and more in knowledge and depth of insight, so that you may be able to discern what is best ... (Phil. 1:9-10).

Decision-making is a process that is often the source of much perplexity. It may influence your future and wellbeing, or that of those whose interests you take care of. It may have a bearing on your business, your personal life or your career. Whatever the circumstances, the fact remains that unless you have a stable and level-headed approach to the problem, you run the risk of being overwhelmed by the anxiety of uncertainty and indecisiveness, and your fear of the consequences of your decisions.

There is no doubt that you need the guidance and wisdom of the Holy Spirit to provide you with clarity of thought and vision. He views matters from the perspective of eternity, while you can only observe the here and now. For this reason, and also so that you can obtain peace of mind, it is essential to pray constantly for the guidance of the Holy Spirit.

To prepare yourself for this you need to have an intimate personal relationship with the living Christ, so that your thoughts can be focused on his will. The more you love Jesus, the closer you will live to Him, thus enabling Him to speak to you through the promptings of his Holy Spirit.

I thank You, Redeemer and Saviour, for the assurance that he who loves You is your child, and can know the God of love.

To love is to admire with the heart, and to admire is to love with the mind.

~ Theophile Gautier ~

---

*I*T IS YOUR RESPONSIBILITY

Come near to God and he will come near to you ... (Jas. 4:8).

*T*he depth and quality of your spiritual life is your responsibility. It may be that you yearn for more faith and plead with God to give it to you, but if you don't practise the faith that you already possess, you cannot expect God to give you more. You may crave a deeper and more realistic prayer life, but only you can silently wait upon God and cultivate an awareness of his holy presence. God planted a yearning for Him in your deepest being. This hunger to know Him better is one of his greatest gifts to you. He is constantly calling: "Come to Me!" and it is in your answer to this clarion call that your Christian perseverance is truly revealed.

To accept your Christian responsibility is a solemn undertaking, and if you accept it in a half-hearted way you are insulting God and depriving yourself of true communion with Him. God demands a devotion that encompasses your entire life, and it is this devotion that many people shy away from. They are unwilling to meet the demands of total commitment, and the unfortunate result is that they end up living in the twilight of an insufficient faith.

God will never require you to give up something without giving you something better in its place. When He asks for your devout life, He gives you eternal life in return, and you step into a dimension you would never have thought you could experience. By accepting the responsibility for your own spiritual growth you continually move closer to your Master and Redeemer.

Holy Father, in your strength I accept the responsibility for my own spiritual development. I want to make use of all the instruments of your grace that You put at my disposal.

It takes a long time for excellence to develop to maturity.
~ Publilius Syrus ~

YOUR DIVINE COMPANION

The righteous cry out, and the Lord hears them; he delivers them from all their troubles (Ps. 34:18).

The dreadful feeling of loneliness is a devastating experience. Many people struggle with loneliness caused by a variety of circumstances: the loss of a loved one; the fear caused by serious illness; struggling with problems all by yourself when it appears as if there are no friends around. These are but a few of the situations in which people threaten to despair in their loneliness, often with disastrous consequences.

It is precisely when you find yourself in these circumstances that you are most vulnerable. It is also then that Satan sows his seeds of doubt, discouragement and despair in your heart. Those who succumb to it feel that there is no future and no hope, and it is not long before they slump into the depths of self-pity and despair.

In the Scriptures as well as in secular history it has been proven time and again that you are never alone, because the hand of God rests upon you. All that you have to do is hold on to his assurance that He is always with you.

When it seems as if life is treating you unfairly, don't give up hope, but rather lay your fears and worries before the living Christ. Open your heart and life to the influence of the Holy Spirit and He will fan the flame of hope yet again, so that the tiny flame that threatened to die out will become a bright light to illuminate your path.

Powerful Redeemer, grant me the strength to keep my hand firmly in yours even under the most difficult circumstances. Lead me from the darkness into your wonderful light.

Man's greatest need is to conquer his isolation and to leave the prison of his loneliness.

~ Erich Fromm ~

*W*HEN LIFE GETS COMPLICATED

(I)n all your ways acknowledge him, and he will make your paths straight (Prov. 3:6).

*S*ometimes life becomes complicated in very covert and subtle ways. Small and apparently inconsequential things are neglected because other things demand your urgent attention. Eventually you are confronted with a whole array of unfinished tasks, irritations and confusions.

To simplify your life and create a blueprint for success, you need a goal towards which you can work. A life with a multitude of goals achieves little, because you waste all your energy without accomplishing anything. Therefore, focus on a positive goal and bring order to your life.

A sure way of complicating your life is to take on a task for which you lack both the time and the energy. There are people who cannot refuse a request, with the result that they leave many tasks unfinished. Determining your priorities is crucial if you want your life to run smoothly and productively.

Creating such a list of priorities should have preference in the planning of your life, and it should be determined in the presence of your heavenly Father. Under the guidance of the Holy Spirit you should consider the demands placed on you, and ask for them to be prioritised in the right order. If you accomplish this, you will live an organised life. Don't forget God when your life becomes complicated.

Heavenly Master, I ask that You will grant me an uncomplicated and inspired life under the guidance of the Holy Spirit.

Man has been created in the image of God and has a purpose: to maintain a relationship with God. Because man forgets his purpose, he forgets who he is and what life means.

~ Francis A. Schaeffer ~

*F*AITH OR WORRY? THE CHOICE IS YOURS

Cast your cares on the Lord and he will sustain you ... (Ps. 55:22).

*I*t isn't hard work that causes mental, spiritual and ultimately physical breakdown – it's worry. Work that is free of worry is stimulating and enjoyable. It gives substance to your daily life, and also confers a feeling of belonging to the human family and contributing to the wellbeing of the human race.

It is worry that exhausts you, because if you are worried you will be unable to achieve anything constructive. Worry alienates the willing worker from his rightful inheritance and the true purpose and satisfaction of life. However, the greatest tragedy of worry is that it estranges you from God. Faith and worry cannot cohabit in the same life. If your faith is a living reality there will be no space for worry, but if worry is the dominant force, faith will wither and die.

Worrying can so easily become an indulgent habit. Only a radical adjustment of your thought patterns can free you from worry. Having a practical faith in the omnipotence of God and his purpose with your life is essential. The conviction that all things work together for the good of those who love God should be the dominant thought in your mind. Then you will experience the renewing power of a living faith, which is the death-knell of all worry.

Merciful Lord, from today onwards I am determined not to allow worry to spoil the beauty of my life or to destroy my faith in You.

When I look back ... I remember the tale of the old man who said on his deathbed that he had had many problems in his life, but that most of them never actually happened.

~ Winston Churchill ~

WHEN YOUR BURDEN BECOMES TOO HEAVY

"Come to me, all you who are weary and burdened, and I will give you rest" (Mt. 11:28).

In these times so many people live under incredible pressure. Tension and stress take their toll on young as well as old. Children and young people are under immense pressure to excel in their studies and their sporting activities. Business people struggle to keep head above water in an extremely competitive environment. The elderly experience an increasingly uncertain future and constantly worry about their security. People of all ages are exposed to all kinds of temptations that promise only disaster for them and their loved ones.

Professional counselling, medical treatment and medication have become common remedies for people suffering from tension. In most cases these are only temporary measures that are merely a crutch to help people stumble through life. And still the tension keeps increasing.

There is only one infallible way of coping with tension and stress, and this is Christ's way. He, who also lived and worked under immense pressure, offers you the peace of God that surpasses all understanding. It is a peace that banishes all anxiety and fear and gives you the ability to cope with life in the strength of the Master. Accept his gift of peace and rest.

I praise and thank You, Lord My God, that the peace and quiet of Jesus fill my life even amidst life's greatest tensions and pressures.

Jesus didn't come to argue away or eliminate our tension and stress. He came to fill it with his peace and quiet.

~ Paul Claudel ~

Disciple and Discipline are Synonymous

Therefore, if anyone is in Christ, he is a new creation ... (2 Cor. 5:17).

There are people who desire to have a religion that suits their personal lifestyle. They seek a church that is broadminded and liberal, and that places few demands on them. Unfortunately these people never experience the impact of a living faith.

If the challenge to discipleship is to be truly effective, it must have an impact on your life. A positive and constructive spirituality should influence every facet of your life. This means that you have to admit the weaknesses in your character to yourself, confess the sins and failures of your past, and realise your dependency on God. It is this realisation of your own inadequacy and frustration that brings about the turning point in your pilgrimage.

When you feel that you can't meet the demands of the Master, and it seems as if your spiritual life is falling apart, you ought to share your unhappy circumstances with God and plead for his help. No one's request for Jesus' help has ever been in vain.

When you accept Christ's assistance, you also accept the responsibility of willing discipleship and discipline. Your mind and spirit should be brought under the dominion of the Holy Spirit. In this way your thoughts become constructive and your character strong so that you can do the will of God and become a disciple who is worthy of your calling.

I thank You, merciful Master, for the strength that You give me through your Holy Spirit so that I can live my life in the way that You expect of me.

A Christian should be like a fruit tree and not a Christmas tree. The excessive decorations of the Christmas tree are hung on it, while fruit grows naturally on a fruit tree.

~ John R. W. Stott ~

*Y*OUR SAVIOUR IS ALWAYS THERE FOR YOU

Because of the Lord's great love we are not consumed, for his compassions never fail (Lam. 3:22).

---

*I*n our lives there are often times when everything seems hopeless and lost. We succumb to illness; adversity descends upon us; fear overwhelms us; or we experience the pain of death's ultimate separation. These things leave us with a feeling of loneliness that borders on despair. What does one do in such circumstances and how do you cope with life?

Some people are extremely fortunate in experiencing the support of their family and friends in such times. Others who are less fortunate are not as blessed. And even though you may have people who stand supportively around you, there are still times when even that support falls away, because they naturally also have their own lives to live and their own families to care for.

When life plunges you into some or other crisis, you should never forget the goodness and faithfulness of God. You are his child, whom He has chosen, and in his Word He time and again reassures you of his perpetual presence. The living Christ is at your side at all times and under all circumstances. He will guide you from the darkness of despair into his wonderful light of hope and peace. Walk with Him and be filled with his love and peace.

Heavenly Companion, even though I sometimes feel lonely, I know that I am never alone, because You have promised never to forsake or abandon me.

People are lonely because they build walls instead of bridges.
~ Joseph F. Newton ~

Your life is secured in Christ

Therefore, there is now no condemnation for those who are in Christ Jesus, because through Christ Jesus the law of the Spirit of life set me free from the law of sin and death (Rom. 8:1-2).

When the ardour of your Christian faith threatens to wane, you easily start looking for all kinds of excuses for the apparent deterioration. Such excuses are not difficult to find, but it seldom happens that you turn the spotlight of truth upon your own inner being. Only if you have the courage to allow the Holy Spirit to reveal yourself to you, will you discover the causes of your spiritual deterioration.

You will discover that your faith is inadequate because you have allowed something or someone to take Jesus Christ's place in the centre of your life. When your awareness of the presence of Christ starts to fade and your intellectual approach becomes confused, your awareness of Jesus starts disappearing.

If you wish to be united with Christ, He has to be the focal point of your faith. Then your faith will once again become a dynamic reality and you will unequivocally know that sin can no longer control you, because you are controlled by Christ. Freedom from sin and the awareness of Jesus' presence will impart a special quality to your life, which cannot be obtained from any other source. This freedom and this special quality constitute more than just an emotional experience. Your entire life changes because Jesus works through you and you are secure in Him.

Saviour and Master, I humbly plead that my life will channel your life into the world in which I live.

If Christ lives in us and controls our personalities, we will leave blessed impressions on the lives of those with whom we are involved. Not because of *our* radiant character, but because of his.

~ Eugenia Price ~

---

*M*ORE CHRIST-LIKE EVERY DAY

Instead, speaking the truth in love, we will in all things grow up into him who is the Head, that is, Christ (Eph. 4:15).

*I*t is a glorious truth that believing in Jesus Christ as your Redeemer and Saviour redeems you from your sins. This is the foundation of the Christian gospel. But you should never forget that after you have accepted Jesus Christ as the Lord of your life, the process of growth should continue. If you ignore the necessity of growth, your spiritual life will start to founder in the ocean of disappointment and despair. There must be growth and development.

In his mercy, God has put many resources for spiritual growth at our disposal, but we should be careful not to let these resources become an end in themselves. Communion with fellow-believers is essential, but communion that is not centred on Christ serves no spiritual purpose. Studying the Scriptures is a source of inestimable inspiration and guidance, but you must remember that the purpose of the Scriptures is to point the disciple to Christ. Good works and helping those less fortunate than yourself are undoubtedly agreeable to God, but these things are only the fruits that spring from knowing Christ. In themselves they do not necessarily lead to Christ.

Spiritual growth can occur only when your ideal is to be more like Jesus. This should be the yearning of every disciple. Spiritual growth transcends emotion and demands your everything in the service of Christ.

Possess me so completely through your Holy Spirit, o Master, that my life will reflect your glory.

Testimony is to remove the various obstacles of our self-love and to allow Christ who lives in us to reveal Himself to our fellow human beings.

~ Paul Frost ~

*A*void unnecessary worry

Out of the depths I cry to you, O Lord; O Lord, hear my voice. Let your ears be attentive to my cry for mercy (Ps. 130:1-2).

*H*ave you ever taken a moment to ponder how patient God is? He continually offers his children love, forgiveness, comfort, encourage-ment, assistance and an array of other gifts that allow us to live a life of comfort and certainty. He promised to be with us always. He has even offered to live *in* us. Despite all of this, how often do we only ask for his help after we have exhausted all other sources? How often do we, like the psalmist, only call to Him from the depths?

The wonder of it is that God – unlike people – never tires of us. He is never impatient and his love remains constant. However difficult our circumstances are, He is always at hand to hear our cries for help and come to our rescue.

People could spare themselves a great deal of worry and fear if they would immediately turn to Christ for help when a problem crops up. There is no point in being reticent or hesitant, because Jesus has in-vited all those who are tired and overburdened to come to Him so that He may give them rest. Do it, and worry will no longer reign supreme in your life.

Beloved Saviour, whether I find myself in a stormy crisis or in the peace-ful sunshine, I bring all my worries to You. You have proved that You have the solutions for all of them.

Worry is the natural result when our hope is focused on anything but God and his will for our lives.

~ Billy Graham ~

*T*HE LIVING *W*ORD REVEALS THE LIVING *C*HRIST

Then he opened their minds so that they could understand the Scriptures (Lk. 24:45).

*T*here are many people who regard Bible study as a bit of a nuisance.
They have been taught that it is a duty, and consequently they struggle
through the pages and breathe a sigh of relief when they have read the
prescribed passage. Others find that they don't understand what they
are reading, or that their daily problems destroy their inclination to
read the Bible. Many people read the Bible only in the evening after a
day's work, when they are tired and cannot possibly take in what they
are reading.

If you are having problems with your Bible study because of these
or other reasons, it might be worthwhile to consider that perhaps you
are spending more time reading *about* God than spending time *with*
God.

It is necessary to know the Incarnate Word personally so that you
can live the life of spiritual abundance that He offers you. In order to
know Him it is necessary to reach out to Him in the silence of your
inner room through contemplation and prayer. And to validate this
activity you should serve Him among your fellow human beings.

If you draw near unto God in this manner, you will find that the
Word starts to assume new life and meaning, because you are no longer
merely reading a book. Instead you are *living* the Word together with
its Author!

Incarnate Word of God, I open myself to You, so that You can fill me
with your Spirit and your Word, and truly live in me.

The word of God is in the Bible as the spirit is in the body.
~ P. T. Forsyth ~

September

Creator-God, in this month of spring we worship You as the
loving keeper of your creation.

We praise your holy Name for the beauty of spring
that erupts everywhere around us.

Thank You for trees that until recently were bare and dry,
and are now suddenly breaking into growth like giant bouquets,
displaying their splendour to glorify You.

Thank You for the thousand shades of delicate, crisp green
that are appearing all around
as if You spoke the words of creation just now!

Your earth is awakening and exult in new life; the winter is past,
the time for singing has come.

Grant that all of us – farmer, painter, poet,
economist, student and teacher –
will see your handiwork behind it all
and will know in wonderment:
You have visited the land.

Saviour, please touch my heart and life too:
bring new growth to my arid heart;
grant that the grain of wheat that fell to the earth and withered
will now sprout, grow robustly and bear fruit.

Let a surging song of praise for spring sound gratefully in my heart.

Praise the Lord, o my soul.

Amen.

*P*raise the Lord for the Miracle of New Life

For by him all things were created: things in heaven and on earth ... all things were created by him and for him (Col. 1:16).

*W*e so easily fail to notice the beginning of spring simply because our love of life has faded. When this happens, it is usually a good time to come to a standstill, take stock, and rediscover the mysticism and meaning of life. If your spirit is no longer moved by the beauty of a sunrise or the sounds of soothing music; if you no longer find joy in the company of trusted friends; or if monotony has destroyed all your ambitions, it has definitely become time to deepen and broaden your concept of life.

To accomplish this it is imperative to deepen your knowledge and experience of the Creator-God. A tried and tested way to do this is to cultivate the art of thanksgiving. Look around you for something to thank God for. It may be something small and unimportant that you have accepted as a given through the years. When you start praising and thanking God, you release tremendous spiritual forces within you.

This praise and thanksgiving should not remain an emotional experience alone. Find someone who is going through a difficult time and offer your assistance. In this way your own life will be enriched beyond your wildest expectations. Count your blessings and thank God for them, be a blessing to other people, and you will rediscover the true spring beauty and vitality of life.

God of new life and growth, help me to discover the true meaning of life by being a blessing to other people.

Inner growth is only possible if we devote ourselves to God as well as other people.

~ Jean Vanier ~

*L*IVE YOUR FAITH

But if I say, "I will not mention him or speak any more in his name," his word is in my heart like a fire, a fire shut up in my bones. I am weary of holding it in; indeed, I cannot (Jer. 20:9).

*A*ny true disciple of Christ will know the ecstasy of having a personal relationship with his Saviour. It creates such an intense feeling of joie de vivre that your heart brims over with joy in the knowledge that the living Christ lives in you.

In many cases people also experience an irrepressible urge to tell others of the wonder of Christ. They bubble over with enthusiasm and give testimony in front of friends and acquaintances, business partners and even strangers. They want to tell everyone of their wonderful Lord and his marvellous deeds of love and grace. Their sincerity is beyond question. In today's world there is a definite need for this kind of testimony to be given and heard.

But perhaps you feel that you are unable to speak about Jesus. Don't be discouraged by this, because there is another, just as important way to share the gospel, and this is through the way in which you live and behave in your interaction with other people. Jesus is the Incarnate Word and if He takes possession of your life, it will be reflected in your deeds. His acts of love and compassion will be evident in your behaviour. Share your feelings of joy with the people you encounter in your daily relationships. In so doing you will lead them to Jesus by your example.

Heavenly Example, come and fill my life, so it will reflect your love.

The world is much more willing to accept the gospel than what Christians are to share it out.

~ George W. Peters ~

*W*ALK WITH JESUS

As they talked and discussed these things with each other, Jesus himself came up and walked along with them ... (Lk. 24:15).

*T*ragic events paralysed Jesus' first disciples. Their spiritual perception was unable to see beyond the darkness of the crucifixion and therefore they could not remember Jesus' promises. Consequently, the road to Emmaus was shrouded in despondent darkness for the disciples.

Jesus joined them on this journey, but they did not even recognise Him. Initially He was only a stranger who astonished them with his ignorance of recent events. But when He started to explain the Scriptures, He became a Prophet to them, and they listened to Him with interest. After they had invited Him to spend the night with them, they recognised Him as the Master they loved.

The events on road to Emmaus were not unique in Christian experience. Many have walked this path in his company without recognising Him. He showered his blessings on them and they did not respond to his love. They may have listened to the gospel for years without grasping its full meaning. They may even claim to have been converted, and yet the joy and reality of true faith have passed them by.

The wonderful truth is that the Master is with you every step of the way. Even when He is regarded as a stranger, He remains your Friend; even when his blessings aren't recognised, He keeps giving; and if you listen to his Word He reveals Himself to you. The living Christ wants to walk the road with you; do you want to walk the road with Him?

Powerful Redeemer, I no longer want to treat You as a stranger, but I accept You completely as my Saviour and Redeemer.

The Bible is a window in this prison-world through which we can see to eternity.

~ T. Dwight ~

LET YOUR LIGHT SHINE

... And [Joseph] reassured them and spoke kindly to them (Gen. 50:21).

Different people respond in different ways to other people's approaches. Some people respond favourably to a friendly approach, while others respond better to a command rather than a request. In some cases discipline causes fear, while in others it brings about respect and efficiency.

No one, not even the most hardened person, can resist friendly reassurance indeterminately. An overview of Jesus' life reveals that He was held in high esteem and treated respectfully by people, even by his worst enemies. Everything that He said and did was characterised by love.

The gospel shows us that even when He firmly admonished people He always spoke in a friendly and charming manner. Whatever He said was always to the advantage of the person He spoke to, and his words sprung from his deepest concern over their welfare. Even at the moment of his gruesome death on the cross his loving reassurance conquered the hardened hearts of the murderer and the Roman soldier.

In your relationships with others it is crucial to follow the example of the Master. Display his love and understanding in the way that you treat them and their problems. Assure them of your interest in them and your concern over their welfare. Let the love of Christ shine through you so that they may find his peace in you. In this way you are following his command to be the light of the world (see Mt. 5:14).

Lord Jesus, may I reflect your perfect love in everything that I say and do.

It is always spring in the heart that truly loves God.
~ John Vianney ~

Why should we praise and glorify God?

... Praise, O servants of the Lord, praise the name of the Lord. Let the name of the Lord be praised, both now and forevermore (Ps. 113:1-2).

Why should God be praised and glorified? Why should we tell Him how almighty, all-knowing and omnipresent He is? Why should we waste time on telling Him things that He already knows? And yet He commands us to praise Him. God never channels our energy into dead-end streets. There is more to praising and glorifying God than simply repeating his divine attributes.

The complexity of the human temperament compels it to reach out to something higher and greater than itself. This yearning can be fulfilled by praising and glorifying God, through which we connect ourselves to Him who knows and understands the desires of our hearts. God can manage fine without our praise, but we cannot manage without the uplifting strength and inspiration that emanates from our praise for Him.

True praise is one of the greatest inspirational forces in life. It raises you up from your spiritual despondency and enables you to live in communion with your heavenly Father. Praise can occur in many different ways: during the excitement of a revival service; during the sanctification of the communion; or in those quiet moments when you are alone with your heavenly Father. The method is of little importance, as long as it allows you to enter into the holy presence of God.

Holy Father, I enter your gates with adulation, with praise I go into your temple court. In so doing I enter into your presence with joy and thanksgiving.

Praise is not a part of the Christian's life; it *is* the Christian's life.
~ Gerald Vann ~

Don't turn back

From this time many of his disciples turned back and no longer followed him (Jn. 6:66).

For Jesus' disciples life with Him was filled with excitement, and they were witnesses to many of his mighty deeds and miracles. They were with the Master when crowds flocked around Him to listen to his words and teachings. As part of his following they must have been swept up in the radiance of the mystery and wonder that surrounded this exceptional Man.

However, at some point their enthusiasm suddenly started waning. For a moment they came to a standstill to think, and inner doubt started gnawing away at them. The excitement made way for worry, which became so overwhelming that many of them decided no longer to walk with Him, as John recounts. How is it possible that such enthusiastic followers lost interest and returned to their old ways of life?

The Master was busy explaining to them exactly what the price of complete surrender and commitment to Him entailed. He emphasised the things which God expects of his people so that they may obtain the abundant life that Christ offers. These expectations were too high for them, and they felt that more was expected of them than what they were willing to give.

The same challenges confront us today and the temptation to turn back is a reality to each Christian. Meanwhile, the devil continues to try and sow the seeds of doubt and discouragement. Don't turn back, but rather open your life to the influence of the Holy Spirit. He will give you the ability to follow Christ to the end.

Leader and Master, I accept the challenge of following to the end. Guide me, so that I will not lose my way.

A Christian is the life of Christ in a man, and a man's life in Christ.
~ Romano Guardini ~

*Y*OUR ATTITUDE IS EXTREMELY IMPORTANT

I do not hide your righteousness in my heart; I speak of your faithfulness and salvation. I do not conceal your love and your truth from the great assembly (Ps. 40:10).

*D*espite appearances to the contrary, we are all endowed with a sensitivity that makes us deeply aware of other people's attitudes towards us. For example, you may be introduced to a person who smiles amiably and has a friendly handshake, and yet you instinctively distrust him. You can't explain your distrust, but it is *there* as a reality and therefore you approach that person carefully.

The fact is that when you meet someone for the first time, your smile and your handshake are not adequate proof of your sincerity. People pick up your invisible, though essential, nature as a radio picks up sound waves from the air, and they instinctively know you.

When you meet someone for the first time, your attitude should be one of goodwill and sincerity. When you are involved in an interview with someone, let your love towards the interviewer replace your fear. Remember the words of the Scriptures: *There is no fear in love. But perfect love drives out fear* ... (1 Jn. 4:18). When you find yourself in a situation where you are expected to venture an opinion, let there be no bitterness in your heart so that love may be the dominant emotion.

What you feel in your deepest being is reflected far beyond your appearance or the personality that you present to the world. Approach all people with an attitude of love, and you will be astonished at the joyful and trusting response that you elicit.

Only through your grace, Lord my God, is my heart filled with your love that is revealed in my attitude towards my fellow human beings.

Nothing is a greater obstacle in your relationships with others than being unable to live with yourself.

~ Honoré de Balzac ~

Transform Your Faith Into Deeds

In the same way, faith by itself, if it is not accompanied by action, is dead (Jas. 2:17).

You may be finding it a problem to transform your religious theories into deeds. Perhaps you spend some time with God early in the morning, and find his presence to be a glorious reality, so that you are able to face the day in the firm conviction that He will be with you at all times.

Then you begin your day with its changing circumstances and continual demands, and hours pass without your giving the Lord a single thought. When you suddenly remember that it has been some time since you have had contact with Him, a feeling of guilt saturates your being. Don't be discouraged. Your mind can handle only one thought at a time, and when you focus on the task at hand, you can't think of anything else. Remember that He is with you even when you are immersed in a task that leaves no opportunity for other thoughts. If you complete a task to the best of your ability you are doing it in his honour, and when your mind is focused on Him once more, you will hear Him saying: " ... *'Well done, good and faithful servant! ... '''* (Mt. 25:23).

The Holy Spirit who lives inside you creates an attitude that makes every ordinary task an act of worship. If your spirit is in harmony with Christ, whatever you do in your practical life will be transformed into an act of practical faith.

Master and Saviour, your immanent presence enables me to express my faith in practical terms.

As the blossom leads to fruit, so faith should lead to good works.
                              ~ Richard Whately ~

REMEMBER WHO YOU ARE!

So God created man in his own image, in the image of God he created him ... (Gen. 1:27).

When it seems as if nothing in your life is working out, when loneliness takes hold of you and despondency descends upon you, it is time to call into remembrance a few spiritual facts.

You were created in the image of God. Yes, this image *has* been damaged and perhaps you *have* forgotten your rich spiritual heritage. But the fact remains that you are irrevocably a spiritual being. Knowing this should let new hope and inspiration flow through your mind and spirit. You were not created to be the plaything of moods that are beyond your control. Because you have been created in the image of God you have also been created for spiritual greatness, and you will know no rest or fulfilment before you live in the awareness of his presence, thus growing and developing spiritually.

This may sound very theoretical, but actually experiencing it brings forth practical results. If you are afflicted by feelings of inferiority, you will find great succour in remembering that you are a spiritual being meant to live in the presence of his holy countenance. If your life is impaired by the stress and tension created by feelings of inadequacy, you will find liberation in drawing on the abundance of God's strength. This will enable you to face life confidently, because you will be assured that his Spirit is working in you.

My Saviour, Jesus Christ, because of my spiritual heritage and the awareness of your living presence I go forward to meet life with confidence.

Our humanity would have been pitiful if it weren't for the divinity that moves in us.

~ Francis Bacon ~

LIFE-ALTERING LIGHT

"Can his forces be numbered? Upon whom does his light not rise?" (Job 25:3).

One of the most wonderful phenomena in this world is the way in which beauty may be experienced in the most unlikely places. An arid desert landscape may be transfigured by the rays of the rising or setting sun. Dreadful precipices may suddenly lose their austerity when they are illuminated by the light of the rising moon. In many parts of the world the barrenness of the land is transformed, almost overnight, into a fairyland of colour and exotic blooms after the spring rains have fallen on the apparently dead earth.

Such is the wonder of God's omnipotence while He continues to watch over his creation. In this way He proves time and again in so many ways that all things are possible for Him. In the same way that He created light from the darkness in the very beginning, so He can still today transform the darkest night into dazzling morning light. Here and now.

These divine wonders are not limited to nature. Jesus also moves in the lives of people, and is prepared to illuminate your darkness if you are only willing to turn to Him and trust Him. In spite of your circumstances you can be sure that the living Christ is prepared to lead you from the darkness of your circumstances into the wonderful light of the presence of God.

Jesus, Light of the anxious heart, You appear and command the darkness to disappear, thus spreading the beauty of your heavenly light.

Light, even when it passes through pollution, does not become polluted.

~ Augustine of Hippo ~

LISTEN TO YOUR CONSCIENCE

... "I heard you in the garden, and I was afraid because I was naked; so I hid" (Gen. 3:10).

There are times in our lives when we are burdened by feelings of guilt. In these times we find it very difficult to live with our conscience. The most common causes of these kinds of experiences include acts based on half-truths, deception, jealousy and envy, but there are many other causes, too numerous to list. Some of these acts may seem trivial, but whatever form they take, the human conscience will reprimand the wrongdoer in no uncertain terms.

Because of these feelings of shame and self-reproach most of us instinctively try and hide from our wrongdoing by turning our backs on it or excluding it from our thoughts. Some people try to justify their behaviour, while others think that an external façade of bravado will calm their inner storms.

One thing is absolutely sure: whatever you do and however hard you try, you cannot hide from God. Whatever you do to erase your footsteps, you can be sure that the blinding light of Jesus Christ will reveal it before your heavenly Father. Never try to hide from God. Be assured of his undying love; confess to Him in repentant prayer those things that cause you shame and fear; then receive from Him the peace of mind that springs from the true confession of your sins. Listen to your conscience!

Lord Jesus, because I am assured of your loving forgiveness, I reveal my soul to You in confession. Thank You for your boundless forgiveness.

Many of us follow our conscience as we follow a wheelbarrow. We push it in the direction we want it to go.
~ Billy Graham ~

We cannot place demands on God

Teach me your way, O Lord; lead me in a straight path ... (Ps. 27:11).

There is an essential difference between laying your requests before God and making aggressive demands on Him. To ensure that God will be present in the inner sanctuary of your heart, you need to be obedient to his demands and rejoice in his answers to your requests. You must believe that He knows what is best for you, and willingly submit yourself to his judgement. This acceptance creates a firm bond between you and your heavenly Father. As your faith grows, you will be increasingly willing to meet the demands that He puts to you.

When you are tempted to approach his throne of mercy with demands, you should remember that sincere humility is a virtue. However strongly you may feel about the matter, you really have no right to demand anything from Him. Irreparable damage has been caused by people making aggressive demands on God that He has chosen to leave unanswered. In such cases it is easily said that people's prayers are not answered because they lack faith.

It is not the person who storms the gates of heaven, but the disciple who in humility lays his requests before God who experiences the joy of God's guidance in his everyday life – those who say: "Lord, this is my humble prayer, but let your will be done."

This is not an approach of blind fatalism, but one of deep trust born from the profound conviction that God knows best and that He wants to do what is best for you.

O Hearer of prayers, help me not to walk my own path, but yours, so that I can come to a deeper understanding of your love and your purpose with my life.

All that we have to strive for in prayer is the correspondence of our will with the holy will of God.

~ Teresa of Avila ~

*F*OR DAYS WHEN YOUR FAITH FALTERS

My soul yearns, even faints, for the courts of the Lord; my heart and my flesh cry out for the living Lord (Ps. 84:2).

*I*f you have experienced the love of God in your life, encountered his power and walked in his presence every day, and have then allowed all these wonders to become nothing more than beautiful memories, then you are truly experiencing a tremendous tragedy.

There are many Christians who look back on the road they have travelled and wonder where they lost the glory and the reality of their faith. They still possess some form of Christian faith, but only they and God know that it is merely an empty shell from which the dynamism has disappeared.

Very few people are really content with this unfortunate situation, because they know what they once possessed, and they are challenged to once again become what they used to be. To know what they are now *and* what they ought to be, causes an intense disappointment with themselves and a deep yearning for a more profound experience of God. People who once experienced the deep waters of God's grace can never be content with sloshing around in the muddy waters of mundanity.

It is not God's will that anyone should be separated from Him. However, to return to God is something that many people find extremely difficult. Nevertheless, be assured that if you return to God He will still be waiting with the outstretched arms of his Son on the cross. If you become estranged from God, it is through your own fault and not his.

Holy Lord Jesus, in simple faith I return to You and ask that the awareness of your love and strength will once again fill my life.

Faith is never identical to piety.

~ Karl Barth ~

Live victoriously for Christ!

This is what the Lord says: "Maintain justice and do what is right, for my salvation is close at hand and my righteousness will soon be revealed" (Is. 56:1).

When casting an eye on the things happening in contemporary society, there are many people who feel that it is simply no longer worth the trouble trying to maintain standards. They see good people suffering while criminals prosper; honesty is not rewarded, but dishonest people get off scot-free. All things considered, is it still worthwhile to maintain Christian standards? So often we are tempted to compromise, abandon our principles and follow the popular opinion rather than Christ's standards.

Despite the fact that it sometimes appears as if everything is turned against the righteous, we should never lose sight of the fact that God ultimately judges everything. We might manage to get away with compromising our principles in this life, but the fact remains that we are also busy preparing ourselves for eternity, when all people will be held accountable for their deeds.

Never tire of doing what is right, and open yourself to the influence and power of the Holy Spirit. He will enable you to weather life's storms and live in victory.

O Holy Spirit, in You I find the strength to live victoriously for Christ. For this I praise and thank You.

Without a struggle there can be no victory; the best helmsman is known in the storm; the soldier proves himself in the war.

~ Cyprian ~

*C*OPE WITH YOUR WOUNDED FEELINGS

You will increase my honor and comfort me once again (Ps. 71:21).

---

*M*any people claim to believe in an almighty God, but their lives do not reflect this faith. They see the wonders of creation or try to fathom the mysteries of their own personalities, and feel that this knowledge is out of their reach. The greatness of God in nature and in wisdom overwhelms them and they recoil into the pettiness of their own personalities. Consequently their perspective becomes confused and narrow-minded.

If your concept of God is large enough, there can be no space for pettiness or narrow-mindedness. If someone hurts you with a snide remark or an unfriendly gesture, you can either take revenge or accept it in the spirit of God's forgiveness. If you take it personally and nurse a grudge, your life will become miserable. However, if you simply accept these incidents against the background of God's omnipotence, they will become inconsequential and you will grow spiritually.

You can only experience mental and spiritual greatness if God is in the centre of your life. It is only when you accept everything that comes your way in the spirit of Him who lives inside you, that nothing can undermine your spiritual stature. In this case God becomes of greater importance than your feelings or desires. If God comes first in your life and you aim to please Him alone, what other people say and think will be of little importance to you.

I praise and thank You, holy Master, that I am able to handle even my injured feelings constructively and positively through the grace that You grant me.

There is no point in burying the hatchet if you are going to put a marker on the place.

~ Sydney Harris ~

What do I owe God?

... "Here I am, living in a palace of cedar, while the ark of God remains in a tent" (2 Sam. 7:2).

The issue of stewardship has, throughout the years, been a thorny one among Christians. People have argued and debated about tithes and offerings, and a variety of different standpoints have been held. Many of the arguments are completely transparent and do little to hide people's unwillingness to give an offering to Christ. On the other hand, there are also people who truly find this matter extremely problematic.

While people continue to argue about whether you should give ten per cent of your nett or gross income to the Lord, and about what is lawfully deductible, the fact remains that the Scriptures are very clear about what the Lord expects of his disciples.

As a Christian you and everything that you own belong completely to Christ. In his grace He has trusted you to be the steward of your life and your possessions. It then follows as a matter of course that you, as a good steward, should be extremely careful to perform your task well. Consequently, God should have the first priority over anything else in your life. Once you have accepted this, you will find that all arguments are pointless, because God's cause must come first. If you honour Him in this way, He will bless you and guide you in how to use your life as well as your possessions.

My Lord and my God, I want to profess my faith anew. May I have a love as perfect as Yours, in body, mind and spirit.

The principle of sacrifice is that we choose to offer that which we would prefer not to offer outside of our love.

~ William Temple ~

*A*LL IS WELL WITH MY SOUL

Why have you rejected us forever, O God? Why does your anger smolder against the sheep of your pasture? (Ps. 74:1).

*T*here are many people who feel that they are abandoned and completely alone in the world. Circumstances cause things in their lives to go wrong; illness and death dominate their thoughts and the only thought in their minds is: "Why?" As far as one can see they seem to live worthy lives, keeping God's commandments, and yet now, in their times of trial and tribulation they feel that God has forsaken them.

It is an absolutely false conception to think that you are abandoned or forsaken by God. He has promised to be with you always and not to forsake you (see Heb. 13:5). He has proved the unfathomable depth of his love in your life by offering his Son on the cross.

God has a divine purpose with all the things that happen in your life. Even when you are the victim of adversity or disappointment, don't despair. He wants to, and can, use these circumstances to bring about his perfect will in your life.

There was a brief moment on the cross when Jesus felt abandoned by God, but the humiliation of Good Friday was transformed into the triumphant victory of Easter Sunday. Know under all circumstances that the living Christ is with you, place your trust in Him, and in his good time you will experience victory.

Be still, my soul, the Lord is on your side. Patiently carry all your sorrow and grief and leave all decisions in his loving hands. When everything else fails us, He remains faithful.

There is no one in the world without some or other problem, whether he be king or pope.

~ Thomas à Kempis ~

Don't be impatient

But grow in the grace and knowledge of our Lord and Savior Jesus Christ ... (2 Pet. 3:18).

When some people commit themselves to Christ, an immediate transformation of their personality takes place. The weakness of their character is replaced by strength and an indescribable confidence fills their entire life. Rebirth can indeed be a joyous experience. But with the passage of time the wonder and enthusiasm of this initial phase sometimes abates, and the spirit that was once aflame for Christ starts to wane. Unfortunately this is not an uncommon occurrence among relatively new Christians.

When one surrenders oneself completely to Christ, one becomes a new creation, but old habits die hard. Even though the freshness of Christianity is a glorious reality to new Christians, they are still infants in Christ, and in the process of growing old habits may easily make their influence felt once again. Therefore it is imperative that the young Christian will begin the process of growth immediately after his conversion to Christ. The excitement of conversion, which is undoubtedly a legitimate spiritual experience, should be strengthened by the foundation of Bible study, prayer, and communion with the faithful. If a piece of coal is removed from the fire it cannot retain its heat.

Without worship, prayer and Bible study there can be no growth. It is God's desire that you will grow spiritually, but the responsibility for actually *doing* it belongs to you.

Thank You, Lord Jesus, for starting me on my Christian pilgrimage. With your help I am determined to work hard at my growth and development.

Spiritual maturity is not achieved by reason, but by submitting yourself to the will of God.

~ D. W. Lambert ~

*F*ind joy in the small things

For everything God created is good, and nothing is to be rejected if it is received with thanksgiving, because it is consecrated by the word of God and prayer (1 Tim. 4:4-5).

---

*M*any people tend to take things for granted. This is an unfortunate attitude, because it causes people's sense of value to be skewed so that they can no longer appreciate the intrinsic value of things. The colours of the flowers, the song of the birds, the beauty of a sunrise or sunset are all things that many people barely notice. They regard these things as mundane occurrences that do not deserve special attention.

It is only when you start pondering a life without these blessings that you begin to realise how drab and mediocre your existence would become. Life without these gifts of God would be colourless and uninteresting. It is difficult even to imagine a situation like this. We ought to cherish and appreciate every blessing in our lives, be it large or small. We should learn to appreciate the wonders of God's creation, especially in nature, because it adds meaning, beauty and purpose to our lives.

We should therefore appreciate everything that God has granted us in his grace, but we should also realise that we must carefully protect and conserve the wonders of creation, because we are its keepers. This is the most practical way of thanking God for his greatness and benevolence.

Heavenly Father, I thank You for the everyday things in my life and for everything that they mean to me.

It is through nature that we encounter the Supernatural.
~ Michael Ramsey ~

---

*T*HE SIMPLICITY OF JESUS' TEACHINGS

Then he told them many things in parables ... (Mt. 13:2).

---

*O*ne of the most marvellous things about Christ is the simplicity of his teachings. He expressed the great truths of his heavenly Father in such a way that illiterate people could understand it. He also confronted the scholars of his time and stunned them to silence with the quality of his wisdom. The difference between Jesus and the scholars who questioned him from time to time was that He was completely practical, whereas they had a theoretical approach to life.

He challenged people to forgive their enemies and spoke of transforming your enemies into friends. In his teachings as well as through his example He conveyed the importance of love, and He clearly showed that a dynamic religion encompasses more than a rigid moral code that leaves no room for love. The simplicity of faith, as He taught it, leads to a practical, devout lifestyle that transcends theological theories. Everyone who was willing to listen to Him and learn from Him understood what He wanted to tell them.

In the midst of clashes between different theological ideologies it is advisable to remember that the simple elements of Christ's teachings are such that everyone can understand and take joy in them. To love Him and to love your neighbour through Him; to experience his strength in your spirit; to know that his immanent presence is with you at all times – these are simple yet profound truths that ultimately become a glorious reality in your life.

Loving Master, grant me the wisdom to develop a faith that is simple yet powerful.

Blessed are those of simple heart, because they will have peace.
             ~ Thomas à Kempis ~

---

*U*se God's gifts

Timothy, guard what has been entrusted to your care. Turn away from godless chatter and the opposing ideas of what is falsely called knowledge ... (1 Tim. 6:20).

*A*s a child of God you are blessed with a precious gift: the ability to reflect the nature of Christ in your life. As is the case with all things of great value, this blessing also involves great responsibility. You have to cherish it, look after it and use it in the way it was intended to be used. After his death and triumphant resurrection Jesus gave his disciples the great commission for missionary work (see Mt. 28:19-20). To enable them to follow his instructions He sent the Holy Spirit to assist them. This gift and the strength of the Spirit are as available today as they were to his first disciples. All that Jesus asks of you is your complete surrender to his sovereignty and your willingness to serve Him in the way that He calls you to.

This may appear to be an immense challenge, and you may doubt your ability to meet its demands. However, remember that history proves that Christ has always provided his disciples with the strength to accomplish their tasks. Allow his Spirit to possess you completely, and you will experience the fullness of Jesus Christ in wonderful ways.

Leader and Master, I dedicate myself to your service, and am grateful that You wish to use me.

The service that really counts is the service that costs us something.
~ Howard Hendricks ~

Joy in the Service of the Master

The seventy-two returned with joy and said, "Lord, even the demons submit to us in your name" (Lk. 10:17).

Those who are familiar with the Scriptures will know how Jesus sent out seventy-two of his disciples. Luke tells how Jesus sent them out to preach the gospel in his Name, and how they returned joyfully to tell of what they had achieved.

People often think of their work in Jesus' Name as a necessary but tedious calling. They do their work with a grumbling attitude, and consequently find no joy in it. Your attitude towards your work for the Master will play an important role in the way that you work for Him. It makes the difference between happiness and unhappiness in his service. Your attitude will have an amazing effect on you as well as on those you serve.

Remember that the living Christ is always willing to be your heavenly partner in everything that you undertake in his Name. If you devote all your time and labour to Him, you will not only go about your work with confidence, but you will also experience the joy that gives you peace of mind, because you are performing your task in his strength and to his glory.

Faithful Lord Jesus, with You at my side I perform every task You entrust to me with joyful self-confidence.

He who works while he prays, lifts his heart to God with his hands.
~ Bernard of Clairvaux ~

The Unseen Things Are Important

So we fix our eyes not on what is seen, but on what is unseen. For what is seen is temporary, but what is unseen is eternal (2 Cor. 4:18).

Many people find that their experience of the beauty of life is spoiled by the narrowness of their spiritual perspective. They cannot appreciate beauty or any form of goodness unless it conforms to their religious convictions. However, a life and character that have been created by inner piety cannot be narrow in either perspective or in practice. The beauty of piety transcends narrow-mindedness and reflects the glory of God in the life of his disciple.

When your thoughts are focused on Christ and you try to live to his glory, your spirit is elevated beyond place and time and you develop a greater understanding of eternal truths. You appreciate love, honour, purity, unselfishness and other noble qualities, despite the fact that they reside in the realities of a rough and often crude life.

As your appreciation for the intrinsic values of life increases, you develop the ability to distinguish between that which is genuine and that which is feigned; between the wheat and the chaff. And then you realise that the things that you cannot see or touch are actually the most important things. He who claims only to believe in what he can see, touch and understand, has a very limited perspective on life, because the great wealth of God does not fall into any of these categories.

Beloved Lord, may I always have a deep appreciation for the value of the spiritual forces that surround me, and which remain unseen and untouched.

Faith is the sight of the inner eye.
~ Alexander Maclaren ~

*G*OD'S STANDARDS

... "A man can receive only what is given him from heaven" (Jn. 3:27).

*I*n today's world material possessions play an important role in most people's lives. Things that used to be regarded as luxuries have become necessities in people's attempts to keep up with the neighbours.

Indeed, over the years things have changed radically, but it would be a foolish mistake to say – especially now, at the beginning of a new century – that life ought to continue at the same pace as a century ago. Progress simply does not allow for this, however much we long for "the good old days".

If we accept that things have changed and will continue changing, we will also have to accept that we now have a new way of life. However, we dare not allow our value system to change. Despite modern progress and changes in lifestyle, the age-old truth remains steadfast and sure: any worthwhile undertaking must have the blessing of God, otherwise it is doomed to failure.

When you are challenged to change your lifestyle, or when you are guided towards a new path of life, you should humble yourself before God before making a final decision. Pray that his way, the only true way, will be made known to you.

Eternal and immutable God, in this changing world I hold on to You in the knowledge that You are God from eternity to eternity.

We must all obey the great law of change. It is the most powerful law in nature.

~ Edmund Burke ~

The art of Christian conversation

Let your conversation be always full of grace, seasoned with salt, so that you may know how to answer everyone (Col. 4:6).

People often underrate the powerful effect of the spoken word. So much depends on the way in which things are said. The tone of voice, the timing and the circumstances in which words are spoken are all of cardinal importance. The same words can be interpreted in many different ways and can create wrong impressions, which can, in turn, cause much damage.

There are few things worse to behold than to see someone snubbed by a sharp reprimand or a condescending remark. Because of experiences like these, shy or modest people rather keep quiet, for fear of being ridiculed or humiliated by words. Insensitive and intolerant people often speak cruel words that do not take other people's feelings into consideration.

Take a minute to ponder how Jesus spoke to the people with whom He interacted. Whether He agreed or disagreed; whether He attacked or defended; whether He addressed friends or enemies; beggars or rulers, there was always a tenderness in his voice – a tenderness not to be confused with weakness. He spoke with authority, but without being dogmatic. He was always understanding, sympathetic and loving. When you speak to other people, follow Jesus' example and you will find that your conversations will elicit responses of love and understanding.

Beloved Saviour, may what I say always be acceptable to You. Please use my words for your honour and glory.

Cold words make people freeze; warm words make them burn; bitter words make them bitter and vengeful words make them vengeful. Friendly words make an impression on people's souls. They comfort and bring peace of mind.

~ Blaise Pascal ~

Are you trying to carry your burden alone?

"I will come down and speak with you there, and I will take of the Spirit that is on you and put the Spirit on them. They will help you carry the burden of the people so that you will not have to carry it alone" (Num. 11:17).

There are many devout and zealous servants of the Lord who serve Him with enthusiasm – to the detriment of their personal health. They never refuse a request to serve on a committee and willingly take on any task, even if they are not equipped for it. Ultimately their responsibilities become so numerous that they can do nothing properly. Their mental and spiritual tension becomes so intense that it affects their health. And yet these people are reluctant to share their responsibilities with others.

Many ministers, pastors, priests and lay preachers are so conscientious and concerned about their God-given tasks that they are unwilling to share it with anyone else, because they are afraid that it will not be done properly. With so many things to do in the limited time at their disposal, nothing can be done effectively and they become frustrated and discouraged.

If God has called you to do a specific task it is your duty and privilege to do it to the best of your ability. This does not mean that you are not allowed to call upon others to help you accomplish the task. Accept your God-given responsibility, but never think that by sharing it with others you are evading your duty towards God. With others' help you may, in fact, serve God more effectively.

Loving Master, when You entrust me with a task, please give me the wisdom to use others' help to accomplish it.

Self-adulation is the death-knell of the soul. It means that we have no desire to change, and then our soul dies.

~ William Barclay ~

RELIVE YOUR MEMORIES

Early the next morning Abraham got up and returned to the place where he had stood before the Lord (Gen. 19:27).

*E*very Christian faces the danger of becoming smug and self-satisfied about his religion. We so easily lapse into a comfortable pattern of worship and personal quiet time with God. It may be a very gradual process, but you will soon see its effects when something of the dynamism starts disappearing from your faith. Your sense of purpose and joy is replaced by apathy and disinterest.

It is therefore beneficial to look back on your pilgrimage from time to time. Remind yourself of the mountaintop-experiences as well as the times spent in the valleys. Relive the time when you were filled with ecstasy in the presence of God; remember those times when it seemed as if you were walking alone through the valleys of despair, and suddenly found yourself surrounded by the love and peace of God.

When you feel that the flame of faith is burning low in your life, turn to God and remember how He helped and encouraged you in the past. Ask that He will once again fill you with his Holy Spirit so that the spiritual strength and purposefulness of your Christian calling will be revived.

Merciful Lord, please keep my faith from weakening and help me to follow You with enthusiasm. Grant me the full measure of your Holy Spirit to inspire me.

Don't be afraid of enthusiasm. You need it; without it you can do nothing effectively.

~ Francois Guizat ~

Be sincere before God

Search me, O God, and know my heart; test me and know my anxious thoughts. See if there is any offensive way in me, and lead me in the way everlasting (Ps. 139:23-24).

There are some people who appear to be very religious, but whose lives do not correspond to the example that Jesus set. They speak in an intimate way about God, and yet they maintain an unforgiving spirit; they ignore the truth that God cannot forgive them their sins before they forgive others theirs; they boast of speaking to God, but cannot speak to their fellow human beings in a loving and civil way.

The fact is that such people may manage to deceive others for a while, but they can never deceive God. He knows their thoughts and emotions and knows just as well as they do that they are living an unsatisfying life. And yet God continues to love them. God's love does not fluctuate and even those who are spiritually immature do not fall outside the sphere of his love.

The tragedy of such "imitation" Christians is that they miss out on the joy and peace of a life in the abundance of Jesus Christ. If people are not sincerely and completely devoted to God, their faith will always be of an inferior quality. God expects you to be honest with Him. Confess everything in your life to Him and all the hidden inhibitions that hinder your spiritual growth will disappear.

Teach me, o perfect Example, to live for You alone, because only in doing so will I find complete satisfaction in my life.

How incredibly difficult it is to be honest with yourself. It is much easier to be honest with others.

~ Edward Benson ~

*B*E POSITIVE IN TEMPTATION

When tempted, no one should say, "God is tempting me." For God cannot be tempted by evil, nor does he tempt anyone; but each one is tempted when, by his own evil desire, he is dragged away and enticed (Jas. 1:13-14).

*T*emptation assumes many guises, but it will always come to you in moments of weakness or when you least expect it. There are many ways to resist temptation. Some disciples try simply ignoring it, but this is seldom an effective solution.

Moments of futility are an open invitation for temptation, and the consequences can be disastrous. Never allow destructive thoughts to take possession of your mind, because they will fester and affect your attitude towards life. Initially all temptations seem reasonable and even acceptable, but do not be deceived: the ultimate goal of all temptation is your spiritual degeneration and destruction.

Prayer, Bible study and contemplation all play an important role in your fight against temptation. In prayer you enter into the presence of God and you can draw on his strength; the Bible teaches you how the heroes of faith resisted temptation through the strength of the Holy Spirit; in contemplation you allow sanctified and constructive thoughts to fill your subconscious.

When you have completed these spiritual disciplines, it is of the utmost importance that you will live them in practice. Keep yourself constructively occupied under the guidance and strength of the Spirit, and you will be able to triumph over temptations.

Lord, my Redeemer also in temptation, make me sensitive to the danger of temptation through the ministry of the Holy Spirit.

The devil tempts man in order to ruin him; God tries man in order to perfect him.

~ Ambrose ~

*G*OD'S GRACE IS SUFFICIENT

The days of the blameless are known to the Lord, and their inheritance will endure forever (Ps. 37:18).

---

*O*ne often hears of people who apparently live a virtuous life and yet are pursued by disaster. They live frugally, are careful with their expenses and make provision for a safe future, and then, through no fault of their own, they are struck by disaster and face financial ruin. There are those who generously give of themselves in the loving and compassionate care of others, and then find themselves or a loved one struck by illness or death. These are but a few examples of virtuous lives that appear constantly to be followed around by disaster.

When you become entangled in such a situation, it is difficult to agree with Paul when he says: *And we know that in all things God works for the good of those who love him, who have been called according to his purpose* (Rom. 8:28). The human reaction is immediately to question God's actions, and to wonder whether it is, in fact, worthwhile to live a virtuous and honourable life.

In such circumstances it is important to remember that God's perspective on life is eternal, and that it is true that He wishes all things to work for your own good. Paul also says that our present suffering does not outweigh the glory that will be revealed to us (see Rom. 8:18). Take courage and let your heart be peaceful: God's grace is sufficient!

I thank You, all-knowing God, that I am always assured of your grace, despite my problems.

Grace cannot be bought or earned. It is a free gift from the almighty God to a humanity in distress.

~ Billy Graham ~

October

God of love and grace,
    today we kneel before You for the sake of the elderly;
    those whose tent-dwellings look more dilapidated day after day,
    but who possess an inner strength and power.
Thank You that when all we seem to see around and in us
    are change and decay,
    You remain the Immutable One!
We worship You as the God who controls our lives:
    our youth with its strength and invincibility,
    its passion for life and its fearlessness ...
    and yet, when we grow older, You bless us with
    calmness, peace, wisdom and maturity.
We praise You for this most beautiful of months that You have created:
    the daybreak and the sunrise;
    the full ripeness of the noontide;
    the glory of the sunset;
    the twilight and the quiet of night-time.
Thank You, good Shepherd, that You remain with us
    even to the very last stretch of our journey;
    that You do not forsake or abandon us, even in our old age,
    that You are with us as You were in our youth;
    that we only become more aware of your eternal arms beneath us.
We pray this in the Name of Jesus, our Saviour and Redeemer.

Amen.

YOUR DIVINE SUPPORT

Immediately Jesus reached out his hand and caught him. "You of little faith," he said, "why did you doubt?" (Mt. 14:31).

There are times in all of our lives when our problems threaten to become just too much for us, and we feel that we are in danger of drowning in the waves of doubt and despair. One moment we are completely sure of our faith, and the next we are overwhelmed by a tidal wave of fear and unbelief. This is especially true when we have experienced Jesus' peace in our personal time with Him, and then suddenly lost our faith when we had to cope with difficult life situations.

Peter had exactly this kind of experience. He was overcome with joy when he saw Jesus walking on the water towards them. In his excitement he left the safety of the boat and walked across the water towards Jesus. Then he was suddenly overwhelmed by fear when he saw the wind and the waves. His faith failed him, and Peter started sinking into the water.

When the storms of life threaten, there is only one thing to do, and that is to follow Peter's example and to call on Jesus for rescue. He will take your hand and lead you safely through it. Place your trust in Him, because He will never disappoint you. Even though you may not be aware of it, Jesus is at your side at this exact moment, ready to help you, should you call upon Him.

My Saviour Jesus, grant that I will retain my faith in You through the work of the Holy Spirit, even in the most trying circumstances.

If we truly believe, we have no choice but to continue.
~ Graham Greene ~

CHRIST'S GIFT TO YOU

But now a righteousness from God, apart from law, has been made known ... This righteousness from God comes through faith in Jesus Christ to all who believe ... (Rom. 3:21-22).

There are, unfortunately, many people who deny themselves the privilege of a Christ-fulfilled life, because they are convinced that they are not worthy at times of it. Because of something they have said or done in the past, or because they have drifted from their faith, they claim that they cannot simply turn to Christ for help. Consequently they deprive themselves of Christ's greatest gift to humanity: God's love.

The greatest wonder of the Christian faith is that, regardless of what you have said or done in the past, God has still chosen you to be his property. Nothing qualified you for this privilege, except for the fact that you believe in Jesus Christ. His love cannot be earned and nothing that you do can make you worthy of it. It is God's gift to you, given in unrestricted grace.

If you find it difficult to understand or accept this fact of salvation, just think back to the crucifixion of our Saviour. A thief, who lived a life of lawlessness and sin, was crucified with Jesus, and at the very last moment he turned to Jesus for mercy. He was accepted and assured that he would be in paradise together with the Redeemer.

Regardless of who you are or what your past involves, the love of the living Christ is God's gift to you, if you accept Christ as your Saviour.

Just as I am, dirty and black of heart, I come to You, Lord, in my distress. You are the One who never rejects any sinner, and therefore, o Lamb of God, I turn to You.

The way to salvation is not to keep postponing, but to come and take hold of it.

~ Dwight L. Moody ~

*L*IVING IN ACCORDANCE WITH *G*OD'S WILL

... Then the Lord said, "Look, I am setting a plumb line among my people Israel; I will spare them no longer" (Amos 7:8).

---

*M*ost of us are just so adept at making excuses. When we are challenged, we will usually find some excuse for what we have said or done. How often do we hear: "I didn't mean it like that" or "I was told to do it"; "You probably misunderstood me" or "I thought you wanted me to do it like that." These are but a few of the well-known expressions that we often hear as excuses.

In your Christian faith there is no room for excuses not to do what God has called you to do. He always specifies exactly what He wants you to do. Just as He, through his prophet, set a plumb line among his people, from which there could be no deviation, so God gave humanity the living example of Jesus Christ to show us the kind of life that every Christian should live. His doctrine is clear and unavoidable and leaves us with no doubt about the standards that He has set for us.

In his great grace and understanding God goes even further. Because He is aware of human fallibility, He gives us the Holy Spirit to equip us for leading this life. Without this assistance we would never be able to succeed, but in the strength of the Holy Spirit we can accomplish anything. Therefore, follow God's path and enjoy a life of abundance in Christ.

Grant me the ability and the will, beloved Father, to live as You wish me to live.

Knowledge of sin is the point of departure for salvation.
                    ~ Epicurus ~

DON'T BE MISLED

See to it that no one takes you captive through hollow and deceptive philosophy, which depends on human traditions and the basic principles of this world rather than on Christ (Col. 2:8).

Some people can be tremendously convincing in stating their particular theories. This is especially true in the case of religious matters, and exceptionally so in the case of the Christian faith. Much unhappiness has been caused by such people, whose attitude is both destructive and divisive. It is all too easy to take a passage from the Scriptures and to use it out of context to support a particular theory. However, the consequences can be extremely far-reaching and disastrous.

In your prayer life, never neglect to ask God for the wisdom to understand certain passages from the Scriptures, and also ask the guidance of the Holy Spirit in assessing the theories and arguments that other people force upon you in their quest to get you to share their views.

Continually develop an awareness of the presence of the living Christ who are with you at all times. In this way you will remain sensitive to the promptings of the Holy Spirit who will guide your thoughts and deeds in his special way. However convincing others may appear, unreservedly place yourself in the care of Jesus Christ, and He will always make his will known to you.

Thank You, o Holy Spirit, for your light and guidance in my understanding of the eternal truths that You impart to me through the Word.

The best and the highest that we can achieve in life is to be still and allow God to act through us.

~ Meister Eckhart ~

*N*EVER UNDERESTIMATE YOUR THOUGHTS

I have considered my ways and have turned my steps to your statutes (Ps. 119:59).

*I*f you are sensible, you will take some time to study the path that you have travelled, and consider the direction in which you are going. If you neglect to do this, you may find, to your chagrin, that you achieve little in life. Eventually your daily routine may become the grave of your ideals and ambitions. There are too many people who blame their circumstances for their lack of accomplishment, and refuse to admit that their circumstances are the direct consequence of their lack of mental power and planning.

The fact is that your thoughts possess an immense power. Negative thoughts not only create an ineffectual life, but can sometimes be extremely dangerous, because they easily cause one to act irresponsibly, without taking into consideration the rights and feelings of other people. Negative and immature thoughts are the basic cause of disrespectful behaviour towards other people.

To think positively is to act creatively in every situation. However dark the future may seem, the positive thinker always plans constructively. Constructive thinkers have developed the ability to look beyond the darkness, and to continue cherishing high ideals. They are not distracted by their immediate circumstances, because they are able to focus on the final goal. This may seem to be an unattainable ideal, but many people have proved that it is possible if we only place our faith in God. A living faith produces positive and creative thoughts.

Leader and Finisher of my faith, in living close to You I always have a positive attitude towards life.

There is no salvation except in truth, and the regal way of truth is through the mind.

~ Martin C. D'Arcy ~

Your strength in difficult times

Let the word of Christ dwell in you richly ... (Col. 3:16).

How do you survive when things go horribly wrong? How do you cope with financial setbacks, family crises, illness or death? Can you maintain a calm and poised attitude, or do you go to pieces in a turbulent sea of doubt, confusion and despair?

Any of the mentioned circumstances can cause you serious anxiety and concern. Your perspective can easily become obscured, and your disorganised thoughts may be unable to handle the situation logically or sensibly. There is a fundamental danger that you will make the wrong decisions or follow an inappropriate course of action, which will ultimately turn out to be nothing but damaging and will leave you with great self-reproach.

In order to live in peace and to be prepared for any eventuality, it is essential for you to maintain an intimate relationship with your Saviour. To know *of* Him is one thing, but for the sake of your peace of mind you should *know* Him personally. Develop an awareness of his presence at all times and in all places. In this way you will ensure that his Spirit will continually work in you and sustain you in your difficult times.

Lord Jesus, You call everyone who is tired and overburdened to You. I accept your invitation with gratitude and praise.

How else but through a broken heart can Christ enter a life?
~ Oscar Wilde ~

DISCOVER GOD'S WILL FOR YOUR LIFE

Now to each one the manifestation of the Spirit is given for the common good (1 Cor. 12:7).

Sometimes it feels as if you are drifting aimlessly through life, and that it doesn't really matter whether you are here or not. Day after dismal day passes without your accomplishing anything worthwhile. The sparkle seems to have disappeared from your life long ago. This unfortunate state of affairs by no means comes about through any fault of God.

To prevent it, you should, in the first instance, relive the glory of your spiritual experience. Then seek God's plan for your life so that you may strive towards a positive goal in your life. When the living Christ takes control of your life and reveals Himself through you, you will cease drifting aimlessly, and become a positive and inspired Christian disciple.

A renewal of your spiritual experience with Christ occurs when you invite the Holy Spirit in and allow Him to take complete control of your life. You will discover that while you are living in harmony with the Spirit, new avenues of service open up to you, and you are guided towards as yet undreamed-of spheres.

When you sense that God is busy guiding you, you should confirm it through continual prayer. Dare to trust God unconditionally. To discover God's will for your life not only requires faith, but also positive actions.

With renewed faith and fervour, o Master, I step into the future with the confidence that only You can give me.

The best thing about the future is that it arrives one day at a time.
~ Abraham Lincoln ~

All things work for the common good

"For there is nothing hidden that will not be disclosed, and nothing concealed that will not be known or brought out into the open" (Lk. 8:17).

One often hears the complaint that it is always the wrong people who achieve success in life. People who are involved in dishonest practices become very wealthy, while honest people struggle financially. People who deliberately harm their bodies never become ill, while health-conscious people contract all kinds of illnesses. Examples of these kinds of situations abound, and the complaint continues to resound: good people suffer while corrupt people prosper.

Before you join this choir of voices, it is necessary to remember that life as we know it is not the end. What we experience now is transient, but the true life to which Christians aspire is eternal and lasting. In the spiritual life, people who cling to their faith and keep to their course will receive their just rewards, not from people, but from God.

Nothing that happens in this world is hidden from God. The most insignificant event is known to Him. We will all be called to account for our lives, in God's own perfect time. So if it seems as if you are ill-used by life, don't be discouraged or succumb to the temptation of throwing in the towel. Renew your trust in Jesus Christ and remember: *"... Be faithful, even to the point of death, and I will give you the crown of life"* (Rev. 2:10).

I praise and thank You, Lord my God, that because of our faith in Jesus Christ everything in life and death will turn out well for us.

The will to persevere is often the difference between success and failure.

~ David Sarnoff ~

Uphold the day of rest

"'... keep the Sabbath day holy, as I commanded your forefathers'" (Jer. 17:22).

The day of the Lord is slowly but surely beginning to lose its importance – and in Christian countries, at that. There was a time when keeping the Sabbath holy was a way of life among Christians. This holiness has gradually been worn away and today there is little difference between the day of the Lord and an ordinary weekday. Shops are open for business, entertainment centres operate, and big sport events are the order of the day.

Many people argue that keeping the Sabbath holy is nothing but the Puritan attitude of some people who are out to spoil other people's fun. They say that because you have worked the entire week, you have earned the right to enjoy life on a Sunday in any way you choose.

We do not want to deny anyone's right to some time of leisure for even a moment. However, remember that the Sabbath calls the completion of God's miracle of creation into remembrance, and as such it should be regarded as a day of rest, used to devote ourselves to praise and contemplation.

It is impossible to remain active for seven days of the week without paying the spiritual, mental and physical price. God set aside a day of rest for you – for your own sake. Uphold it as such!

This is the day the Lord has made; let us rejoice and be glad in it (Ps. 118:24).

If you want to kill Christianity, do away with the Sabbath.
~ Francois Marie Voltaire ~

Dynamic Christianity is more than a Feeling

So then, just as you received Christ Jesus as Lord, continue to live in him, rooted and built up in him, strengthened in the faith as you were taught, and overflowing with thankfulness (Col. 2:6-7).

The experience of the living Christ residing inside your spirit provides you with inspiration and strength for your everyday life. This experience initially changes your entire way of life and fills you with an indescribable joy. There is something very attractive about a Christian with a joyful spirit. Many of Christ's more conservative disciples feel that something essential is lacking from their spiritual lives because they are not as demonstrative as some of their fellow believers.

The danger of such an extroverted faith is that it feeds on emotion. In times of despondency or failure it is shown to be insufficient, because it lacks those qualities that fortify the basic needs of the spirit and the heart. There are many who started out on their Christian pilgrimage with great joy and enthusiasm, but once the initial excitement faded, they started to drift and eventually became spiritual wrecks.

Emotion is based on your physical state and your temperament, and fluctuates according to your feelings and your responses to your environment. We dare not put our trust in them. Dynamic Christianity transcends feeling and emotion. It is obedient to God's call for a life of complete devotion and surrender to his will. It means that you will never lack the Christian qualities of goodness, forgiveness, tolerance, understanding and humility. Ultimately everything you do is dedicated to the glory of God.

O Lord, grant me a faith that is sensitive to the voice of the Holy Spirit, and practical in the application of his message.

It takes so many years before we are able to believe in what we feel that we never really know what the feeling is.
~ W. B. Yeats ~

True Love

Love must be sincere ... (Rom. 12:9).

The word "love" is probably the most used and least understood word in any language. Through the years it has been used to express people's feelings towards art, food, leisure and relaxation. On a personal level it is used to express one's feelings of affection. It is even used in connection with clothes and other material possessions.

When you are professing your love towards people, it would be beneficial to take a moment to consider the actual depth of your love. To what lengths would you go and what sacrifices would you be willing to make for the sake of love?

Jesus Christ came to demonstrate to us the meaning of true love when He willingly gave his life for you and for all of humanity. To redeem mankind of its sin He was willing to die for all of us, and to take our punishment upon Him. As Jesus said: *"Greater love has no one than this, that he lay down his life for his friends"* (Jn. 15:13).

True love involves making sacrifices for the sake of another. It is tolerant, patient and understanding, even in the most trying circumstances. It comprises forgiveness and giving of yourself for the benefit of others. It means to love others as Jesus loves you.

Loving Lord Jesus, help me to distribute your love in the world around me.

Love seeks only one thing, and that is the good of the beloved. Therefore love is its own reward.

~ Thomas Merton ~

The Power of the Spoken Word

... and how good is a timely word! (Prov. 15:23).

Words possess a dynamic power. If used correctly they can inspire and provide courage; they can supply hope and encouragement; they can express understanding. But words are also neutral. It is the way in which they are used and the emphasis which they are given that convey their meaning and influence communication. "I love you!" can wound and hurt if it is said in sarcasm or insincerity. Words are extremely personal and to a large extent emanate from the personality who uses them.

The receiver of the spoken word is either blessed or tormented by it, but the speaker is similarly influenced by words. If you regularly disparage yourself in front of others or belittle everything you do, you will eventually believe your own words, and your low opinion of yourself will become a conviction. Words give power and purpose to life. You become what you say.

If you are experiencing a time of discouragement and are feeling despondent, admonish yourself with these words from Scripture: " ... *Be strong and courageous; do not be terrified; do not be discouraged, for the Lord your God will be with you wherever you go"* (Josh. 1:9). Repeat this to yourself out loud, so that it becomes indelibly imprinted on your mind. Always consider the power and the influence of the spoken word. Think before you speak and ask yourself whether that which you are about to say is true, friendly and sensible.

Holy Master, let the words I speak be good in your sight.

Hold on to the words of God that you hear with you ears, because they are nourishment for the soul.

~ Pope Gregory I ~

---

*G*UARD AGAINST PRIDE

Humble yourselves, therefore, under God's mighty hand, that he may lift you up in due time (1 Pet. 5:6).

*I*n Proverbs 16:18 Solomon says: *Pride goes before destruction, a haughty spirit before a fall.* This is an irrefutable truth about life. Throughout the ages there have been many people – in widely diverse circumstances and from all walks of life – whose lives attest to this truth. Their own bitter experience has confirmed the truth and the caution of these wise words.

There are many occasions in life when you feel compelled to stand upon your dignity or to maintain an attitude of cool aloofness. The circumstances in which you choose to act in this manner may serve as justification for your behaviour. Whatever the situation, it would be sensible to say to yourself: "There but for the grace of God go I."

Jesus' humility was a salient feature of his earthly existence. Even in his death and resurrection He moved among all classes without pride or superiority. Follow the Master's example. Even in those moments when you stumble, He will be there to support you and guide you towards the right path.

Beloved Lord and Saviour, help me never to think too much of myself, so that I will not come to a fall.

Pride is the soil from which all other sins grow, and the parent from whom all other sins are born.

~ William Barclay ~

God's Silences

Yet when he [Jesus] heard that Lazarus was sick, he stayed where he was two more days (Jn. 11:6).

There are many devout Christians who, like Peter, constantly want to remain on the mountaintop with Jesus. When they occasionally become despondent, they feel that they have somehow disappointed God. The Christian life is lived by ordinary people who are subject to the fluctuations of the human spirit. There may be times of mountaintop-experiences, shortly followed by a plunge into the valley of despair. As a matter of course we tend to link our spiritual peaks to the presence of God, and our depths to his absence. This need not necessarily be the case.

Whatever your changing moods, God remains unchangeable. The question you should ask yourself when you are in the depths of despair is: "What is God trying to tell me or teach me in this situation?"

Many of God's most devout followers on earth have found that his will became known to them when they were struggling through the dark valleys. Never regard yourself as a spiritual failure just because you are passing through a time of despondency. Become still in the midst of your sorrow and self-pity and try to understand God's will for your life. Don't become afraid in those times when God is silent and appears to be distant. In these moments He is just as close to you as when you were with Him on the mountaintop.

Ever-present God, help me always to experience the reality of your presence, even when I feel far away from You.

It is in silence that we get to know God, and in mysteries that He reveals Himself to us.

~ Robert H. Benson ~

Trust in God

... "My grace is sufficient for you, for my power is made perfect in weakness" (2 Cor. 12:9).

There are very few people who have not upon occasion experienced the inadequacy of their own resourcefulness, and who feel that they simply cannot continue. These feelings may be the result of illness, death, loneliness, financial insecurity or any of the numerous setbacks that can have a destructive influence on the human spirit and emotions.

In so many cases people regard their situation as hopeless, and then they run the risk of becoming completely discouraged. Whatever the predicament in which you find yourself, and however dark the outlook, never underestimate the scope of God's love for you and the expanse of his grace.

Take a moment to consider the innumerable instances in the Bible and in world history when God transformed despair into hope, and defeat into victory through his grace. However desperate your circumstances may seem to you, always remember that God loves you with an eternal love, and that He is waiting for you to turn to Him and trust in Him. Your faith will be rewarded, and in his own wonderful way He will deliver you.

Faithful God and Father, through the years You have proved Yourself to be faithful, even when I found myself in extreme difficulties. Therefore I will hold on to your hand in the future, because your grace is sufficient for me at all times and under all circumstances.

Grace is not sought, bought or earned. It is a free gift from God to a humanity in distress.

~ Billy Graham ~

*E*FFECTIVE CHRISTIANITY

... (W)e have been released from the law so that we serve in the new way of the Spirit, and not in the old way of the written code (Rom. 7:6).

*W*e might as well say it once again: there are many people who are disillusioned by Christianity. Or maybe it would be more accurate to say that they have become prejudiced against the Christian faith because of the way in which it was presented to them, because no level-headed person could reject the basic tenets of the living Christ. When zealotry and hypocrisy taint the principles of the Master and transform them into a fixed set of rules from which his love and compassion are absent, the love and power of Christianity become a mere stereotype.

Effective Christianity only emerges when the words of Romans 5:5 ring true: ... *God has poured out his love into our hearts by the Holy Spirit, whom he has given us.* It cannot be limited to religious formulas, but must be free and validated by the Holy Spirit.

It is the Holy Spirit that breathes life into Christianity, because without the Holy Spirit our religion becomes a set of dogmatic percepts that lack inspiration and are virtually impossible to follow. Therefore true Spirit-filled Christianity is intensely personal. It is a matter of the heart and lies between you and God. While your mind is certainly important in the formation of your concept of God, the full power of your faith is not revealed unless your emotions are touched, unless you have transcended the theory of your faith and lost yourself in the wonder, love and praise of God, brought about by the Holy Spirit.

Holy Spirit, open my life to your influence so that my faith may be meaningful and vital.

Sanctity is not an optional extra of the process of creation, but rather its entire purpose.

~ Donald Nicholl ~

Inner discord

For what I do is not the good I want to do; no, the evil I do not want to do – this I keep on doing (Rom. 7:19).

To a greater or lesser extent, everyone is familiar with the inner conflict of a divided personality. There are times when you are possesed by an overwhelming desire to live an honourable and uncompromising life. In these times spiritual matters have a strong appeal for you. You are confident that you will harbour no mean or unworthy thoughts, and you experience God as a reality. It may be precisely while you are experiencing these feelings of ecstasy that your spiritual defences start to relax and religious pride and conceit start to undermine your faith in your heavenly Father. You start to weaken spiritually and no longer enjoy the spiritual strength you once experienced.

Under such circumstances it is difficult to maintain your spiritual enthusiasm. You know what you have to do, but you find it impossible to do it. Your baser nature is engaged in a struggle with your mind, wins the battle and turns you into a slave of sin. An endless battle between right and wrong may ensue in your spirit, and it will only be settled if Christ is in complete control of your life. Once you have completely surrendered to Him and live in the assurance that his living presence belongs to you, his unifying and triumphant power will be at your disposal, and you will become a fully integrated personality.

Lord Jesus, through the guidance and inspiration of your Holy Spirit I become a completely integrated personality.

The first step to the restoration of the soul is the knowledge of our own sin.

~ Seneca ~

---

*H*OLD ON TO YOUR PRINCIPLES

"The day of the Lord is near for all nations. As you have done, it will be done to you; your deeds will return upon your own head" (Obad. 1:15).

---

*B*ecause of the events taking place around us, there are many people who question whether it is worthwhile to live a virtuous and honourable life. They give examples of people who achieve success through dishonest practices. They refer to criminals who manage to evade justice, and to their victims who have to endure the suffering inflicted upon them. They draw attention to the violence, oppression and injustice of the world. And then they want to know why it appears as if injustice reigns supreme.

It is extremely important not to give in to temptation, and not to allow yourself to be influenced by these circumstances. You must never compromise with the evil one or give up on your Christian principles. What happens around you is of a transient nature, but God's will remains eternal. Therefore justice will ultimately prevail and evil will be conquered by good.

Seek your strength in Jesus and take a stand against an evil world. Open your life to the influence of the Holy Spirit so that He may empower you to stand firmly and to be strong in your faith. In the strength of the living Christ you can and will triumph. If you remain faithful to Christ, the day will come when you will experience victory together with Him.

Holy Jesus, I so much want to receive the victor's crown from your hands. Help me through your Holy Spirit to hold on to my Christian principles.

It is easier to fight for your principles than to live according to them every day.

~ Alfred Adler ~

The Never-Ending Quest

"If only I knew where to find him; if only I could go to his dwelling!" (Job 23:3).

Man's inborn yearning for God may be revealed in a multitude of different ways. The first indication of spiritual hunger is a restlessness that refuses to be appeased. It often manifests itself in dissatisfaction with a church that has served you faithfully and well for many years. When this happens you run a fundamental risk of becoming a spiritual drifter who fruitlessly seek ... *the peace of God, which transcends all understanding* (Phil. 4:7).

One of the encouraging facts about our spiritual hunger that is often overlooked or ignored, is that God is always waiting to fulfil every person's spiritual hunger and yearning. It is not the Father's will that any of his children should drift from the sphere of his love and become unhappy with the lives that He granted them.

The message of the gospel is precisely that our heavenly Father is waiting to receive every one of his children into a full and enriching union with Himself. This is his fervent desire for all people, and it is for this purpose that He sent Jesus Christ to earth. In order to experience this profound unity it is essential to turn away from your stubborn disobedience to God and to accept the gift of Jesus the Saviour in faith. Allow God's Spirit to enter your life so that Jesus can live in you. It is the only way for your hunger or yearning for God to be appeased.

By unconditionally accepting You in my life, Lord Jesus, I enter into a spiritual union with my heavenly Father. For this I praise and thank You.

Religion is the first and the last thing: before man has found God and has been found by God, he has no beginning and no end.

~ H. G. Wells ~

TRUE CHRISTIANITY

Examine yourselves to see whether you are in the faith; test yourselves. Do you not realize that Christ Jesus is in you ... (2 Cor. 13:5).

*M*any people perceive Christians to be generally weak, prosaic and ineffective. Christians are often regarded as a species living in an isolated world of their own, removed from the realities of life. They are seen to be banding together in excluding the world while spending their time in prayer and Bible study. Of course, this is a complete misconception of the Christian faith.

There was nothing weak, prosaic or ineffective about Jesus Christ. The Scriptures, and especially the Gospels, are witness to his humanity and his divinity; to his firmness and his tenderness; to his courage as well as his humility; and above all, to his love, even when He was subjected to bitter hatred and barbaric torture and death.

This is the example that our Leader set for all Christians to follow if we wish to be faithful to our highest calling as Christians. It is an accepted fact that you cannot accomplish it in your own strength. Therefore God granted us the Holy Spirit and if you give Him complete control of your life, the transformation that He brings about will undoubtedly reveal you as a true Christian to the world.

Thank You, heavenly Father, that we are more than conquerors in your Son and through your Holy Spirit.

An essential fact of Christendom is that God regarded all people worthy enough to sacrifice his Son for them.

~ William Barclay ~

CONFLICTING PERSONALITIES

A hot-tempered man stirs up dissension, but a patient man calms a quarrel (Prov. 15:18).

No two human personalities are exactly alike and therefore it is inevitable that we will experience a conflict of personalities somewhere along the road of our pilgrimage through life. The vast majority of God's heroes of faith had to contend with someone who was difficult to love – and most of us are not heroes of faith!

How does one handle such people and at the same time maintain one's Christian testimony? The first important step is to pray for people who you find difficult to live with in love. Praying destroys the destructive power of hate that has such a negative effect on your spiritual life. After you have prayed for the person, only speak well of him to others, and never be destructively critical. This may sound idealistic and even hypocritical to you, but it is really just common sense. Acting in this way destroys bitterness and hate and addresses the problem of human relationships in a constructive way.

When you, as a disciple of Christ, find that you dislike someone, do not disparage him. Do as much good unto that person as you possibly can. In so doing you will discover that you can transform enemies into friends. It is the practical application of the Christian faith. While people are easily critical of the Christian faith, they can also not deny its efficacy, because they see it every day in the practical lives of devout disciples.

Loving Teacher, teach me to apply your wisdom in every human relationship in which You place me.

Personality is that being that has control over itself.
~ Paul Tillich ~

The Lord will provide

The desert and the parched land will be glad; the wilderness will rejoice and blossom. Like the crocus, it will burst into bloom ... (Is. 35:1-2).

Throughout the ages people and nations have experienced difficult times. The future often seems dismal and hopeless and the outlook appears grim. The reasons for these difficulties are too numerous to mention, but the consequences can be extremely destructive, because many give up hope and see no possibility for the future to improve. In these circumstances many lives may be adversely affected.

We must always remember that God loves his creation. He loves the world and He loves humanity; man is, after all, created in his image. The love of God is so vast that He sacrificed his only Son so that those who believe in Him may be saved from despair and death and be assured of eternal life. It is because of this great love that God has always restored the ruined hopes and expectations of people. He takes pity upon his people, answers their prayers and provides in their need.

The living Christ is your faithful Friend to whom you can turn in your moments of distress. If you are worried or have struggled through some unpleasant times, place your trust in Him and lay your needs before his throne of grace. Do not despair, but trust Jesus to lead you from your present darkness towards light and hope for the future. Remember, He promised never to forsake or abandon you (see Heb. 13:5). Hold on to this promise and believe that the Lord will provide.

Benevolent Father, I place my trust steadfastly in You, and step into the future in the knowledge that You will provide.

We sleep peacefully in the arms of God if we surrender ourselves to his providence.

~ Francois Fenelon ~

The only true God

"Who among the gods is like you, O Lord? Who is like you – majestic in holiness, awesome in glory, working wonders?" (Ex. 15:11).

From the earliest times people with different religious convictions have worshipped a variety of different gods. Some of these gods are feared, while others have to be placated with gifts and sacrifices. We encounter these idols in all shapes and sizes and every one of them is supposed to possess its own unique power. However, one thing that is true of all of them is that they are dead, lifeless objects. They possess no feeling or love and are feared by those who worship them.

There is another kind of idol, which is created by man. Anything to which man becomes addicted assumes the stature of an idol. Many people's souls are enthralled by the accumulation of wealth and possessions, power and status; others become drug addicts. If you find that you cannot manage without any of these or other things, you can be sure that you have created an idol that demands your faithfulness above all other things – and this may eventually lead to your destruction.

On the other hand, Jesus offers you life in all its abundance as reward for your surrender and commitment to Him (see Jn. 10:10). He offers you love, forgiveness and hope, redemption and eternal life. The Lord gave you the free will to make your own choice.

Once you have accepted the living Christ as your Saviour, you will experience a rich fulfilment and joy. Ultimately no other form of worship or devotion will be acceptable to you, because you have met the only true God.

Holy God, I worship You and only You.

We easily fall into idolatry, since we are naturally inclined to it; and because we receive it through heredity, it seems pleasant to us.
~ Martin Luther ~

*W*HEN THINGS NEED TO BE SAID

For in him you have been enriched in every way – in all your speaking and in all your knowledge ... (1 Cor. 1:5).

*W*e often find ourselves in a situation where something needs to be said. Our words may express encouragement or sympathy; they may be words of admonition or of praise; we may be expected to deliver criticism. Whatever we say, it may have far-reaching consequences for our relationships and our feelings, and therefore we have a profound responsibility to choose the right words and the right time when we speak.

Our words should also carry the hallmark of honesty and should be spoken in the spirit of sincere Christian love. Love without honesty is mere sentimentality, and honesty without love can border on brutality. Unless the occasion requires us to comment in public, our conversations should always take place in private and should always occur at the most appropriate time.

There is only one way to ensure our adherence to these basic rules, and that is through a steadfast relationship with Jesus Christ. If we have such a relationship with Him we become sensitive to the promptings of the Holy Spirit who will guide us in all our relationships. In so doing we can be sure that all our words will be inspired by Christ and spoken in love.

Holy Spirit, Teacher and Leader, guide my thoughts and restrain my tongue so that I will never intentionally hurt someone.

Freedom of communication, also in a Christian society, not only requires integrity, but also love.

~ Jack Dominian ~

Let your love be practical

Dear children, let us not love with words or tongue but with actions and in truth (1 Jn. 3:18).

True love is not something that can be fathomed by the human mind or experience. It cannot be sufficiently explained, and yet it is the most important and dynamic human emotion.

Because of the unique quality of love and the ineffectuality of human attempts to express it in distinct terms, words remain incapable of explaining it. Compassion, goodness, tenderness and many other beautiful and highly emotive words cannot succeed in describing the strength and power of love. However, there is an unfortunate tendency to equate love with sentimentality, and then this dynamic force becomes weak and ineffectual.

The foundation of true love is complete identification with the beloved. The same joys, sorrows, temptations and failures are experienced. True love entails sacrifice and often includes sadness. The quality of love transcends sympathy and comes to expression in loyalty and faithfulness, even if the whole world should turn against the beloved.

Love in action is more than just the performance of good deeds, even though such deeds may be an expression of love. True love is deep and unselfish and encompasses qualities such as faithfulness, trust, noble principles and many other similar values that enrich the mind and spirit. It cannot be bought, and it is precisely for this reason that love is so precious.

Eternal God of love, help me to love without calculating the cost.

Only love can transport people to perfection, because it is only love that can take possession of them and unite them with what is hidden deep inside them.

~ P. Teilhard de Chardin ~

*Y*our heavenly Leader

... "You must serve faithfully and wholeheartedly in the fear of the Lord" (2 Chr. 19:9).

---

*I*t is a great source of frustration when your careful planning goes awry. You are deeply disappointed when your best attempts come to nothing and all your hopes are dashed. Often you become disillusioned as a result of this kind of experience, and sometimes you become so discouraged that you threaten to throw in the towel. You are convinced that everything you undertake is doomed to failure.

It is scant consolation to say that you are not alone in going through this kind of experience. However, the solution to your problem does not lie in accepting your failure, but rather in finding the reasons for it. And then it is a good time to ask yourself: "Where does God fit into my planning?"

When you embark on a venture, however minor or insignificant it may appear, you dare not underestimate the importance of seeking the will of the Lord before proceeding with your project. He knows what is best for you, and though it may initially seem as if his will does not fit in with your plans, you have to realise that his perspective on your life is eternal. Therefore He is able to lead you into a future that may be unknown to you, but is perfectly clear to Him.

You would not risk venturing blindfolded into the street unless you had a trustworthy guide. Make Jesus your partner and your leader in everything that you undertake. If you do, you can be assured that you will ultimately achieve success.

Heavenly Leader, in the past I have tried to choose my own path, but now I am guided by You.

Success consists in getting up just one time more than what you have fallen.

~ Oliver Goldsmith ~

Your calling to be Christ-like

"On that day you will realize that I am in my Father, and you are in me, and I am in you" (Jn. 14:20).

The life and teachings of Jesus Christ pose the greatest challenge that anyone can accept. Many people who accept Him as their perfect example try to follow Him by committing themselves to good works. They make great sacrifices in the hope that this will help them to become like Him.

While all disciples should have a sincere desire to be like Jesus, all the effort and toil in the world will not help them to achieve this goal. Being Christ-like must have its origins in the heart and mind. It is only here where the awareness of the presence of the living Christ is to be found; where He becomes the Source of the strength that enables them to grow spiritually in strength, beauty and truth. Unless the presence of Christ is a living reality in their hearts, it is impossible to reflect his personality in their lives.

The challenge and call to be more Christ-like is intensely personal. It is a challenge to a deeper and more intimate relationship with the Master, in which you allow Him to reveal Himself through your life.

Holy Master, through your great grace and immanent presence I grow every day to become more like You.

It would barely be necessary to preach dogma if our lives were reflections of Jesus. If we were to live like true Christians there would be no heathens.

~ Pope John XXIII ~

Scrutinise yourself thoroughly

"When he came to his senses ... " (Lk. 15:17).

Few people have the courage to engage in some painfully honest self-examination. They defend their own weaknesses and are always quick to justify their own shortcomings. They even ignore their sins in an attempt to evade the consequences thereof.

An honest evaluation of yourself is the first step towards spiritual and moral renewal. The picture that you see when you look at yourself honestly may be very discouraging. Hidden sin, pettiness, jealousy, greed, lust, and a multitude of destructive forces that only you are aware of, are revealed in the hidden depths of your soul. And you are standing in the bright, white light of God's perfect holiness. It is an experience known only to those who have enough courage to be completely honest with God and with themselves.

Fortunately God not only sees you for what you are, but also for what you can become through his grace and the work of the Holy Spirit. When you have reached this low-water mark, you should look up and see yourself as God sees you. It is an astonishing sight! You realise that you are his child, who was made for the mountaintops of faith and not for the valleys of sin. Through Jesus you are redeemed from the power of sin, your love for Him intensifies and you view life from a completely new perspective. You suddenly discover that you are a new creation through the strength of the immanent Christ.

I rejoice, merciful Father, because I am your child and nothing and no one can tear me from your hands.

Focus your attention on God when you attack the roots of sin. Desire Him more than the sins to which the devil draws your thoughts.

~ Walter Hilton ~

Make a Right Judgment

"Stop judging by mere appearances, and make a right judgment" (Jn. 7:24).

There are so many people who think that they can determine the quality of a person's character from a brief encounter: "I liked him from the beginning" or "I mistrusted him from the moment I met him." These are common expressions, but it is often foolish to judge in this hasty fashion.

As a Christian disciple you should not judge people according to outer appearances. If you do, you are bound to be prejudiced when you meet an apparently unpleasant person. If you have a sensitive spirit and remember that precious diamonds are often found in mud, you will first spend time in prayer and contemplation before criticising someone. Always try to discover the hidden personality.

Our Master had the marvellous gift of penetrating beyond the external façade to meet the true person inside. When He touched someone's inner being He was never judgmental, but only showed love and compassion. In doing so He restored people's self-respect.

During your journey through life you are constantly forming opinions about people and classifying them in your subconscious. Ask the Master to impart to you his gift of perception so that you will be able to see people not according to your own judgment, but rather in the same way as the heavenly Father sees their potential. After all, He is able to see the human heart.

Merciful Father, help me to assess and judge others in the light of your love and compassion.

Man's judgment of another is based more on his own passion than on the behaviour of the one being judged.

~ Paul Tournier ~

---

*T*HE BEAUTY OF A LIVING FAITH

Let us not become weary in doing good, for at the proper time we will reap a harvest if we do not give up (Gal. 6:9).

*I*t is sad to see what some people do to their faith. God has intended it to be a life-giving force, but they allow it to degenerate into a limiting, depressing and dismal burden that warps their life into an atrocious lifestyle, and then they believe that this is God's will for their lives. God intended faith to be an experience of his love, strength and immanent presence.

  If the Christian faith has lost its allure for you, it is time to contemplate the matter honestly. Jesus created something that should radiate beautifully in you. It touches your deepest being and impels you to spritual growth. It enriches your personality. It is not the product of emotion or superficial thought, but the result of steadfast devotion and continual prayer.

  The experience of the living Christ in your deepest spirit brings forth a quality of life which is so genuine that it can convince sceptics of the authenticity of Christ. A colourless and lifeless faith is a catastrophe that is of little value to both you and God. A dynamic, living faith glorifies God and blesses the person who possesses it.

Lord my God, preserve me from the laziness and the happy-go-lucky attitude that are the causes of a drab and ineffectual faith.

Faith requires the whole truth.
~ P. Teilhard de Chardin ~

*C*ome, let us pray

... and there on the beach we knelt to pray (Acts 21:5).

---

*O*ne is often reminded of the saying that there is a time and a place for everything. It is also often applied to religion. In many segments of society the matter of a person's faith is regarded as a taboo topic of conversation. Furthermore, there are also people who believe that prayer should be limited to the church or to the privacy of your inner room. They regard any form of public prayer in the run of daily life with uneasiness or even disapproval.

Prayer is as much a form of communication as is conversation. The difference is merely that conversation is a form of communication between people, while prayer is a conversation between us and our heavenly Father. There is nothing more natural than this.

There are moments in our lives when it is both essential and desirable to draw near unto God. In these circumstances prayer is normal and appropriate as a form of communication.

While you should never be too shy to pray, it is also necessary to be careful and discreet in terms of the time and the place where you choose to pray. Trust in the guidance of the Holy Spirit and your prayers will at all times be a blessing to you as well as others.

O Hearer of prayers, thank You that I may draw near to your sacred throne at all times and under all circumstances, and know that You will always listen.

Let us not forsake one another in interest, support and practical assistance; but above all, let us not forsake one another in prayer.

~ Michael Baughen ~

November

All-knowing Teacher,
    during this month we worship You as the Source
    of all true wisdom and knowledge.
Thousands of students will write examinations in this month –
    but thousands of others will also struggle with
    the examination of life.
Please give all of them your peace in these days;
    the peace that is beyond all human comprehension.
Strengthen them physically and make them calm
    when they are under pressure.
Be in their hearts, so that they will be calm and peaceful
    when they are required to give account.
Be in their eyes so that they will be able to
    read and understand with discrimination.
Be in their thoughts so that they will be able to
    think logically and orderly.
Be in their hands and make them strong and steady
    so that they will be able to do what is expected of them.
Be, now and forever,
    the road they have to travel;
    the truth they have to know;
    and life in all its fullness.
In the Name of Him who makes everything possible,
Jesus, the living Christ.

Amen.

*P*EACE IN THE STORM

You will keep in perfect peace him whose mind is steadfast, because he trusts in you (Is. 26:3).

---

*I*f you allow your thoughts to dwell on the things that happen in the world today you run the risk of being caught up in a maelstrom of hatred, bitterness, fear and a multitude of negative things. God definitely does not expect this of you.

To enable you to remain steadfast in these changing times and to surmount personal fear amidst wars and tidings of war, God has given Himself to you as a wonderful gift. He grants you his eternal life; because He is love, He plants his love into your heart and gives you the peaceful assurance that this love can never be destroyed – not even by the combined forces of hatred.

When disturbing influences threaten your faith, He gives you the power to believe that all things are working for the good of those who love Him. If you focus your energy on God and surrender your life to Him, his peace will be your glorious possession at all times and under all circumstances (see Jn. 14:27). This peace is the direct result of trust. When your faith in God exceeds your faith in anything else, you possess an inner calm and balance that imparts equilibrium to your life. Put God first in all things and you will know his peace and joy even in the most trying circumstances.

Almighty God, with You at the centre of my life I fear no storms, not even those that grow into hurricanes.

If we want to enjoy true peace, we will have to give it a soul. The soul of peace is love and love comes from God alone, and is expressed in our love for our neighbour.

~ Pope Paul VI ~

Identify your fear

The Lord is my light and my salvation – whom shall I fear? The Lord is the stronghold of my life – of whom shall I be afraid? (Ps. 27:1).

Fear in any of its dreadful forms is a powerful and negative force in the lives of many people. It may be caused by economic and social circumstances, racial tension and a multitude of other factors that are too numerous to list. However, it is an undeniable fact that fear causes irreparable harm to many people's lives.

Somebody once remarked justly that there is nothing to fear but fear itself. If fear is casting its shadow over your life at the moment, ask yourself honestly what the source of your fear is. If it is a passing fear, it will disappear before long without causing too much damage. However, if it is a fear that gnaws at your spirit and confuses your mind, it is essential to deal with it immediately.

In order to manage fear effectively, you have to identify it properly. It could be caused by a vague influence that is casting a dark shadow over your spirit, thus rendering you someone suffering from habitual fear. If this is the case, now is the time to ask God to help you to rid yourself of this destructive ailment through his Holy Spirit. By becoming aware of the mighty presence of God, your fear will gradually be allayed. Allow Him to erase the dominance of fear from your thoughts. He will control your fear and guide you towards a peaceful life without fear.

Almighty God, with your guidance and through the influence of the Holy Spirit I will conquer all the destructive fears in my life. For this I praise and thank You.

In a storm, the wise man does not pray for safety from danger, but for release from fear. The inner storm is the dangerous one, not the outer one.

~ Ralph Waldo Emerson ~

The Litmus Test of Your Faith

"My command is this: Love each other as I have loved you" (Jn. 15:12).

Fanaticism is a common sin among spiritually attuned people. They have fought their way through many problems to reach a state of faith, and then they suddenly believe that they are the only ones to have found the full truth. Their faith is the product of their personal thinking and possibly also of their individual experiences. However, when they claim to be the only ones to possess true faith and knowledge while denying other people the same privilege, their lives are no longer receptive to God's love. Their fanaticism and narrow-mindedness prevent the love of God from spreading to their neighbours.

It is vital to know exactly what you believe in. If not, you could easily fall prey to deception. But it is even more important that your love for your neighbour will transcend any dogmatic differences. For the Spirit of the living Christ to live in you and for you to realise that He can also live in those who differ from you, love has to be the dominant emotion in your spiritual experience: *"By this all men will know that you are my disciples, if you love one another"* (Jn. 13:35).

Unless we have become a channel for Christ's love and unless we possess the ability to embrace people who differ from us, love has not yet been perfected in us. Then we will not be able to serve God and our fellow human beings. Love that is manifested caring and service is the divine test for those who want to be his disciples.

God of love, your Holy Spirit teaches us that love is the key to each problem and each human heart. Let your love fill my life and allow me to reveal it to my fellow man.

Love is perfect; it has no flaws. All flaws are caused by a lack of love.
~ William Law ~

Missed Opportunities

... "If you, even you, had only known on this day what would bring you peace – but now it is hidden from your eyes" (Lk. 19:42).

*F*ew people can claim to have no regrets over some kind of missed opportunity, even just the opportunity to do a good deed or to offer a word of encouragement. Hardly a day passes without the opportunity to encourage someone who is depressed, to console someone who is experiencing profound sorrow or simply to offer a heartening word to someone who is on the verge of succumbing to the struggles of life.

To be aware of the distress of others and to do your utmost to relieve that distress is one way of avoiding feelings of regret and self-reproach when it is too late to do something about it. Turning away from someone who needs your help and empathy is more impoverishing to you than it is to that person. It is a law of life that you cannot bring rays of light into the lives of others without also basking in those rays yourself. To give yourself to others in love and service is a privilege that belongs to those who are disciples of the Master. It is also a certain way of building a more profound relationship with God.

Don't keep glancing over your shoulder and harp on missed opportunities. It is nothing but a waste of time. Ensure yourself of a better present and bright prospects for the future. Commit yourself to serving others with an enthusiasm born of your sincere gratitude for God's great love for you.

God and Master, teach me never to miss an opportunity to encourage or bless others.

He who refuses to grasp an opportunity that offers itself to him, misses the prize as certainly as if he had failed.
~ William James ~

Awe-Inspiring Miracle

... God was reconciling the world to himself in Christ, not counting men's sins against them. And he has committed to us the message of reconciliation (2 Cor. 5:19).

One could ponder the question of which miracle you find most awe-inspiring. In the New Testament there is a large variety of miracles from which to choose: the feeding of the five thousand; wine from water; cripples who walk and blind people who see; Lazarus who is woken from the dead. All of these could be regarded as great miracles.

Your answer to this question may be more personal. The Master may have healed you; your prayers may have been answered in a wonderful manner; your life may have been changed irrevocably by the love of the Redeemer and the working of the Holy Spirit. You might view this as the biggest miracle of them all.

Could there ever be a bigger miracle than the breathtaking fact that you have received a new life from Jesus Christ? Jesus is the biggest miracle of all. All the other miracles derive their power and inspiration from Him. He came from God and revealed the heavenly Father to common people. In Him people saw what God is like. After his time on earth he physically ascended to heaven and bestowed the Holy Spirit upon his faithful followers. Even though two thousand years have passed since, He is still alive and active in the lives of his disciples.

Jesus Christ belongs to eternity and can therefore not be limited by time and space. He is the most awe-inspiring miracle of all ages and is as real today as when He lived on earth.

I praise You, holy Lord Jesus, for everything You mean to us, your modern disciples.

All miracles are but dim lights that light the way to the total light of the resurrection like beacons.

~ Jacques Ellul ~

Give me patience, o Lord

Be still before the Lord and wait patiently for him; do not fret when men succeed in their ways, when they carry out their wicked schemes (Ps. 37:7).

Sometimes you rush hurriedly and unthinkingly into an endeavour only to be disappointed deeply because your plans have been foiled. It is scant consolation to know at such times that your experience is not unique. Many people pay dearly for their impulsiveness. Consequently they become despondent, lose self-confidence and their enthusiasm dwindles.

The cause of this situation is your inability to lay your problems before God and wait patiently for his guidance. It has been proved repeatedly in the Scriptures as well as in secular history that God's timing and methods are perfect. We only witness the temporary scene while God views matters from the perspective of eternity. We are bound to the here and now, whereas God opens eternity to us.

Before making any decision or executing any plan, first submit the matter to Christ in prayer and ask for the guidance of the Holy Spirit. Wait for Him patiently and humbly and be sensitive to the voice of the Holy Spirit. Evetually you will become aware that He is guiding you on a particular path. Walk this path in faith and with the knowledge that in all things God works for the good of those who love and serve him (see Rom. 8:28).

O Holy Spirit, grant us the ability to become quiet before God and to wait patiently for his guidance.

We have to wait for God, tirelessly, humbly, in wind and rain, cold and dark. Wait and He will come. He never comes to those who refuse to wait.

~ Frederick W. Faber ~

Serve Christ joyfully

"If you love me, you will obey what I command" (Jn. 14:15).

Many people regard their surrender to Christ as a strict discipline that adds an unbearable burden to their lives. They feel that the cost of being a disciple is too high a price to pay. As the demands of their faith increase, their grip on Christ weakens until they completely lose it and relapse. They consequently lead an unsatisfying spiritual life that lacks fulfilment.

You must never regard your attachment to the cause of Christ as a burden. Your life in Christ should be joyful, and as you grow in Christ, your joy should increase. If you are truly devoted to Christ, your highest desire will be to get to know Him better and serve Him more effectively. As you grow in faith you will constantly strive towards ways of serving Him better because you want to, not because you have to.

To reach this point in your pilgrimage, you have to get to know Him increasingly better through Bible study and wholesome Christian literature. However, you also have to know the living Christ personally by conversing with Him through prayer. Strive to be with Christ, and the more He becomes an inseparable part of your life, the more joy you will experience in his service.

I rejoice in your service, o Lord, and thank You for this wonderful privilege.

There is no truer religion than human service. To work joyfully for the sake of your fellow man is the highest testimony of your faith.
~ Albert Schweitzer ~

Don't be prejudiced

... (W)here the Spirit of the Lord is, there is freedom (2 Cor. 3:17).

The vast majority of people view life through the glasses of prejudice. Their opinions are shaped by their race, colour, philosophical and religious convictions, and their views are influenced by the community in which they live. Even if they speak as individuals, their words are actually the expression of their group. This often makes it difficult for them to communicate effectively with people of another group.

Prejudice limits our spiritual and intellectual perspective. It closes our minds to the truth and smothers our spirits' yearning for God. Freedom from prejudice should be the glorius experience of every person who has felt the liberating Spirit of Christ in his life. When you have the Holy Spirit you also receive the assurance that you belong to God's family. When this happens, all people, regardless of their race, colour or language, become your family in Christ. You are connected with them through the unique qualities of Jesus Christ.

To be liberated from the taint of prejudice is to experience a form of intellectual broadening and enrichment in every aspect of your life. You no longer wear the blinkers of hatred or pettiness, your love is no longer limited by sectarian convictions, but is extended to those who differ from you. Through the freedom from prejudice which Christ gives you, you can attain a fuller, freer and richer spiritual life.

Holy Lord Jesus, through your Spirit who lives in me I am freed from prejudice in all the spheres of my life.

Very few people take the trouble to use their minds as long as their prejudices are in full working order.

~ Roy L. Smith ~

*T*HE REASSURING PRESENCE OF CHRIST

While they were still talking about this, Jesus himself stood among them and said to them, "Peace be with you" (Lk. 24:36).

*A*fter the terrible events of that first Good Friday, Jesus' followers were flabbergasted. Without their beloved Master they were scared, confused and without a leader. Their dreams had been shattered and life had lost all meaning for them. All their hopes and expectations were destoyed when they had to witness how the One they regarded as the Messiah was humiliated by his shameful death. Dejected and disheartened, this sad group of people sought the consolation of each other's company – when Jesus suddenly appeared in their midst.

The transformation in the lives of those people was nothing short of a miracle. Examples of the powerful deeds that they performed in the Name of the Master, abound in the Scriptures. The presence of Jesus brought new impetus and drive to their lives.

All of this happened two thousand years ago, but the resurrected and living Christ still has the same impact on the lives of people today. If you are depressed or disheartened; if you are in danger of giving up hope; if you are under the threat of fear; when you experience misfortune and problems that threaten to become too much; then it is time to invite Jesus into your life and to ask Him to support you. Trust Him unconditionally and allow Him to change your despair into hope and your sadness into joy.

I plead of you, beloved Redeemer, to send your Holy Spirit to change my life so that I will constantly be aware of your holy presence.

During his life, Christ was an example; in his death He was a sacrifice; in his resurrection He was a conqueror; in his ascension a king; in his prayers a high Priest.

~ Martin Luther ~

The Way to Peace

Jesus said to the woman, "Your faith has saved you; go in peace" (Lk. 7:50).

Doubt, fear and worry are factors that are notorious for the havoc they can wreak on a person's spiritual, emotional and intellectual well-being. Even stable and clear-headed people can be reduced to confused wrecks through acute anxiety.

How often have you, or someone you know, been confronted with an unmanageable situation? There are simply no obvious solutions and consequently a feeling of helplessness and despair develops. In times like these you are in danger of acting abnormally, usually to your own detriment. In order to handle situations like these and to prevent stumbling over the obstacles of poor advice, you have to trust Christ unconditionally. Lay yourself and your concerns before Him and allow Him to guide you in his way.

Perhaps you think that it isn't in your power to do so – and you are perfectly right. However, with God everything is possible, and as you come to live more intimately in Christ, you will find that He will guide you safely through each crisis. He will give you his peace, the peace that is beyond all human comprehension.

I bow in grateful worship before You and thank You for your peace, which You give to your faithful children.

Where there is peace, there is God!

~ George Herbert ~

*B*RIDGE THE GAP

I pray that you may be active in sharing your faith, so that you will have a full understanding of every good thing that we have in Christ (Phlm. v. 6).

---

*D*ivision in the church is as old as the church itself. If you read in the book of Acts about the history of the founding of the first church, you will also find an account of the first division. It remains a sad fact that the gap between the different denominations has only become bigger and bigger with the passage of time. This division has resulted in long and bitter debates, unhappiness, enmity and even terrible hatred.

Obviously, all of this proclaims nothing but a victory for the Devil in his merciless attack on the church of Jesus Christ. The logical conclusion is that we, as followers of Christ, are duty-bound to surmount this division, so that we can present a strong and united front in Christ against the great seducer.

It is only natural to have differences of opinion in the church. Discussions resulting from these differences can be very meaningful. A stereotype, agreeing whole would be very dreary and would inevitably result in a bland way of life. Nevertheless, the important thing to remember is that the Christ we all worship sacrificed Himself for all of us. We must never forget this. In all your interactions with other people, regardless of how much your opinions may differ, you must never allow the love of Jesus Christ to be denied – a love He has called us to share with each other. It is this love that will bridge all gaps and heal all wounds.

Lord Jesus, You died for us because You and your Father loved the entire world. Please let me live in this love.

In the dusk of our lives we will be judged on our love.
~ Johann Wolfgang von Goethe ~

Restoring Good Relations

"Therefore, if you are offering your gift at the altar and there remember that your brother has something against you, leave your gift there in front of the altar. First go and be reconciled to your brother; then come and offer your gift" (Mt. 5:23-24).

Christ's message can so easily be overshadowed by religious convictions fuelled by profound emotion. When your Christianity becomes so personalised and limited that it simply ignores the evil of broken human relationships, it does nothing but ridicule the high moral standards of Christ. Irrespective of how passionate your worship may be; of how enthusiastic you may be about matters of the kingdom of God, your praise and enthusiasm remain useless if you retain an unforgiving attitude in your heart and mind.

If there is bitterness between yourself and another person, you will be unable to appreciate the true freedom of worship inspired by the Holy Spirit and the joy and power of the living Christ in your spirit. It may be that these poor relations are not of your own making. If you have done everything in your power to mend the breach, and forgiveness is still withheld, you must be careful not to harbour thoughts of revenge. You have to make sure that you not only forgive the person, but also continue to pray for him.

When your prayers are answered and the breach has been mended, you will experience great peace and joy because you have proved once again that reconciliation is an indispensable part of being a Christian.

God of love, through forgiveness and praise I live in peace with You and my fellow man.

Everyone claims that forgiveness is a wonderful idea until there is something they themselves have to forgive.
~ C. S. Lewis ~

Choose your words carefully

There is a time for everything, and a season for every activity under heaven (Ecc. 3:1).

*T*ruly fortunate are those who are able to find the right word for the right occasion. There are many people who boast that they are frank, truthful and get to the bottom of things. They say what they think without considering the consequences for themselves and for others. They tend to forget that words uttered without love lose their force, because they lack the ability to heal a broken spirit, console those who mourn, raise the spirits of someone who is depressed, or give hope to those who are despondent.

If you have been placed in a responsible position where the happiness and welfare of others are in your hands, you must take care to choose your words carefully, as well as the circumstances under which they are uttered. This is particularly true if the people you talk to cannot reply without fear of reprisal. Sarcasm used towards people who are not in a position to talk back simply attests to spiritual immaturity and narrow-mindedness.

The words you use reflect the quality of your spirit. Petty and bitter words result from a small-minded spirit. Harsh and sharp expressions are the fruits of a mind twisted by disappointment and frustration. If you intend your words to convey the conviction of truth, you have to live in harmony with the Spirit of truth. The Holy Spirit lives in the hearts and minds of those who open up their lives to Him.

Gracious God, give me the wisdom to choose my words carefully and always to speak with love in my heart.

Don't always say what you want to say, unless you want to hear what you would not like to hear.

~ Seamus MacManus ~

Actions without plans

The Lord said to Satan, "Where have you come from?" Satan answered the Lord, "From roaming through the earth and going back and forth in it" (Job 1:7).

Active lives are not necessarily the most constructive lives. You may be frantically busy from morning until night, but if this is not accompanied by definite direction and positive purpose, you are wasting a lot of energy. This could result in a feeling of futility.

Many factors contribute to this meaningless kind of activity: the suppression of a guilty conscience; the evasion of responsibility; a form of escape from a significant challenge – all these things could lead to futile activity. Make sure that everything you keep yourself busy with is part of a purposeful plan that inspires and empowers you to achieve your goal. Once again this will require an intimate relationship with God through prayer and contemplation. God's joy generates positive thinking and creative action.

Activity without planning is useless. Consequently, it is wise to make time to plan your way of living in partnership with God. You will discover that your way will be the right way only if it corresponds with the way of God: in fact, God's way is the only way. Make time to discover God's way for your life. If you do your life will become less frantic, but it will definitely also be more productive.

Lord Jesus, guide me on your way so that my life can be constructive and purposeful.

Life, with all its stress and activities, requires relaxation, because that gives us time for recreation and renewal; a time to contemplate our lives and to plan.

~ Neil C. Strait ~

Don't undermine your faith

Brothers, do not slander one another (Jas. 4:11).

One of the biggest disservices you could do the cause of the Master is to put down the work of a fellow servant of the Lord. Destructive and negative criticism of another servant of the Lord is often uttered, usually based on theological or dogmatic differences. The result is inevitably a weakening of faith in one of the two persons. This in turns creates doubt in the minds of the spectators, because should the foundation of Christian faith not be love?

Everyone has the right to an opinion and this fact must always be respected. You don't necessarily have to agree with everyone, but it is essential for Christians to handle differences constructively and to avoid vicious arguments. Too often people are carried away by their obsession with their own viewpoint, and consequently the command to love each other is discarded.

In all our dealings with others we have to remember that we serve the same God and that our ultimate goal is to glorify God, even if our methods differ. This cannot take place in an atmosphere of bitterness. If, however, you bear in mind that you are always in the presence of Jesus, and if you want to remain true to your faith, you dare not neglect to act in love.

My Example and Leader, Jesus Christ, help me always to see You before me in my dealings with other people.

If slander were a snake, it would have had wings – it flies and it crawls.
~ Douglas Jerrold ~

*S*PIRITUAL PRIDE

The Pharisee stood up and prayed about himself: "God, I thank you that I am not like other men … " (Lk. 18:11).

---

*S*piritual growth often goes unnoticed by those in whom it is taking place. When a disciple attempts to determine his spiritual quality by comparing it to the spiritual development of other people, he is in danger of becoming self-centred. The religious leaders in the time of Christ suffered from this ailment: they thought that they were spiritually superior and consequently they let themselves in for the judgment of Christ.

Be careful not to become self-centred and smug, irrespective of how faithful you are to God. Sincere humility and self-obliteration will keep you from becoming conceited over your own spiritual importance. If Christ is in you it is testimony of your true spirituality.

The most important testimony you as Christian can show to the world is to be filled by Christ to such an extent that you are no longer aware of the self. This means that your thoughts must be inspired by the Holy Spirit and that all your deeds must be done to the glory of God and in the service of others.

To live a Christ-centred life is to forget yourself in the reality of Jesus Christ. The more you elevate Him in your life, the more you will discover the true meaning of life.

Keep me, merciful God, from exulting in anything but the cross, especially not in my own humility.

In the presence of God no man can see himself unless he is on his knees.

~ Francois Mauriac ~

Your greatest asset

Timothy, guard what has been entrusted to your care. Turn away from godless chatter and the opposing ideas of what is falsely called knowledge (1 Tim. 6:20).

As you proceed in your spiritual life, you accumulate valuable assets that can only be obtained through experience. The exuberant joy of being born again begins to wear off. Your experience with Christ, even though it is still genuine and dynamic, becomes deeper as you practise a disciplined and meaningful prayer life. You become increasingly aware of the permanent presence of Christ, and the more time you spend with Him, the more real He becomes in your life.

If you are not continually growing closer to the Master in your spiritual life, it is because of a lack of prayer and contemplation of God's miracles. Spiritual failure usually doesn't occur suddenly or dramatically, but laziness and the absence of essential spiritual discipline gradually diminish your love for the Master and your loyalty towards Him.

As soon as your love for Christ begins to wane, you may find that you begin to defend yourself with explanations and arguments in an attempt to explain the shortcomings of your love. What you need is an ever-increasing capacity for love. This is your single biggest spiritual gift: Christ's love for you and your love for Him. If you treasure this gift as a dynamic power in your life, your spiritual growth will bear witness to this fact.

Teach me, o Holy Spirit, throughout my spiritual life, to be controlled by the essential matters and not by insignificant things.

That which grows makes no noise.
~ John Henry Newman ~

Verbal Gymnastics

Some have wandered away from these and turned to meaningless talk (1 Tim. 1:6).

It is essential to be able to give an intelligent explanation of your faith. If not, your faith in God becomes a matter of emotion without substance, making you susceptible to any passing spiritual fad. There are so many spiritual butterflies who flit from church to church, because their convictions are not founded on solid dogma.

However, there are others for whom dogma is the alpha and omega of their faith. Their biggest task is to involve others in religious arguments in an attempt to convert them to their own opinions. They make use of religious generalisations and clichés; they refer to profound theological terms; they quote the Scriptures out of context. It is easy to win an argument with uninformed people, but eloquence won't impress anyone unless the Spirit of Christ is evident. It is possible to agree with your mind while your heart remains untouched.

In your attempts to explain to others what your beliefs concerning Jesus are, begin by ensuring that you know Him as your personal Saviour and Redeemer. If this is absent from your testimony, your words will be nothing but words, nothing more than verbal gymnastics. To know Christ personally is much more important than knowing all the dogma concerning Him.

My humble and sincere prayer, Lord Jesus, is that my words will be filled with profound conviction whenever I talk about You.

Truth has never been nor will it ever be contained in any dogma.
~ Mary Augusta Ward ~

*F*OLLOWERS OF CHRIST

Do not conform any longer to the pattern of this world, but be transformed by the renewing of your mind (Rom. 12:2).

*T*he difficulties and problems of this world have a marked influence on our lives. But people are also influenced by times of prosperity and peace. In times of war or economic depression people tend to become pessimistic and depressed. In good times they are light-hearted and cheerful.

As a responsible citizen you should feel at least parially responsible for world conditions. However, there is always the danger of being tempted to allow circumstances to affect your judgement on events in your own life as well as in the lives of those who depend on you. If you depend on world conditions for your decisions in your domestic, spiritual and business life, you are looking for trouble.

To be able to live a well-balanced life and evaluate every situation calmly and sensibly, you require clarity of vision and mind. Surrender your life to Him unconditionally, and allow his Holy Spirit to guide you in everything in which you are involved. If you do this, you will live your life according to God's perfect will for you and not according to the dictations of a changing world.

Glorified Lord Jesus, I want to be your follower every day and under all circumstances. Therefore I open my life to You and your Holy Spirit.

God has placed both good and evil within our power and gave us absolute freedom of choice. He does not hold back the unwilling, but embraces those who are willing.

~ John Chrisostimus ~

Reflect the presence of Christ

When Moses came down from Mount Sinai with the two tablets of the Testimony in his hands, he was not aware that his face was radiant because he had spoken with the Lord (Ex. 34:29).

People often claim that each picture tells a story, and this also applies to a person's facial expression. Often it is possible to tell at a glance what kind of person you are dealing with, which emotions he is experiencing and whether this is the type of person you can trust – all by merely looking at a facial expression.

However, we often judge other people wrongly, with the result that we are often disappointed. There are also those who formed a wrong impression only to regret it later, because their perception was based on a misconception. But you never have to doubt a person who has an intimate relationship with the living Christ. It will always be evident, because the love and compassion of Christ is visible in that person since he looks at you through the eyes of Jesus.

If you cultivate an intimate relationship with Jesus, you will become more and more like Him, because his Holy Spirit is working in you and reaches out to others through you. Allow Him into your life and allow his love to flow through you to others. Then you will live a life of plenty, which only Jesus can give you (see Jn. 10:10).

Lord Jesus Christ, grant me the privilege of being an instrument of your peace.

O God, make us children of the silence that belongs to You and the heirs of your peace.

~ Clement of Alexandria ~

What many forget

... "Watch out! Be on your guard against all kinds of greed; a man's life does not consist in the abundance of his possessions" (Lk. 12:15).

People without wealth are often the ones who belittle it. Wealth itself is neutral. It can become a blessing or a curse, depending on the priority it has in your life. It is tragic when the acquiring of great wealth becomes the driving force in a person's life.

When money is an idol it becomes so demanding that it destroys everything that is beautiful and worthwhile in terms of character and personality. Friendships are often destroyed when the suspicion exists that it is only based on personal gain. Being wealthy often causes people to become contemptuous of those who have nothing, and such people often become hard-hearted towards charity.

If money is kept in the right place on our life's agenda and if it remains a servant, it can be a great blessing. Still, it cannot buy those qualities that are essential for true life. It might cushion some of life's blows and make your life more comfortable, but there are assets that come without a price tag and that are essential for true life.

We have to remind ourselves constantly that money can buy books, but not intellect; a bed, but not peaceful sleep; food, but not appetite; entertainment, but not happiness; luxuries, but not culture; a Bible, but not heaven. People often forget that the most valuable things in life are free.

Beloved Saviour, keep me from allowing money to become my master and make it a servant through your grace.

Obsession with possessions, more than anything else, prevents people from living freely and nobly.

~ Bertrand Russell ~

Make your prayers positive

So, if you think you are standing firm, be careful that you don't fall! (1 Cor. 10:12).

There are many devout people whose thoughts contradict their prayers. They mouth prayers of thanksgiving, but fail to appreciate God's daily blessings. With beautiful phrases they tell God how wonderful and great He is, but their perspective on life remains pitifully narrow and they are unable to understand that setbacks are merely opportunities that must be accepted eagerly. They praise God's greatness and believe that he is omnipresent, yet they mourn their loneliness. Their prayers never inspire them to confront life bravely.

Prayer should inspire us to positive action. Many Christians pray and then sit back and wait for God to perform miracles. Of course God can perform any miracle, but when you pray you open yourself to the guidance of the Holy Spirit and allow Him to work through you. In this way you become an active partner of God in the answering of your prayers.

If you are in financial trouble and ask God for help, He may first expect a sense of responsibility from you in the way you spend your money. Meaningful prayer will enable you to consider every aspect of your life positively and creatively.

Prayer is not intended as an escape mechanism from the realities of life, and it should not be reserved for those times when all other attempts have failed. Prayer makes you a partner of your heavenly Father, and surely this is the greatest miracle of them all.

Through your perfect guidance, o Holy Spirit, prayer becomes a practical way of life to me.

What is important in prayer is that God is such an integral part of life that spontaneous conversation with Him becomes second nature.

~ Cliff Richard ~

Do you understand yourself?

I do not understand what I do. For what I want to do I do not do, but what I hate I do (Rom. 7:15).

It is a sad fact that there are many people who do not understand themselves. They spend long and agonising hours in self-examination; they study psychology or regularly visit psychologists to arrive at a better and more profound understanding of their personality. Unfortunately their studies only cause more confusion, sometimes even resulting in spiritual disaster. Psychological self-examination can lead to self-centredness, which in turn results in frustration and dissatisfaction with the quality of your life.

In order to understand yourself, you have to accept and appreciate the fact that God created you in his image. This realisation will bring you in harmony with yourself. If Christ Jesus is Lord of your life and if you give Him priority over everything else in your life, you will discover that your personal life acquires meaning and purpose because of your intimate relationship with Him. Consequently you will also experience the fulfilment of getting to know your true self. Under the authority of Christ and the guidance of his Holy Spirit, it becomes possible to understand yourself.

It is impossible to have daily communion with Christ through prayer and contemplation and still to feel confused and lonely. By getting to know Christ, you also get to know yourself.

Holy Lord Jesus, through your Spirit who lives in me I have come to know my true self. I thank You for this.

A humble knowledge of yourself is a truer way to God than the most profound search for knowledge.

~ Thomas à Kempis ~

Think before surrendering to temptation

The truly righteous man attains life, but he who pursues evil goes to his death (Prov. 11:19).

No one has the ambition to become an alcoholic, a criminal or a failure. Every alcoholic used to be a moderate drinker; every criminal thought that he could cheat and steal without being caught out. People who commit social sins always try to hide them.

Harmful and eventually destructive habits do not assault your character brutally. If they did, you would immediately reject them. They begin with a minor and harmless gesture that has pleasant results. As the pleasure increases you may think that you are still in control, until you suddenly realise that it has become impossible to resist the temptation in your own strength.

It is important to identify an addictive habit in advance. This is also where the acceptance of the living Christ is invaluable in your life. His Holy Spirit gives you the perception that makes you sensitive to the habit-forming powers of the evil one and He also gives you the spiritual power to enable you to say "No!" to the slightest indication of evil.

When temptation beckons the first time and offers you illicit pleasure, pause a moment and ask yourself where this will lead eventually. Don't collude in matters that could cause your downfall. Reject them while you still have the strength to do so, and remain true to God as well as to yourself and those who love you.

Holy Spirit of God, I know that I can only resist and conquer temptation through your immanent presence.

Praying to be protected from temptations and then still rushing into them is like putting your finger in the fire and praying that it will not burn.

~ Thomas Secker ~

Good Intentions

Do not merely listen to the word, and so deceive yourselves. Do what it says (Jas. 1:22).

*I*f all our good intentions were fulfilled, the world would be a wonderful place. Unfortunately words have no power if they are not expressed in deeds. Good intentions are seldom fulfilled and the good that could have been achieved remains undone.

Be realistic when you express your intentions: keep them within the realms of possibility and leave flights of fancy to those who dream dreams knowing full well that they will never be fulfilled. Begin with the simple things. If you planned to write a letter of condolence or apology, do it now. If you are aware of someone who is in need of encouragement and you are in a position to provide it, why not do it immediately? If you don't transform your intentions into actions they will become meaningless.

In the spiritual life the failure of good intentions is evident in the lives of many people. We will only know in eternity how many people "intended" to follow Jesus at some time or another. They admire, respect and even love Him, but they withhold their full surrender to Him. In the meantime everything remains only good intentions, merely serving to quiet their conscience.

The Master demands of you as Christian to execute your good intentions in practice. If not, the vision you once had of the good you could do, will die.

Living Lord Jesus, through your wisdom and power all my good intentions become glorious realities.

The awareness of good intentions is our biggest consolation in times of hardship.

~ Marcus Tullius Cicero ~

From Appearance to Reality

When Jesus saw him lying there and learned that he had been in this condition for a long time, he asked him, "Do you want to get well?" (Jn. 5:6).

It's amazing how much energy people waste in pretending to be what they are not. They go through life and interact with their fellow human beings, all the while holding up a façade to make them acceptable to others. Behind their masks they may hide feelings of inferiority, frustration or suppressed anger, but all these emotions are obscured by a veil of pretence that is only lifted for brief moments.

Of course, if everyone expressed their true feelings, the world may have been an even more unpleasant place. However, life can become extremely stressful for those who hide behind masks. The answer to this unfortunate situation is that your inner character should be of such high quality that it would be unnecessary to live a life of pretence. The outer and inner person must form a close unit.

The teachings of Christ proclaim the completeness of the human personality. It emphasises the fact that the inner person must be in complete harmony with the heavenly Father. If a person's soul is in harmony with the Holy Spirit it becomes unnecessary to pretend, because your outer life will be nothing more than a reflection of your profound spiritual experience of Jesus Christ.

Merciful Lord and Master, in your strength and with the aid of the Holy Spirit I undertake to be as devoted on the inside as on the outside.

Hypocrisy is the worship that sin brings to virtue.
~ Francois de la Rochefoucauld ~

*C*ONQUER DEPRESSION THROUGH FAITH

"But for you who revere my name, the sun of righteousness will rise with healing in its wings ... " (Mal. 4:2).

*D*epression and pessimism are ailments that destroy the soul. Apart from the fact that depression is an illness of the mind, it also affects your physical and spiritual well-being, limits your vision of the future, and negatively influences your general attitude to life. The causes of depression are numerous and include fear, anxiety, illness, financial instability and loneliness, to name but a few.

You may attempt to fight the condition with man-made medicines, but their effect will only be temporary. Sooner or later the effects will wear off and your condition will return, often with a vengeance.

The only way to fight such an emotional disruption effectively is to turn to Christ and to open yourself to his love and healing influence. Accept Him as the Lord of your life and unconditionally put yourself in his care. This will require immense faith, but when Jesus takes control of your life and guides you on the path you have to take, you will find that, because of your obedience to Him, you will be filled with a sense of self-confidence and well-being that only He can award you.

I cling to You like someone who is drowning, Lord Jesus, in the knowledge that nothing in this life can disturb me as long as You are with me.

Defeat is never more certain for an individual than when he accepts it.
~ O. A. Battista ~

Spiritually Underprivileged

"What good will it be for a man if he gains the whole world, yet forfeits his soul? Or what can a man give in exchange for his soul?" (Mt. 16:26).

The average person wishes to achieve something with his life and wants to feel that his life was not in vain. To accomplish this aim he sets certain goals for himself and works towards achieving what he regards as success. He accumulates everything that might award him money and prestige. But in spite of all this, many people who have surrounded themselves with all the good things in life cannot get rid of the nagging suspicion that they have missed out on something significant.

Any person who has neglected his spiritual life, irrespective of how successful he might be in the eyes of the world, is short-sighted and foolish. He has convinced himself that gold (and everything it represents) is more important to him than God; that the visible things are more important than the invisible; and that a false balance sheet is preferable to integrity and honesty.

No person who pushes God from his life can be truly successful. Only when our spiritual life is in harmony with God and when we continually grow towards a fuller and richer maturity will we have a sound understanding of the meaning of life. To rob your spiritual life of the awareness of Christ's immanent Spirit is to live under the spiritual breadline. Then you are truly underprivileged.

Heavenly Father, I realise the importance of my spiritual life and know for certain that your Holy Spirit achieves purposefulness and depth in my life.

God instructs the heart, not with ideas, but with pain and contradictions.

~ Jean Pierre de Caussade ~

*Y*OU ARE WATCHED CONTINUALLY

A good name is more desirable than great riches ... (Prov. 22:1).

*U*nless you are a hermit you constantly live under the scrutiny of many people. You are part of a family circle or of a business world in which you deal with different kinds of people. You live as part of a community and you may even be part of a sports group. Wherever you are and whatever you do, there are always people who are forming an opinion about you, and therefore you are constantly busy building up a character. There are people who say that they don't give a hoot about what others say about them, but this is often nothing more than a shield for a bruised spirit and feelings of inferiority. Serious and sensible people, however, are deeply aware that reputation is a valuable asset and therefore they work hard at making their name synonymous with truth, honesty and integrity.

Establishing and developing an honourable name seems like a time-consuming and tiresome task to some people. The values of society make it appear to be an impossible task and an unattainable ideal, but the truth of the matter is that it is the most rewarding task you can ever undertake. It brings you peace and creates a feeling of well-being and peace of mind, because such a life is pleasing to God.

Make honour more important than profit; honesty more noble than cheap popularity. Remember that a good name is worth more than great riches. Then you will make the exciting discovery that an honourable life is the most rewarding life that can be lived, because it is to the honour of God.

Holy Lord and Master, help me always to hold my character and reputation more dear than wealth and popularity.

Character is who you are in the dark.
~ Dwight L. Moody ~

The Path of Prayer

"And when you pray, do not keep on babbling like pagans, for they think they will be heard because of their many words ... for your Father knows what you need before you ask him" (Mt. 6:7-8).

Stereotyped and repetitive prayers may be a good discipline to contain the spirit of prayer, but the Master makes it abundantly clear that prayer becomes ineffective when it deteriorates into the mere recital of pretty phrases. Many prayers have failed because the beauty of their phrasing exceeded their actual substance.

True prayer is more than words. It is an orientation of spirit and mind that reaches out to the eternal God. When you pray you must be convinced in your soul that you are willing to be used by God to answer your own prayers. Too often we lay our needs before Him and then disappear from the scene, instead of remaining ready for and sensitive to hearing and obeying his voice. Prayer is a two-way process. You tell God what you want from Him and He reveals to you what He expects from you.

Prayer is not a series of empty words that are divorced from life, but rather an increasingly profound relationship with the heavenly Father and a sincere desire to do his will. When He reveals his will to you, you will be moved to the kind of praise and worship that will be reflected in the quality of your life.

God and Father, grant me the true spirit of prayer so that my communion with You will become more and more profound and meaningful in practice.

Whether we like it or not, the rule of the kingdom is to ask.
– Charles H. Spurgeon –

DECEMBER

Holy God and our loving Father in Jesus Christ,
we look forward expectantly to another Christ-feast.
Let our perspectives on Christmas be pure and Christ-centred.
Cleanse our spirit from all bitterness and hatred;
our will from unworthy motives,
and our soul from practices that dishonour You.
Let each gift be accompanied by true love and let each greeting card
profess our faith in You.
We long, o Father, for the simple beauty of Christmas:
unadorned by the tinsel and shiny lights of the world.
Give new meaning to each familiar Christmas melody.
Let us rejoice in the knowledge that God became man –
a Child in a humble manger –
so that people could be reconciled with God
and call Him Father once again.
May it also bring reconciliation between person and person.
May the peace of which the angels sang not remain
a vain dream or impossible ideal to us,
but become a glorious reality to the honour of God.
Grant that the goodness and tenderness of Christmas will not only
remain in our hearts for a brief time, but that it will stay there when
we return to the harsh realities of life.
We pray this in the Name of Jesus who came to be our Saviour;
to be Emmanuel to us – God with us!

men.

The Gospel in a Nutshell

"For God so loved the world that he gave his one and only Son, that whoever believes in him shall not perish but have eternal life" (Jn. 3:16).

Jesus Christ had an exeptional ability to express the gospel in the simplest terms possible so that even the simplest person could understand it, and yet, the profound nature of the message was never lost. The main topic of his message was always the eternal and constant love of God: ... *God is love. Whoever lives in love lives in God, and God in him* (1 Jn. 4:16).

In order to be allowed to share in this love, we must first open our hearts to Him: ... *"If anyone loves me, he will obey my teaching. My Father will love him, and we will come to him and make our home with him"* (Jn. 14:23). Love for God presupposes obedience to Him, and allowing his Spirit to reign over each aspect of your life and to be central to your thoughts and deeds.

To declare: "God is love!" is much more than a simple and possibly sentimental confession of faith: it requires a particular way of life which has to be a confirmation of that unspoken faith in the immeasurable love of God that was confirmed by the coming of Jesus Christ.

Consequently we must once again ponder the birth of our Saviour during every Advent-time; we must purify our festivities so that it will truly be a Christ-feast, and we must once again devote ourselves to the Child of Bethlehem.

Holy Father, I want to joyfully experience this Christ-feast in the knowledge that You are my Saviour and Redeemer. May this impart a special character to my Christmas joy.

The coming of Jesus Christ to this world was the final and incomprehensible proof that God cares.

~ William Barclay ~

Close to God through Jesus Christ

... you who once were far away have been brought near through the blood of Christ (Eph. 2:13).

Christmas-time is Advent-time! The term "advent" derives from the Latin word "adventuske", which means "arrival" or "appearance". In the terminology of the church it is used to refer to the four weeks preceding Christmas: the joyous time when we commemorate the coming of Christ to this world of humanity. The Light Christ became "flesh", but without sin. We are also flesh, but in our case the word carries the blemish of our "sinful nature". From the Word – and from experience – we know that the flesh is in a constant battle with the Spirit. Paul says in Romans 8:7 that the mind set on the flesh is hostile to God.

For Christ, however, the blemish of sin falls away. As human being He was without sin, but still human and in the tarnished form of a servant. He became our equal in everything except in sin. This is the glorious message of Christmas: Emmanuel! God with us! God visits man personally. He descended from heaven in his Son to prepare the way for humankind to be restored in the favour of the Father. He came to be the Redeemer of a lost world.

First it was God above *God far from us*, then it became, in Christ, *God with us*, and then, through the Holy Spirit, *God in us*.

This is the secret of the divine Christmas Eve and the reason for our inexpressible joy at Christmas. May the time of Advent truly be a feast of Christ for you.

Heavenly Father, my mind reels before the mystery of the incarnation in the flesh of your Son, my Saviour, Jesus Christ.

You can never truly enjoy Christmas before you have looked up into the countenance of God and honestly told Him that you have accepted his Christmas gift.

~ John R. Rice ~

*T*HE PROMISE OF A NEW LIFE

A shoot will come up from the stump of Jesse; from his roots a Branch will bear fruit (Is. 11:1).

A long time ago the royal house of David stood in the centre of the entire country like a proud tree-trunk with a high top. But all this beauty was felled in the fullness of time. The house of David was dilapidated and its glory had waned. All that remained was to be found in Mary, in whose veins the ancient, noble blood still flowed, but who was reduced to such a state of humiliation in the world that she could not believe that God would esteem her enough to make her the mother of his Son.

And yet, through God's omnipotence and mercy, a shoot came up from the meagre remains of the once powerful house of David. This "shoot" that Isaiah prophesies of is no one else than Jesus Christ. This humble shoot became an ineradicable and mighty trunk which spread out its branches to the ends of the earth. The Child in the manger grew up to become the way, the truth and the life. He brandishes the sceptre over the entire earth and his reign knows no bounds.

With the approaching Christ-feast we must once again assess our personal relationship with Christ. We must first humble ourselves over our spiritual decay and confess our sins before the Lord. From the stump of Jesse He brought forth new life, a new dispensation, a new period of spiritual growth for those who had slid back: *He who was seated on the throne said, "I am making everything new! ... "* (Rev. 21:5).

Lord God, in these days bring forth new life from the half-withered stump of my spiritual life, to your glory and through Jesus Christ.

Conversion may occur in a flash, but the process of moving from a life of sin to a new life may be a long and laborious path.

~ Charles Kolsen ~

Live Like Royal Children

For you did not receive a spirit that makes you a slave again to fear, but you received the Spirit of sonship. And by him we cry, *"Abba, Father"* (Rom. 8:15).

There is a world of difference between confessing that you are a child of God and living a life as child of God. Many people profess faith and yet live in constant fear. They suffer from a destructive sense of inferiority and they are unable to deal with life's problems. There is such a gap between what they should be and what they really are that they tend to become despondent and to abandon their principles.

When God called you to become his child and when you reacted to his call with joy, a new life began for you. Your sins were forgiven and since then you have stood in a new relationship to the King. Through his grace you become part of his kingdom. Because his Spirit now lives and works in you, your behaviour towards people and your total way of life have been revolutionised.

The Advent-time reminds you once again that you should face life with conviction and without fear. Your Father is the King of all kings. Knowing that He loves you and cares about you should give you inner peace. The streadfast faith that He will guide you safely if you obey Him and return his love should be your comfort in life. Through Jesus Christ He invites you to call Him "Father".

Father, thank You for the indescribable grace of being allowed to talk to You, which Jesus Christ obtained for me.

Even if Jesus Christ were born in Bethlehem a thousand times, but is not yet in my heart, Christmas is a meaningless event.

~ Martin Luther ~

*Y*OUR SALVATION IS HERE!

The Lord has made proclamation to the ends of the earth: "Say to the Daughter of Zion, 'See, your Savior comes! ... '" (Is. 62:11).

---

*D*uring the Advent-time we commemorate the coming of Christ. However, we must never forget about the coming of Christ to our souls and into our hearts. His appearance in the flesh was not everything. We must never be content simply to testify that He came to take the curse of our sins upon Himself as Lamb of God. It is a glorious testimony, but it means nothing if we don't yet personally share in the salvation. Then it is a Christmas carol sung out of key. Then it is only a feast around us, never inside of us.

If we want to experience the joy of Christmas in the true sense of the word, Christ has to arrive in and inhabit our hearts with his salvation and peace. Christ's coming to the world is the objective event; his coming to my heart the subjective. We thank God that his coming can be a subjective reality in the heart and life of everyone who believes in Him.

He came to find and redeem what was lost, and He gave everyone who accepted Him the right to become a child of God (see Jn. 1:12). Do you believe this? Do you believe that He comes to where you stand worried and overwhelmed by your own sin? He comes to you with his hands filled with grace and forgiveness and blessings; He comes to convert your sadness into joy. Christmas is essentially a feast of salvation, because your Saviour came!

Jesus, my Saviour and Redeemer, thank You that I may relive the all-surpassing joy and happiness of someone who has been redeemed.

The simple shepherds heard the song of the angels and discovered their Lamb; the wise men saw the light of a star and found their Wisdom.

~ Fulton J. Sheen ~

Our Fears Allayed by a Child

But the angel said to her, "Do not be afraid, Mary, you have found favor with God" (Lk. 1:30).

With this message, God wants to free Mary, and through her all of humanity, from fear, and to replace this fear with exultant joy. That is why the angel said on that first Christmas Eve: ... *"Do not be afraid. I bring you good news of great joy ... "* (Lk. 2:10).

This world has become a maze of fear. And it all began with the Fall when Adam said: " ... *I was afraid ... so I hid"* (Gen. 3:10). And on the day of judgment sinners will still plead in a last, terrified prayer meeting ... *"'they will say to the mountains, "Fall on us!" and to the hills, "Cover us!"'"* (Lk. 23:30).

Fear is not merely a figment of man's imagination. From the cradle to the grave it remains a terrible presence. We fear the unknown as a child fears the dark. We fear for our health, for loneliness, for old age, and then for that fear of all fears: death. Everywhere and in everyone there is a constant fear for thousands of threatening things.

At Christmas-time God once again sends his messenger to bring us tidings of great joy: the love of God expels all fear because the source of fear, namely sin, was conquered by Jesus Bethlehem. In each terrifying storm of life He is with us to tell us: "Don't be afraid. Emmanuel, I am with you!"

Shepherd of my life, even though I walk through the valley of the shadow of death, I will not be afraid, because You are with me.

We must fear God with love and not love Him with fear.
~ Jean Pierre Camus ~

*C*HRISTMAS: FEAST OF THE CHILD

... and she gave birth to her firstborn, a son. She wrapped him in cloths and placed him in a manger, because there was no room for them in the inn. (Lk. 2:7).

---

*A*t Christmas-time we all become children once again. In our hearts we relive the timeless adventure of unquestioned faith, where all things are immediately possible and where the child Jesus is in the centre of everything. The stable is transformed into a palace and kings from the east kneel in worship before the King of kings.

For a short time, as in a dream, we leave our predictable way of life and walk the path of rich imagination, of amazement and exciting joy, while we freely rejoice in the immeasurable love of God. Even the staunchest spiritual realist experiences stirrings in his heart upon hearing the age-old tale, almost smelling the fragrances of incense and myrrh.

On the other hand, Christmas-time is also as real as the gifts that we give and receive; as real as the candles we light and the lights that charm us; as real as the bread we break in love with our dear ones; as real as the songs that we hear everywhere during this wonderful time. In experiencing the mystery surrounding Christmas as well as the concrete reality thereof we are all touched by the wonder of God's love – and all our dreams of peace and joy are rekindled.

If we have forgotten how to experience Christmas like a child, with joyful and excited expectation, we have to learn anew to discover the enchantment of Christmas.

I thank You, Lord Jesus, that I may experience the remembrance of your birth like a child and that I can therefore see the gates of your kingdom open before me.

It is good sometimes to become a child again, and never better than at Christmas, the time when our mighty Creator Himself became a child.
~ Charles Dickens ~

Christmas: also a feast for the elderly

Moved by the Spirit, he went into the temple courts. When the parents brought in the child Jesus to do for him what the custom of the Law required, Simeon took him in his arms and praised God ... (Lk. 2:27-28).

The pious and just Simeon was already an old man when he held the Messiah in his arms. He could talk to God and listen to God. In fact, Simeon's name means "the one who hears". God blessed him with the sight of the Messiah because he had been faithful in his meetings with God. Because he was present in the temple, he could take the Christ-child in his arms. In so doing Simeon received God's wonderful gift and by implication also accepted Christ as his Saviour and Redeemer.

In old age you and I should also learn to wait for God, to listen to his voice, so that we too can receive his wonderful gifts. You must know that Christ was also born for you. That is what faith is: to see the invisible every Christmas. This is the type of faith that will compel you, like Simeon, to proclaim the message of Christ with jubilation in your old age: *"a light for revelation to the Gentiles ... "* (Lk. 2:32).

This is the miracle that God works with Christmas: He puts the Child of his love in your arms. And with this you receive his love, his salvation, his blood, his body, everything that is necessary for your redemption. What an incomprehensible gift this is. But with Christmas we also have to do something from our side. We must embrace Jesus and accept Him just as Simeon took the Child in his arms.

Help me, o Child of Bethlehem, to take You in my arms and heart as the aged Simeon did, so that Christmas can truly become a Christ-feast to me.

Life is a country seen and inhabited by the old. Those who still have to travel this country can only learn from them.

~ Joseph Joubert ~

---

*I*T IS ADVENT-TIME FOUR TIMES IN OUR LIFE

"Behold, I am coming soon! ... " (Rev. 22:7).

*T*he first Advent was when Jesus came to the earth in the flesh as mankind's Saviour. He descended from the glory of heaven to the indignity of the manger and the cross. His earthly path would pass through great depths so that He could elevate a lost humanity to the heights of salvation as his glorified children.

His work, which began in humility during the first Christmas Eve, will be completed with his glorious second coming to harvest the crop. It will be a triumphant coming in majesty and honour. It will be the day of all days, the great Advent awaited in supplication by the true congregation of Christ. At Christmas-time we once again hear his voice saying: ... *"Yes, I am coming soon ... "* to which we answer with a deep yearning: ... *Amen. Come, Lord Jesus* (Rev. 22:20).

There are four Advent-times in your life: the coming of Christ in the flesh to earn redemption for; a coming in the Spirit to give me a personal share in his redemption; a coming in my death to transfer me from the sphere of time into eternity; and finally Christ's second coming in glory to conclude the history of mankind, which will be followed by eternal life.

Hence, Christmas-time is rich in divine consolation. We see Christ always and everywhere: in his struggle to save me; in my heart where his grace worked; in my hour of dying that gives me victory in Christ; and any moment in the second coming of my Saviour in glory and majesty.

I praise and thank You, holy Master, for the great blessing of the Advent. Make me ever ready for your second coming.

We are not a post-war generation; we are a pre-peace generation. Jesus will come again.

~ Corrie ten Boom ~

Don't stop at the stars

After Jesus was born in Bethlehem ... Magi from the east came to Jerusalem (Mt. 2:1).

The Magi persevered in their search for the King whose star they saw. God called them in a special way and in terms of what they knew: through the appearance of a star. They were, after all, astrologers, magi, learned priests of their people. Their fatherland was Mesopotamia, situated between the Euphrates and the Tigris, the old land of paradise from which Adam and Eve were expelled. Now they are following the star to worship and bring homage to the second Adam, Jesus the Messiah.

To them the star was the beginning of the light, because they were still children of darkness. In obedience they followed the star and God prepared for them a vision of what was hitherto unseen by human eyes, unheard by human ears and unknown to the heart of man.

The star enchanted them so that they could find the Child. God indeed calls and searches in many ways: He calls the wise men with a star; He calls the shepherds with heavenly choirs. God's love for sinners gives us stars to guide us and we thank God for these stars. But we may not remain standing in amazement before these stars. They are only the beginning of the path of salvation. We must proceed from the star to the Word; from the word of God in nature to the Word of God in Scripture.

Bethlehem star, please guide me also to the Jesus-child!

Ideals are like stars: we never reach them, but like sailors we set our course by them.

~ Carl Shurz ~

*F*ʀᴏᴍ ᴛʜᴇ ꜱᴛᴀʀ ᴛᴏ ᴛʜᴇ Wᴏʀᴅ

Your word is a lamp to my feet and a light for my path (Ps. 119:105).

*T*he wise men were initially guided by a star, but when they arrived in Jerusalem, the Word of God lighted their path to Christ. In Jerusalem everyone was expecting a King, but they did not know where to find Him. The teachers of the law were reflecting on the meaning of the Word of God. This must have seemed like regression to the wise men: away from the shining star to the mouldy study of books.

We find the wise men with their star but without a Book, and the people of Israel with the Word but without their King – a King without an address. So they returned to the Word with its irrefutable authority. In Micah 5:2 this particular prophecy is presented: *"But you, Bethlehem Ephrathah, though you are small among the clans of Judah, out of you will come for me one who will be ruler over Israel ... "* To Bethlehem then – to the small city of great things.

The star is therefore subservient to the Word. When the gilt is gone; the truth and reality is still there in the Word. Emotion and romanticism evaporate and the Word of God triumphs. Hence the final journey to Bethlehem is always a journey based on the Word of God. We love the stars and it is hard to part with them. But we must! We need the Scriptures: the, at times, disillusioning, provocative, tormenting, but always purely prophetic Scriptures. The stars without the Scriptures leave us with an insatiable longing for eternity *and* without the correct address of our King. The Word guides us to the true gold-reef, to Bethlehem, to the stable, the manger and the King.

Jesus of Bethlehem, keep me from becoming so enchanted by the stars that I lose the address of the Child.

People may gather knowledge, but wisdom is a gift that comes directly from God.

~ Bob Jones ~

Can you truly celebrate the Christ-feast?

... Then they opened their treasures and presented him with gifts of gold and of incense and of myrrh (Mt. 2:11).

The Magi from the east finally understood the true meaning of Christmas: to give. God gave with Christmas: He gave his best, his most valuable, his Son. He gave out of love (see Jn. 3:16). And the Child of Bethlehem also gave: He gave Himself; He continued giving even in his death on the cross.

You must first learn to forget what you did for others in order to remember what others did for you out of love. You must learn to forget what you expect from others and rather ask what you can do for them. For once you have to rid yourself of the idea that the world owes you something and start to think about what you owe the world. You must be able to relegate your demands to the background and to place your responsibilities prominently on the foreground.

You must discover that your fellow man is as sincere as you are and be able to see the heart hidden behind the exterior – a heart that yearns for love, friendship and compassion. You must be able to close your book of charges and complaints against life and look around you to find places where you can sow seeds of happiness and love.

If you are willing to do these things, even if only for one day, then you have brought *your* gold, incense and myrrh. Only then can you truly celebrate the Christ-feast.

Loving Master, I begin this Advent-time by giving myself to You renewedly so that You can use me as and when You please.

It is easy to want gifts from God without wanting Him. The gift is never greater than the Giver!

~ Augustine of Hippo ~

*A*ᴛᴛɪᴛᴜᴅᴇꜱ ꜱᴜʀʀᴏᴜɴᴅɪɴɢ ᴛʜᴇ *C*ʜʀɪꜱᴛ-ꜰᴇᴀꜱᴛ

Then Herod called the Magi secretly and found out from them the exact time the star had appeared (Mt. 2:7).

*C*hristmas is firstly and foremostly an attitude of the heart. There are many people who share in Herod's attitude. He is the prototype of those people who live in sin and in enmity with God; people who would like to eradicate the Good News; people with strong personalities and many talents, but who want to banish Christ from their lives. They hide their disapproval behind a mask of hypocrisy. They also want to go to worship the Child. They also celebrate the Christ-feast, but in reality their hearts do not belong to Him. Their motives are impure as they search for the Child: they want to use religion to advance their careers and to keep the crown on their own heads.

The Advent-time proclaims the following message to these Herods: Christ can be found in Bethlehem, but only by those who have the right attitude in their hearts and whose worship is true in spirit.

This is the attitude of the wise men. They came from a distant land, in the same way that we have to come from the distant land of sin as lost sons and daughters. They persisted in their search and did not allow anything to distract them from their purpose. Jesus Himself promised that those who seek Him will find Him. The wise men stipulated no conditions. They expected a palace and a golden cradle – what they found was a stable and a humble manger. Like them, everyone who seeks can experience the joy of finding what God intended for each of us during this Christmas-time.

I thank you, o Holy Spirit, that I not only found the stable and the manger, but also the Child of Bethlehem, my Saviour and Redeemer.

Whoever takes one step in the direction of Jesus will find that He takes two steps in his direction.

~ Moses Mendelsson ~

Christmas and Children

... "I tell you the truth, unless you change and become like little children, you will never enter the kingdom of heaven" (Mt. 18:3).

Christmas is the pre-eminent feast of the family and the child. It is difficult to express the excitement and expectations in the heart of a child during Christmas. Grown-ups are different: we are mostly negative – we expect to fail, and then we do fail; we expect to be unhappy, and then we are; we always anticipate the worst, and then it happens.

Advent is a time for recovering the lost glory of our faith in life and eternity. It is a time to believe that God can work the miracle once again: that Christ can be born again in our life and thoughts. It is a time to devote ourselves anew to God and to rejoice in the fact that his Spirit wants to live in us.

Christmas allows us to obtain new insights into the place of the child in the family. On that first Christmas Eve a Child was at the centre of that holy tableau. Similarly, Jesus taught us that the child is at the core of the family. We are not allowed to remove the child from the centre, simply because we have other interests and responsibilities.

The Christ-feast repeatedly brings us back to the secret of true happiness and joy: mother, father, child – and God! May Christmas lead us to a renewed resolution to maintain the sanctity of the family. Then Christmas will bring you too the happiness and peace of family bliss.

We praise You, Lord Jesus, for bestowing a new and particular significance on the family.

The unity of the family lies in love, and love is the reconciliation of authority and freedom.

~ Robert H. Benson ~

*A*DVENT JUBILATION — WITH A FALSE NOTE

... "Say to the Daughter of Zion, 'See, your Savior comes! See, his reward is with him, and his recompense accompanies him'" (Is. 62:11).

---

*A*t Advent-time we commemorate the coming in the flesh of Christ to the world. However, we must not forget the coming of Christ to our souls, to our hearts. We dare not stop at the material appearance of Christ in the world as if this is the only important event. We must not only testify with our mouths that He came to the world to take the burden of our guilt and curse upon Him as Lamb of God. It is a wonderful testimony, yes, but what good does it do if we do not truly partake thereof? Then it becomes a Christmas jubilation with a false note.

It may be a celebration around us but never inside of us. If we truly want to experience the joy of Christmas, Christ has to come to our hearts with his salvation, peace and joy, and completely inhabit us. Martin Luther clearly states this: "Even if Christ has been born in Bethlehem a thousand times, but not yet in my heart, then I am lost."

Christ came to this world so that his love and grace could become a reality in the heart of everyone who believes in Him. He came to find and save those who are lost, and everyone who accepts Him has the right to become children of God. Do you believe this? Do you believe that He comes to where you stand, overwhelmed by your own sin? He comes to you with his hands filled with grace and forgiveness. He comes to convert your sadness into joy; to take the false note out of your Christmas joy and to make you sing the pure song of salvation.

Heavenly Father, we are once again on our annual pilgrimage to the manger in Bethlehem. Satisfy us with the true Bread and Water of life.

Salvation does not simply look back at the manger. It looks ahead to the freedom in which redeemed people stand. Therefore we have to be God's people.

~ Leon Morris ~

The Sun Shines, but I am Blind

"But for you who revere my name, the sun of righteousness will rise with healing in its wings ... " (Mal. 4:2).

The sun shines in glory and majesty, high in the firmament, far and inaccessible in its reign. The eye cannot look at it directly without being blinded. As the sun is, so is our God. Elevated high above the earthly turmoil, He reigns over the entire world. Even though I try to shield my eyes from his splendour, He remains there. Like the sun that brings light, warmth and growth with its comforting rays, God also comes to us in the Advent-time. But unlike the sun, God is also still close to us in spite of his untouchable splendour.

We cannot go to the sun, but the sun can reach down to us. God sends his light to illuminate our dark minds, warm our cold hearts and turn the night of our sins into the day of his grace. In Jesus Christ the Sun of justice descends upon us. God from God, Light from Light. Zechariah sings the praise of the Child of Bethlehem by describing Him as the rising light that visits us to shine on those who are overwhelmed by darkness and the shadow of death. So many are lost in the dark maze of sin. The sun shines, but they are blind. But, says Malachi, there is healing in his rays. He takes our ailments upon Him and carries the burden of our grief.

After Christmas, we have to return to everyday life and carry the light we receive from Him into a dark world.

Sun of justice, thank you for reminding us in this Advent-time that we have a calling to be the bearers of light in this world.

Our task as laymen is to live our lives in such surrender to Christ that it will be contagious.

~ Paul Tournier ~

The core truth of the Christ-feast

This is how God showed his love among us: He sent his one and only Son into the world that we might live through him (1 Jn. 4:9).

*T*he most astonishing truth about Christmas is that God loves us. God is love and He loves us with a love that gives only the best and most valuable, as with Christmas when He gave us his Son. He also loves us with a love that forgives and cares. We dare not leave such love unanswered.

... (S)ince God so loved us, we also ought to love one another, says the apostle John (1 Jn. 4:11). Love must triumph in our everyday lives: in our marriages, in our home lives and in our relationships – not only with words, but with deeds of love.

However, it is also true that Christ did not remain in the manger; He grew to become a Man of sorrow in Gethsemane and at Golgotha. Therefore we, as his followers, may not remain infants in faith or become stuck in a faith centred only on the stable. We must grow to spiritual maturity.

Like the shepherds we must also be loving witnesses and praise God for everything we have heard and seen. We must proclaim the wonder of love: redemption, grace and peace. The gate is always open to everyone who wants to enter – this is the love-truth of Christmas.

Loving Father, thank You for revealing Yourself and the fullness of your love to sinners like us at Christmas-time.

God doesn't love us because we are precious; we are precious because God loves us.

~ Fulton J. Sheen ~

"Soul, do you have room for Jesus?"

"In my Father's house are many rooms; if it were not so, I would have told you. I am going there to prepare a place for you" (Jn. 14:2). [A]nd she gave birth to her firstborn, a son. She wrapped him in cloths and placed him in a manger, because there was no room for them in the inn (Lk. 2:7).

*H*ad the people of Bethlehem known who these visitors were, they would probably have tried to "make" room for them. Mary would become the mother of the Messiah generations of Israel had been waiting for. Every devout Israelite would have liked to give up his own room for Him. But God does not come to this world in greatness and splendour. He comes in the shape of a servant and is placed in a manger.

Will this Christmas once again proclaim to you that the Lord could not find a place in your life either? If this is the case then, your guilt is bigger than that of the people of Bethlehem. After all, we know that He is the Christ, the Saviour. We dare not be Christians who have no room for Christ. The wonder of God's grace is that He does not repay us according to our sins. Although there was no place for Him on earth, He went to prepare a place in heaven for every repentant sinner. A "no vacancy" sign is never posted.

Our Christmas deed should be to make room for Christ in our hearts and lives. Then we have nothing to fear because we know: for me too a place has been prepared by the Lamb Himself so that I may take my place at the feast of the Lamb. Hallelujah! Praise the Lord!

I want to make room for You in all spheres of my life, Lord Jesus. I thank You for the room You make for me now and in eternity.

Heaven will be the endless reward for everyone who has heaven in his heart.

~ Henry Ward Beecher ~

Nature, Scripture and flesh

The Word became flesh and made his dwelling among us. We have seen his glory ... (Jn. 1:14).

*O*f all the ways in which God reveals Himself to us (in nature and in the Scriptures), the revelation of God in the flesh is the most wonderful. This is the source of all our Christmas joy: Christ became man!

The Christmas drama reaches a climax when the Magi bow down to bring homage to the Child. Now, for the first time, they see God in the flesh. Up until this moment they searched for Him in nature, in the stars. But the enchantment of the stars is past. The light of God shines through triumphantly when they finally stand before the incarnate Word: the shining Morning Star!

Together with the Magi we have to look beyond the stars to the Word in the stable, where we surrender ourselves unconditionally in worship: the gold of our love; the incense of our prayers; and the myrrh of our offerings. In the stable we learn what the stars cannot tell us: that the earth became the centre of the universe on Christmas Day.

And when the stars die out one day, the eternal day of God will dawn. Then God will no longer address us through the stars, nor through the Word, but will speak to us eternally and uninterruptedly through the incarnate Word: Jesus, Emmanuel!

Holy and awe-inspiring God, guide me beyond the stars this Christmas, through the holy Word, and to the Child in the manger, so that I can worship in spirit and truth.

You can no more diminish the splendour of God than a possessed person can wipe out the sun by carving "darkness" on the walls of his cell.

~ C. S. Lewis ~

Christ-feast!

... "Do not be afraid. I bring you good news of great joy that will be for all the people" (Lk. 2:10).

To many people Christmas has become a feast without Christ. He has been eliminated in a subtle manner to make room for other things. It is the task of the Christian to rectify this misconception.

We must confront the worldly tensions of Christmas as mature Christians. We must guard against all God-dishonouring commercialisations of the feast. It must not degenerate into cheap tinsel, shining lights and superficial emotions.

We must not allow ourselves to be swept up in the mad rush before Christmas to such an extent that it leaves us so exhausted on Christmas Day that we are unable to sing a song of praise in his honour. We must penetrate beyond the exterior trappings to get to the core of Christmas, so that the Light of the world can become a reality to us.

We must contribute to making Christmas a true Christ-feast. This does not mean that we should be spoilsports; Christians do have a reason to celebrate, as the fields of Bethlehem resounded with joy on that holy night. Without Christ there can be no true Christmas joy.

We must experience the true glory of Christmas in our hearts and not look for it in shops and places of worldly entertainment. At Christmas the world must clearly see who we belong to: in our Christmas cards; in our Christmas tree that points to the tree of the cross; in our worship; in our gifts to people and our offerings to God – our gold, incense and myrrh.

Holy Spirit of God, guide me this Christmas past the external trappings to the true inner joy that can only be found in Christ.

Let us bring Christ the great, universal offering of our love and pour out our most profound praises and prayers before Him.

~ Paul Frost ~

*B*ethlehem: house of bread

"But you, Bethlehem Ephrathah, though you are small among the clans of Judah, out of you will come for me one who will be ruler over Israel, whose origins are from of old, from ancient times" (Mic. 5:2).

*A*s Micah predicted, Christ was born in Bethlehem – a small town approximately thirteen kilometres south of Jerusalem. It was also called Ephrathah in ancient times. The name Bethlehem means "house of bread". The town is situated among fertile wheat farm-lands, which makes this name very appropriate.

Bethlehem has a long history. Jacob buried his wife, Rachel, there and erected a memorial pillar next to her grave. Ruth was living there when she met Boas and married him, and on a clear day she could see her country Moab across the Valley of the Jordan. Bethlehem was also the town of David's youth. David yearned for the water from the well of Bethlehem when he was a fugitive from the wrath of Saul.

From the ancestry of this David, God would bring forth his Son to become the Saviour of this world. He would become the Bread of life for millions; the Fountain of living water to quench the eternal thirst of humanity.

When a pilgrim wants to enter the birthplace of Christ in Bethlehem today, he has to bend down low to pass through the opening that serves as door. Similarly, all of us will have to bow down during this Advent-time before the Child of Bethlehem so that we can bring Him the true homage that belongs to Him.

Come all you faithful, cheerful and with joy, o come in the spirit to Bethlehem! Praise that Child born for our salvation – come kneel there in worship before Jesus, the Lord.

He who has been wounded requires medicine. Our wound is sin and for that we require the Bread of life.

~ Ambrose ~

Tender Comfort at Advent-Time

When anxiety was great within me, your consolation brought joy to my soul (Ps. 94:19).

There is a lot of sorrow surrounding Christmas-time: some people are gravely ill; others have to come to terms with the effects of old age; for others Christmas will never be the same again because the family circle has disintegrated irreparably through separation or death. There is much grief because death performs its grim task mercilessly on our roads particularly during this period.

There are parents who long painfully for their children who will not be home for Christmas because they have emigrated, or live too far away to be able to be home for Christmas, or because estrangement has set in, threatening to break the hearts of parents.

There are countless reasons why these days hold little joy for many. One of the most terrible is the loneliness of those who will miss a loved one this Christmas, due to death. Who can truly express or comprehend this longing?

The Child of Bethlehem had to travel these dark roads Himself as a man on earth, and therefore He is one with us in our grief and pain. He too had to sob for his loneliness at one time. He cares for you and He understands. He is mighty to touch your heart with consolation. Remain close to Him and you will experience the joy of victory, because his love will pull you through.

God of the lonely and sorrowful, thank You for also bringing us comfort for our pain.

Comfort in tribulation can only be obtained on the certain grounds of faith in the Scriptures and the teachings of Jesus Christ.
~ Sir Thomas More ~

*T*HE SIGN OF *G*OD'S LOVE

"This will be a sign to you: You will find a baby wrapped in cloths and lying in a manger" (Lk. 2:12).

*A*s with the arrival of a baby in a family, thousands of people yearned for the coming of the Child of Bethlehem: the prophets and the Old Testament believers; his parents and the devout people of his time – Simeon and Anna; Zechariah and Elizabeth. Similarly we look forward to the annual commemoration of his coming with the honest prayer: "Grant us in these days a true Christ-feast!"

God speaks to man in a thousand voices: on Sinai the thunder roars; in Sodom and Gomorrah God speaks with fire and brimstone; in the life of Job God speaks through loss, illness and tribulations. But at Christmas God speaks through a Child who beckons us back to the heart of God from a mother's arms and from a manger. God becomes a child and speaks to us in a language everyone can understand.

The Child of Bethlehem speaks to us about God's immeasurable love, and tells us exactly how much God loves the world! Will this love not compel us to love our children more and to desire their salvation? Having children always places us before a choice: to love and comfort them, or to neglect and sadden them. The Child of Bethlehem puts us before the same choice: will we love Him or will we sadden Him?

Holy Father, I gratefully accept your Miracle and my heart chooses You as King for all eternity!

Because of God's love for humanity, Jesus Christ became what we are in order to make us what He is.

~ Irenaeus ~

God with us

" ... and they will call him Emmanuel" – which means, "God with us" (Mt. 1:23).

Christmas reminds us of the fact that God is with us, so that our imperfect love may be purified. Christmas teaches us the truth of self-sacrificing love. Christ came to his own property and his people rejected Him. Nevertheless, He gave everyone who accepted Him the right to become children of God.

There was no room for Him in the inn. Still, He guarantees everyone who loves Him and follows Him a place in the house of his Father.

He was despised and deserted by people. Still, He invites everyone who is exhausted and burdened to find rest with Him. He had the power to come down from the cross and destroy everyone who mocked Him. But He died on the cross for all our sins. The vengeful world begrudged Him his life, but He lovingly and mercifully promises eternal life to everyone who believes in Him. This is the language of Emmanuel – God with us.

There is so much lovelessness and hatred in today's world. It sours the relationship between man and God, and between man and man. But Christmas repeatedly tells us that love will triumph. Because God is love He sent us his Son. If God loves us so much, we must also love one another. Let us profess our love anew this Christmas: to God, to our parents, to our marriage partner and to our fellow man. Then it will truly become a Christ-feast.

Thank You, God of love, for allowing your love to be embodied in Jesus Christ. Give us even more love through the work of the Holy Spirit.

Our love for God is tested by the question whether we desire Him or his gifts.

~ Ralph W. Sockman ~

*C*HRIST IS BORN!

... Jesus was born in Bethlehem in Judea, during the time of King Herod ... (Mt. 2:1).

---

*I*t is an irrefutable historical fact that Jesus was born in Bethlehem. Through this physical birth God revealed Himself to all of humanity. The fact that humanity found it hard to accept this fact does not affect the authenticity thereof.

He who was born in Bethlehem more than two thousand years ago is still being born in the heart and life of modern man. This simple but overwhelming truth is often lost in the agitation of our busy lives.

In spite of the world's festivities around Christmas-time, it remains true that if you have not experienced the birth of Christ in your personal life, you will never know the true joy and peace of Christmas. Only Christ gives depth and peace to the joy of Christmas. The birth of Christ in Bethlehem is a mere historical fact and nothing more than that, until He is born in your life. Then you not only know Christmas, but also the Christ of Christmas.

If you want to experience true Christmas joy, Christ must be born in your life and you have to place Him in the centre of your entire life. When his holiness permeates your life, it becomes "a merry Christmas" in the true sense of the word.

I thank You, holy Child of Bethlehem, for being born in me so that I can become part of your Spirit, and so that my entire life can be a celebration in your honour.

The Word that is God became man, so that we could learn from a Man how to become more like God.

~ Clement of Alexandria ~

The Afterglow of Christmas

The shepherds returned, glorifying and praising God for all the things they had heard and seen, which were just as they had been told (Lk. 2:20).

The shepherds from the fields of Ephrathah witnessed the miracle of that first Christmas Eve. Each of us experiences something of the miracle of Christmas every year, in the Christmas carols, colourful lights and in the gifts that we receive. There is a spirit of love and goodwill everywhere. However, the spirit of Christmas discarded on the garbage heap together with the wilted Christmas tree is useless. It makes a mockery of the deeper meaning of the Christ-feast.

Would it not be wonderful if we could preserve the special Christmas spirit in bottles, like seasonal fruit, and then open one bottle a week for the entire year? After the song of the angels have died down, after the star has disappeared from the skies, after the wise men have returned to their home in the east, and the shepherds have returned to their flocks, only then does the real work of Christmas begin.

Because we were at the stable in Bethlehem and relived the first Christmas Eve, because we met the Christ-child, therefore the afterglow of Christmas must remain in our lives. With the glow of love in our hearts we must continue to have compassion for our neighbour even after Christmas. We must continue to help rebuild the world, to bring peace among people, and to fill the world with the music of his eternal love.

We worship You as the God of the Christ-feast, but also of each day of the year. Help us to continue singing the love song of Christmas throughout the year.

We should love God because He is God, and the measure of our love should be to love Him each day without measure.

~ Bernard of Clairvaux ~

*L*IBERATING INTROSPECTION

Search me, O God, and know my heart; test me and know my anxious thoughts. See if there is any offensive way in me, and lead me in the way everlasting (Ps. 139:23-24).

*I*t is once again that time of year when we have to take stock and do introspection. It is only fitting that we pray the above prayer together with David during these days.

Some prayers make no demands on the one who prays. They lull the conscience. However, to pray meaningfully and in such a way that it also pleases the Holy Spirit, a prayer must be wholly truthful and it must be accompanied by a sincere willingness to engage in thorough introspection.

Requesting God to know your heart and to test your thoughts can be an experience that completely re-creates you. It strips you of all egotism, superficiality and hypocrisy. You see yourself as God sees you, and you may not always like what you see. It is humbling, but it can also be liberating.

Testing and evaluation in your spiritual life is an urgent necessity. It is the condition for service: if we cannot pass God's test, He cannot employ us in his service. Only when the Holy Spirit compels us to do introspection do we become useful instruments in the hands of the Lord, and only then do we work for his honour. Then we no longer fear the future, but we place our weak hands in his almighty hand and walk purposefully towards the unknown future.

Holy Father, make me willing to submit myself to the testing of the Holy Spirit, and shape me for your service.

Introspection never means to give up anything, because something you give up is a loss. The Lord only asks us to give up the things of the world in exchange for things that are much better.

~ Fulton J. Sheen ~

Joyous Christianity

" ... My soul glorifies the Lord and my spirit rejoices in God my Savior ... " (Lk. 1:46-47).

Many people view their religion as a heavy and sometimes even unbearable burden. They easily frown upon any semblance of light-heartedness in spiritual matters. They stoop sombrely under the heavy burden of their spiritual conscience. This is definitely not what God intended.

The faith of the Christian should be a joyous experience. Your Father takes joy in and is interested in your life. He is happy when you are happy; He consoles you in sadness and grief; He supports you when the burden becomes too much for you; He helps you up when you stumble over obstacles; He enjoys your successes as you enjoy them yourself.

Christianity does not eliminate joy and happiness from life. On the contrary, it returns happiness to your life. Through your communion with the living Christ you realise the blessing of his presence every day. The more you praise and thank Him, the more happiness you glean from your spiritual life.

Happiness is the fruit of the Holy Spirit (Gal. 5:22). Your surrender and devotion should be such that the joy of the Lord is revealed across the entire spectrum of your life. Then every day becomes a joyous Christ-feast.

Dear Lord Jesus, I continually delight in the knowledge that You are with me always.

When I think about my God, my heart is so filled with joy that the notes dance and jump from my pen; and because God has given me a joyful heart, you have to forgive me if I serve Him with a joyful spirit.
~ Franz Josef Haydn ~

CHRIST IS ALWAYS AVAILABLE

" ... And surely I am with you always, to the very end of the age" (Mt. 28:20).

One of the glorious truths of the gospel is that Christ is always available for his followers who need Him. This is a comforting knowledge in these last days of the old year, when we are often overcome by an inexplicable melancholy.

The comforting truth is that the Master is with you wherever you are. While you strive to get to know Him better, and while you try to break through your doubt and uncertainty, He is at your side in your struggle. It is as if He wants to tell you: "Stop struggling with your self-made doubt and fear and come to Me. I am the One who will give you calm and peace."

Christian pilgrims know that if they accept this merciful invitation, they will have to relinquish all their pet sins, which have become part of their lives. Unfortunately, there are those who want to claim the presence of the living Christ on their own conditions. This can never happen, because his presence can only be experienced and enjoyed if you meet *his* requirements.

The basis of your Christianity is your acceptance of the living Saviour. Without that your faith has no foundation and you will be unable to venture into the new year. Together with Christ you also accept the Holy Spirit. Through the working of the Holy Spirit you become aware of the presence of Christ with every step that you take.

Thank you, loving Father, that You are always available and that I may experience your presence every day of my life.

If we remain alert and vigilant, God reveals Himself continuously to us and we will rejoice in everything that happens to us.
~ Jean Pierre de Caussade ~

GOD'S PERFECT METHOD

... "He has done everything well," ... (Mk. 7:37).

Most people want to conclude the year that has come to an end in the presence of God, and enter the new, unknown year under the guidance of his merciful and loving hand.

God speaks to us in many ways, but He speaks most clearly to us through his Son and through his Word. With the Word before us, we have to look back on the road we have travelled and beg his friendly light to illuminate the road stretching out ahead of us. On New Year's Eve we are not allowed simply to contemplate the transience of life. The mere thought of our mortality is enough to upset us. But the content of the year behind us is much more important than its duration.

In the past year the Lord has done so much in our lives, giving it meaning and quality. All of this is undeserved grace. We do not deserve what we have achieved. We can merely confess: "Everything He does is good." The year did not bring only joy, but that is not necessarily bad. Sometimes God tests us with grief, but this too is for our own good.

When we reach the end of the pilgrimage, as we have reached the end of this year, we will clasp our hands together in amazement and humbly confess that He did everything well. With this knowledge we can take our leave of the old year with peace of mind.

Leader and Finisher of my faith, I rejoice in the knowledge that through Jeus You work everything that happens to me for my good.

All the living knowledge of God rests on this foundation: that we experience Him in our lives as the will to love.

~ Albert Schweitzer ~

*P*EACE UNTIL THE END

"I am the Alpha and the Omega," says the Lord God, "who is, and who was, and who is to come, the Almighty" (Rev. 1:8).

*A*nd so we reach the last day of the old year, through his grace. There are many things we are ashamed of, but there are also many things we are thankful for. There are so many reproaches for so many missed opportunities, but we have also received so much grace from God. The year brought joy, but also grief; victory, but also defeat; sunshine, but also storms.

However, we may still call God "our Father", the biggest privilege a humble human being can expect. Let us therefore count our blessings today, in the knowledge that He remains constant – yesterday, today and in all eternity.

You are richer today than you were yesterday if you smiled often; could give something of yourself to others; could forgive your enemies; make new friends; convert your problems into opportunities. You are richer today than you were yesterday if you made time to notice God's handiwork in everyday things; if you learned to distinguish the essential things in life; if you had a little more patience with others' faults.

You are wealthy today if a small child smiled at you, or if a stray dog licked your hand; if you sought out the best in others and if you gave the best of yourself to your fellow man and to God. Then you begin the new year secure in his love.

Eternal and immutable God, I thank you for guiding me through another year and for giving me the knowledge that You will never abandon or forsake me.

The grace of the Lord Jesus will be with everyone.
                    ~ The Apostle John ~